OXFORD STUDIES IN M

VOLUME 1

Oxford Studies in Medieval Philosophy Volume 1

Edited by

ROBERT PASNAU

UNIVERSITY PRESS

Great Clarendon Street, Oxford, OX2 6DP,
United Kingdom

Oxford University Press is a department of the University of Oxford.
It furthers the University's objective of excellence in research, scholarship,
and education by publishing worldwide. Oxford is a registered trade mark of
Oxford University Press in the UK and in certain other countries

First Edition published in 2013

Impression: 1

Published in the United States of America by Oxford University Press
198 Madison Avenue, New York, NY 10016, United States of America

British Library Cataloguing in Publication Data
Data available

Library of Congress Cataloging in Publication Data
Data available

ISBN 978–0–19–966184–8 (hbk.)
ISBN 978–0–19–966185–5 (pbk.)

As printed and bound by
CPI Group (UK) Ltd, Croydon, CR0 4YY

Note from the Editor

The present volume, the first in an annual series, takes its place between two other Oxford series, one devoted to ancient philosophy and one to the early modern period. The aim is to publish the best of current research in medieval philosophy, understanding that category quite broadly, so as to include all aspects of philosophy in its modern sense, to range from late antiquity to the Renaissance, and to cover all of Europe, North Africa, and the Middle East.

The richness and diversity of all this material, spanning a dozen centuries, is astonishing, but what is more astonishing still is that it has, for so long, been neglected. The term 'mediaeval' was coined to facilitate setting aside a long line of centuries felt to be uninteresting, those middle ages between ancient and modern. But what a wealth of material to leave unaccounted: the Christian philosophy of ancient Rome; the classical philosophical tradition in Islam and Judaism; the Carolingian renaissance; the philosophy of Byzantium and of the European monasteries; the first four centuries of academic philosophy at Paris, Oxford, and elsewhere. What others haven't wanted, we take gladly, like a box of gifts still unwrapped after all these years.

Robert Pasnau
Boulder

Contents

Boethius on the Problem of Desert*

Peter King

Boethius opens his *Consolation of Philosophy* with a problem of sorts: the Prisoner[1] has been arrested and sentenced *in absentia* to death. Yet while this is a pressing problem for the Prisoner, it is not, or not obviously, a *philosophical* problem. Death might be problematic for any number of non-philosophical reasons.[2] For instance, death might prevent someone from doing something he wants to do, or it might be painful and unpleasant, or the circumstances in which it occurs might be degrading or ludicrous. The Prisoner does object to his imminent death on all these counts, but there need be nothing philosophical at stake in his objections—closure, avoiding pain, and dignity are perfectly good reasons for each of these counts, comprehensible to anyone; they do not of themselves force any philosophical questions on us. Even if we take these objectionable features to be moral evils, as the Prisoner does, there is still no reason to think that their moral evil is thereby problematic. The victim of an injustice has been wronged, but the mere existence of an injustice does not *eo ipso* pose a philosophical problem, be it about the nature of justice, the possibility

* All translations mine. The Latin text is supplied when it is not readily available. References to the *Consolation of Philosophy* are to its prose sections. An earlier version of this paper was delivered as the 2009 Pepys Lecture at UCLA.

[1] The Prisoner is the dramatic character (*a.k.a.* "Boethius") who narrates and appears in the *Consolation of Philosophy*, as distinct from Boethius, the historical person who lived and died in the late Roman Empire and wrote the *Consolation of Philosophy*—a distinction worth keeping in mind.

[2] Death need not be problematic. It could be a blessed relief from pain and suffering, or the honorable response to the circumstances, or justified in a good cause, or a morally irrelevant side-effect of doing the right thing. And if death is not a problem, it is *a fortiori* not a philosophical problem. (Put aside the quibble that death is some sort of event or process or transition rather than a "problem" strictly speaking; we often call a situation, such as widespread poverty, a moral problem, and the same sense of "problem" is at issue here.)

of evil, or anything else. To suffer an injustice may be a tragedy but it need not be philosophy. Plato, in contrast to Boethius, made a similar situation into an explicit occasion for philosophy in his *Crito* when Socrates, tried and sentenced to death by his fellow Athenians, was given an opportunity to escape. As soon as Crito made his offer, Socrates declared that they "must therefore examine whether we should act this way or not" (46B23), touching off a discussion of fundamental moral principles and their application to his case. But there is no such offer or circumstance at the outset of the *Consolation of Philosophy* to spell out what the philosophical question at stake might be. Nor does the Prisoner seem to think that death poses a philosophical problem in general, part of the human condition, the way Sartre held that we are brought face-to-face with the absurd in an existential encounter with death wherein questions about the meaning of life and the ground of moral value are inescapable. Instead, the Prisoner dwells on his own particular death, objecting to its particular features in a long litany of complaints. What the Prisoner seeks for these complaints, as the title of the work makes clear, is consolation. Yet this fact is as unhelpful as it is indisputable. There is no initial reason to think that the Prisoner will find consolation through addressing a philosophical problem or set of problems. Quite the contrary; consolation comes in many non-cognitive forms. We might be consoled by the mere presence of a friend, for example, or by a gift as a "consolation prize". And even if consolation may be a by-product of understanding (though it need not be), the problems for which one receives consolation might not be philosophical problems; after losing my job I might be consoled by the recognition that many people have lost their jobs recently, which is an economic rather than a philosophical problem. If we throw up our hands and insist that there must be a philosophical problem lurking in the area because the title of the work is "the consolation of *philosophy*" (assuming that it was meant to have a title and that it has the title it was meant to have), we may be correct but we are still not a single step closer to identifying the philosophical problem or set of problems at issue.[3]

[3] There was an established genre of consolation-literature in antiquity, much (though not all) of it written by philosophers. Yet even this historical fact is not conclusive. Philosophy in antiquity addressed many topics we no longer think of as part of philosophy—biology, chemistry, economics, and other disciplines are obvious examples. Consolation likewise might once have been taken as part of the philosophical enterprise but which we now think is addressed to non-philosophical issues, dealt with today in a variety of non-philosophical venues: self-help books, grief counseling, therapy, pastoral advice, and so on. Indeed, the idea that *philosophy* could console someone on Death Row might seem improbable. Joel Relihan, *The Prisoner's Philosophy: Life and Death in Boethius's "Consolation"* (Notre Dame: University of Notre Dame Press, 2007), 48–9,

There is a common alternative view, one which philosophers seem to have adopted recently. The *Consolation of Philosophy* has been recognized as a classic of world literature ever since it was written, and its literary aspirations are as undeniable as its literary virtues. It is no accident that the work opens with the Prisoner trying to find consolation in artistic pursuits. The *mise-en-scène* in which Lady Philosophy confronts the Prisoner after chasing away the Muses—"those painted-up whores" (1.1.8: *has scenicas metriculas*)—might serve merely to set the stage for their joint investigation of several loosely interrelated philosophical issues: the unity of virtue, the nature of the good, the existence and providence of God, the relation of free will and foreknowledge. The discussions of these problems are sufficient to cure the Prisoner of his mental torpor (1.2.5: *lethargum patitur*); his recognition of God's governance and goodness is consolation enough. The Prisoner's impending death, on this reading, has a literary rather than a philosophical point, providing a handy introduction to Boethius's philosophical travelogue, which moves "from Stoic moralism to Platonic transcendence" as one scholar says.[4] There is no philosophical problem which the *Consolation of Philosophy* addresses, according to this view, only a series of philosophical topics, the discussion of each occasioned by the dramatic (literary) setting.

I think this alternative view, common as it is, is mistaken. Boethius's *Consolation of Philosophy* is indeed a literary masterpiece, but it is also a philosophical masterpiece, dominated by a philosophical problem that gives it structure and unity.[5] The problem is posed not by the mere fact of death, nor by the precise circumstances or manner of the Prisoner's

for instance, tells us that "the reader" expects a consolation to include "assertions of the immortality of the soul, descriptions of the rewards of the blessed, and visions of eternity"; there being none of these or any mention of "a beatific vision" in the text, Relihan concludes that we are meant to regard the *Consolation of Philosophy* "as not-a-consolation; in short, as a parody" (!).

[4] Henry Chadwick, *Boethius: The Consolations of Music, Logic, Theology, and Philosophy* (Cambridge: Cambridge University Press, 1981), Ch. 5.2.

[5] Well, perhaps two philosophical problems. I follow the mediæval Latin commentary tradition in taking the discussion of free will and divine foreknowledge in Book 5 to address a problem in philosophical theology, while the remainder of the work is a treatise on ethics (with a bit of metaphysics as its underpinnings)—and I follow the same tradition in taking Book 5 to have a problematic status, a view also defended by Hermann Tränkle, "Ist die *Philosophie Consolatio* des Boethius zum vorgesehened Abschluss gelangt?" in *Vigiliae christianae* 31 (1977), 148–56. The recent *Cambridge Companion to Boethius* (ed. John Marenbon, Cambridge University Press, 2009) implicitly endorses the distinction by including precisely two articles on the philosophical content of the *Consolation of Philosophy*, one on Books 2–4 (John Magee) and the other on Book 5 (Robert Sharples). I also hold that the literary merits of the *Consolation of Philosophy* are, at least for the most part, secondary to Boethius's philosophical agenda.

impending death, but rather by the turn of events that led to the Prisoner's unfortunate current condition. Boethius is, I think, quite clear on this score. But modern readers have a hard time recognizing the philosophical problem he is addressing for two reasons. First, the problem itself is not commonly discussed in its own right, traveling under its own name, so to speak, the way more familiar philosophical problems often do: the problem of universals, Newcomb's Problem, the Problem of Evil. Second, not all of the background assumptions entering into the problem are accepted widely nowadays. Yet for all that there is, I maintain, a clear philosophical problem at the heart of the *Consolation of Philosophy*, one that Boethius lays out with clarity and precision. Once we identify the problem we can then consider how Boethius solves it and whether his solution provides the Prisoner with the consolation he seeks—questions which have unexpected answers.

Boethius opens by rejecting the common alternative view. As noted, the *Consolation of Philosophy* begins with the Prisoner seeking solace in literature, composing a poem about his unhappy plight, when Lady Philosophy appears and chases away the Muses (1.1). Shorn of its artistic trappings, Boethius's point is that literary art is not the proper response to philosophical problems, and furthermore that the ensuing work is primarily philosophical rather than literary (which means that its literary qualities in the end subserve its philosophical agenda). After some minor stage-setting, Lady Philosophy asks the Prisoner directly in 1.4.1 why he is weeping and wailing. Again, if we "un-translate" her query from its literary and dramatic context, the question raised here is the very one with which we began: what philosophical problem is posed by the Prisoner's situation? Put another way, what philosophical problem is at stake in the Prisoner's admittedly unhappy circumstances? Boethius recognizes that the problem is not evident and that it needs to be properly introduced. Lady Philosophy's query prompts the Prisoner's long litany of complaints. Modern readers lose track of Boethius's philosophical point in the welter of details in this litany. They do not recognize that the Prisoner adheres strictly to the rules of classical rhetoric, following a pattern which would have been familiar to Boethius's audience.[6] In particular, classical readers of Boethius

For discussion of these matters see Peter King, "Boethius: The First of the Scholastics," *Carmina philosophiae* 16 (2007), 23–50.

[6] The Prisoner's lament follows Quintillian's fivefold structure for effective oratory: (*a*) the *exordium* or *prooemium*, an introduction designed to make the audience well-disposed to the case, 1.4.2–9; (*b*) the *narratio*, the recounting of the facts, 1.4.10–15; (*c*) the *probatio*, describing the false accusations, 1.4.16–21; (*d*) the refutatio, rebutting the accusations, 1.4.22–4; (*e*) the *peroratio*, 1.4.25–46.

would have known that the Prisoner's case is encapsulated in the closing remarks of his peroration (1.4.46):

> I seem to see criminals in their hideaways wallowing in joy and pleasure, the most abandoned of them scheming to renew false accusations, whilst good people are prostrate with terror at the sight of my plight; evildoers, one and all roused by their impunity to venture on wicked deeds, and to see them through for their rewards, whereas innocent people are not only deprived of their safety but even of their defenses.

In short, the wicked prosper and the good suffer. The Prisoner's death is a case of something bad happening to someone good (1.4.34):

> Instead of being rewarded for my genuine virtue, I am punished for a counterfeit crime.

It is not merely that the Prisoner is facing death, or even that he has been sentenced to death for a crime he did not commit; it is that his actions merit reward rather than punishment, which is precisely what has gone awry when the good suffer and the wicked prosper—the generalized version of the Prisoner's case. Boethius confirms that this is indeed the philosophical problem at stake at the next point in the dialogue where the issue could sensibly be raised, the beginning of Book 4. Lady Philosophy has devoted Books 2–3 to "curing" the Prisoner of his delusions and "reminding" him of the Supreme Good (God). The Prisoner acknowledges the truth and value of what Lady Philosophy has told him, and then states explicitly that the central cause of his unhappiness (4.1.3: *maxima nostri causa maeroris*) is as follows (4.1.4):

> While wickedness reigns and prospers, virtue not only goes unrewarded but is enslaved and trodden down by criminals, made to pay the penalties in place of the wrongdoers.

Neither virtue nor vice receives its due. Lady Philosophy recognizes the problem—that is, Boethius declares that it is indeed a legitimate philosophical problem—and, as Lady Philosophy begins to sketch her solution, she calls the results established in Books 2–3 "preliminaries" (4.1.8: *decursis omnibus quae praemittere necessarium puto* . . .). The circle is then closed: the problem raised in 1.4 can finally be addressed in 4.1, all the necessary preliminaries to its solution having been dealt with. The philosophical material in Books 2–3, then, is merely subordinate to the central philosophical problem addressed in the *Consolation of Philosophy*. Call it the *Problem of Desert*: Why do people not get what they deserve?

The Problem of Desert is the appropriately generalized form of the problem Boethius takes to be raised by his own downfall from Master of Offices to convicted conspirator, Boethius regarding himself as a clear example of a morally virtuous person and thus someone who did not deserve his fate. (Much of the Prisoner's Lament in 1.4 is devoted to examples of his moral goodness.) The Problem of Desert is logically posed by any instance of an undeserved fortune: someone virtuous not being rewarded, someone vicious doing well. The Prisoner often speaks of "the good" suffering and "the wicked" prospering, but this is no more than rhetorical shorthand; Boethius knows perfectly well that good people are sometimes rewarded for their virtues and that wicked people are sometimes punished for their vices. Indeed, the Problem of Desert is posed by even a single instance of an undeserved fortune. Yet Boethius is not interested in this minimal logical possibility. Instead, he is interested in what he takes to be the actual case, the real world, in which people's fortunes are strictly independent of their deserts and are distributed more or less randomly across people and their lives, a view he sums up vividly in his image of the Wheel of Fortune (described at length in Book 2). If worldly success and failure are indeed governed by "the blind goddess Fortune," so that chance is the only factor, then everyone's fortune is strongly independent of what they (morally) deserve—and the Problem of Desert has been sharpened to a razor's edge.

Once sharpened, the Problem of Desert naturally gives rise to a related but distinct philosophical problem. Why be moral? If worldly fortune is strongly independent of morality, as the Wheel of Fortune would have it, or even if common wisdom is right that nice guys finish last (and the wicked thus prosper in virtue of their wickedness), why would—indeed, why *should*—anyone toe the moral line? Lurking behind the Problem of Desert is the specter of the moral defector. Failure to give a satisfactory answer to the Problem of Desert makes non-moral behavior that much the more appealing, and seriously impairs the prospects for a convincing explanation of why we ought to be moral. Conversely, a compelling solution to the Problem of Desert might provide everything needed to motivate moral behavior; although it is not the same problem its solution may be transferable.

It might be objected that the Problem of Desert is no more than a specific form of questions about justice and injustice, fairness and unfairness. Yet this is not quite right, strictly speaking. It may well be unfair or unjust for someone not to get what she deserves, but such considerations of justice and fairness are logically posterior to the issue of who deserves what (and why), which is the heart of the Problem of Desert. Claims about desert are usually taken to justify further claims of justice and injustice, not to be such claims themselves. For example, one might think that an injustice has to be the result, direct or indirect, of moral agency; a virtuous person who dies young in an earthquake does not get what she deserves but is not, or not obviously, the victim of injustice, since the earthquake was not the product of moral agency.

The Problem of Desert is often confused with the traditional Problem of Evil.[7] They are not the same. The Problem of Evil questions how the existence of a benevolent and omnipotent God could be compatible with the existence of evil, whereas the Problem of Desert questions (roughly) the distribution of evil in the world; clearly explaining how it is possible for some phenomenon to exist is logically prior to explaining how and why it is distributed in some way. (It is one thing to explain the existence of social wealth and another to explain its distribution.) The Problem of Desert, of course, is logically dependent on a solution to the Problem of Evil, since evil must exist in order for there to be some (perhaps morally objectionable) distribution of it. Again, a solution to the traditional Problem of Evil might well leave the Problem of Desert unresolved, since we might have reasons to accept the existence of evils and nevertheless ask why they fall upon the good rather than the wicked. Most importantly, Boethius himself explicitly says that the two problems are distinct. The Prisoner summarizes the traditional Problem of Evil in 4.1.3: "Despite the existence of a good Ruler of the world evils can exist and go unpunished," a fact "that surely merits great astonishment."[8] He immediately goes on to say that there is *another* problem which logically depends on the Problem of Evil (*huic aliud maius adiungitur*), a problem even greater than the Problem of Evil, the Problem of Desert (4.1.4):

> But the [Problem of Evil] leads on to an even greater problem, [namely the Problem of Desert]: While wickedness reigns and prospers, virtue not only goes unrewarded but is enslaved and trodden down by criminals, made to pay the penalties in place of the wrongdoers.

Since there is an analytical distinction between the Problem of Evil and the Problem of Desert, and since Boethius is careful to distinguish them and give greater importance (or at least have the Prisoner give greater importance) to the Problem of Desert, we are entitled to conclude that the

[7] This confusion has led commentators to identify the philosophical problem addressed in the *Consolation of Philosophy*, at least in part, as the Problem of Evil; so John Magee in "The Good and Morality: *Consolatio* 2–4," in J. Marenbon (ed.), *Companion*: "The second [task], which is made to appear as a kind of afterthought and fits within the confines of Book 4, is... to explain how evil can exist in a world that is universally governed by the Good" (184). Joachim Gruber, *Kommentar zu Boethius: De consolatione philosophiae* (Berlin: Walter de Gruyter, 2006 [second edition]), introduces Book 4 by speaking vaguely of "der Frage nach der Theodizee" (315/316) as the question at issue, not recognizing the clear statement of the Problem of Desert in 4.1.4—seeing fit to comment on that passage only that the notion of "reward" is discussed in 4.3.1–8.

[8] There is a brief allusion to the Problem of Evil in 1.4.30 as well.

Problem of Desert is the central philosophical problem of the *Consolation of Philosophy*, not the Problem of Evil.

The modern response to the Problem of Desert is to reject it on the grounds that it poses an unanswerable question. There is no reason to hold that there is or should be a general answer why a variety of people meet with the variety of fortunes they do. Perhaps there is no reason to discover even in individual cases: someone just happened to be in the wrong place at the wrong time, that's all. It might be true that Mary did not deserve to be run over by a drunk driver, but there need not be any reason why she was undeservedly run over—only reasons why she was run over, which is not at all the same thing, and even in combination with reasons why she did not deserve it do not amount to an explanation of why she was undeservedly run over. To be sure, there are cases in which someone clearly deserves or does not deserve what happens: the hard worker whose perseverance pays off in the end, the criminal who profits through his crime. Particular cases may have particular explanations. But blind chance may still be the best "answer" for most cases of fortune.

Whatever the merits of this modern response to the Problem of Desert, Boethius tries to forestall it. He devotes Books 2–3 to establishing the nature of goodness, the existence of a Supreme Good, and, finally, the governance of the world by the Supreme Good. The Problem of Desert, like the Problem of Evil, gets its bite from the background assumption that a benevolent deity providentially rules the world,[9] and Boethius is well aware of the need for this assumption. After the Prisoner presents the Problem of Desert in 4.1.4, describing how people seem not to get what they deserve, he immediately continues (4.1.5):

> No one could possibly be amazed and upset enough that these things should happen under the rulership of a God Who is omniscient, omnipotent, and wills only good things!

"These things" are the wicked prospering while the good suffer. If we do not accept the background theistic assumption, we have no reason to think that the Problem of Desert poses a general problem. Much that happens just happens. But if God is in His Heaven and all is right with the world, then there must be a reason why Mary was undeservedly run over by a drunk driver, a reason why the Prisoner undeservedly faces a grisly

[9] A Principle of Sufficient Reason might guarantee that there is a reason why the distribution of goods and evils is the way it is, but the further assumption of a benevolent deity is required to motivate the only solution acceptable to Boethius, namely that people get what they deserve. (A malevolent deity might arrange things so that people get only what they do not deserve.) The usual philosophical theism will do the trick for Boethius.

execution. Boethius, of course, not only accepts the theistic assumption, he has spent the greater part of Book 3 trying to establish it as a conclusion, to make it more than a mere assumption.

Take stock. The Problem of Desert is the central philosophical problem addressed in the *Consolation of Philosophy*. The Prisoner addresses the problem directly to Lady Philosophy, taking care to distinguish it from the Problem of Evil and to lay out its theistic background. Lady Philosophy declares that the philosophical results attained in Books 2–3 are all the preliminaries required (4.1.8), and that they can now proceed to resolve the problem, sketching how she will do so (4.1.6–9), thereby giving the Prisoner "wings" with which he can "soar aloft" and "return to his native land." Removed from its dramatic context and put as starkly as possible, the Problem of Desert asks why people do not get what they deserve, a problem made acute by the seemingly random distribution of fortune in a theistic universe. So stated, there seems to be a straightforward and well-known answer to it. The fact that Boethius does *not* give the straightforward answer, and indeed barely gives it a passing mention, is one of the most surprising things about the *Consolation of Philosophy*. (As we shall see it is also a point on which some later thinkers found Boethius wanting.) The oddity of his omission will be apparent.

Call the straightforward answer the *Afterlife Solution*. It is founded on the following two claims:[10]

[A1] Everyone deserves to suffer in this life, as a consequence of Original Sin.
[A2] In the Afterlife, rewards and punishments are distributed in accordance with desert.

[10] See for example Augustine, *City of God* 19.4, which says that Christian faith "holds that eternal life is the highest good and eternal death the worst evil, and that we should live rightly in order to obtain the former and avoid the latter"—a passage typical of many. Similar remarks can be found in Athenagoras, Tertullian, and others among the early Church Fathers, though none are as strident as Augustine, who devotes Book 21 of his *City of God* to the eternal damnation and suffering of sinners in Hell, and Book 22 to the eternal happiness of the blessed in Heaven, as their just deserts. (But see the next note.) In addition to these theologians, the Bible itself offers a wealth of direct support for the Afterlife Solution. With regard to [A1], Ps 51:5, for example, says that we all come into the world as sinners: "Behold, I was brought forth in iniquity, and in sin my mother conceived me." With regard to [A2], Jesus says in Mk 9:43–49, for instance, that sinners are cast into the unquenchable hellfire directly as a consequence of their sins, whereas in Lk 16:32 he says that Lazarus was carried by angels as one of the righteous to the bosom of Abraham; Paul writes in 2 Cor 5:10 that "we must all appear before the judgment seat of Christ, that every one may receive what is due him for the things done while in the body, whether good or bad."

Now [A1] is compatible with people getting undeserved rewards, for it holds only that any rewards they are given are *ipso facto* undeserved, not that people (who do not deserve them) cannot be given them. More to the point, [A1] tries to sidestep the Problem of Desert by claiming that we all deserve to suffer; that being so, no sufferer has a legitimate complaint about her suffering (since it is deserved), even if another person, who also deserves to suffer, does not suffer. The Wheel of Fortune can therefore have full sway over this life. The Afterlife is another matter, for [A2] is central to Christianity itself: Heaven and its joys for the devout, Hell and its torments for the sinner. The import of the Afterlife Solution is clear. People do not always get what they deserve in this life, but in the long run—taking the Afterlife into account—people *do* in fact get what they deserve. Eventually, moral conduct has its due reward and immoral conduct its due punishment, thereby vindicating the justness of God's rule. To this basic framework can epicycles be added: our time in this life is a test, some evils are unforgivable and some can be expunged—but the Afterlife Solution encapsulated in [A1]–[A2] includes all that is necessary for an answer to the Problem of Desert, at least in outline.[11] Its application to the Problem of Desert is straightforward, even if the doctrine of Original Sin underlying [A1] is not. What is more, the Afterlife Solution offers a clear and compelling answer to the Problem of Desert. We only need to take the long view and trust in Divine Justice, and everything will be as it ought to be.

Boethius rejects the Afterlife Solution. It is mentioned once by the Prisoner and brusquely dismissed by Lady Philosophy in the sole direct mention of the Afterlife in the *Consolation of Philosophy*, in the following exchange (4.4.22–3):

"Well, I ask you: Do you not reserve any punishments for souls after the death of the body?"

[11] There are complications and subtleties. Augustine seems to deny [A2], since he takes the doctrine of God's grace to entail that rewards and punishments are *not* distributed in ways proportionate to desert, except in the broad sense that all humans deserve the torments of Hell as a consequence of Original Sin, as [A1] maintains; to think that reward and punishment are parceled out according to desert is to subscribe to the Pelagian heresy. This blocks a solution to the Problem of Desert, since God's distribution of postmortem fortunes is (literally) gratuitous—which replicates in the Afterlife the very problem the Afterlife Solution was introduced to resolve. Yet as mentioned in the preceding note, Augustine wholeheartedly endorses the Afterlife Solution. Whether the two are logically consistent is an open question, but there is no question that Augustine thought they were, and no indication that Boethius was aware of the philosophical difficulties for the Problem of Desert lurking inside the Augustine's doctrine of grace.

"Indeed, considerable punishments: some I think will be imposed with penal harshness, and others with merciful cleansing. But it is not part of the plan to examine these matters now."

As with punishments, so with rewards, though here the interlocutors speak only of punishment. But the remarkable feature of this exchange is Lady Philosophy's claim that the Afterlife is not up for discussion in the context of answering the Problem of Desert: *nunc de his disserere consilium non est.* Literally, such issues are *irrelevant* at the present time, or, to remove the point from its dramatic context, Boethius is declaring that the Afterlife is irrelevant to a solution of the Problem of Desert. And indeed, Lady Philosophy immediately returns to address the Problem of Desert in 4.4.24, having dismissed the Afterlife Solution. But a mere dismissal, no matter how brusque, seems hardly enough, especially given that the Afterlife Solution is common enough to occur to anyone.

Boethius has, I think, two reasons to set the Afterlife Solution aside. The first is suggested by the dramatic action of Lady Philosophy's dismissal, namely that matters pertaining to the Afterlife are not relevant to *philosophy.* For Boethius did know about and accept the Afterlife, complete with its rewards and punishments, as his brief summary of Christian dogma, *The Catholic Faith,* makes clear.[12] He may have thought of the Afterlife as an article of faith, not accessible to philosophy. Some confirmation that this may have been his view is provided by the literary context in which Lady Philosophy offers her brusque dismissal. For the passage in which it occurs is otherwise heavily indebted to Plato's *Gorgias* 523A–527A. If we look back at Boethius's source, what follows upon Socrates's exchange with Callicles is an eschatological myth, and the rejection of the Afterlife by Lady Philosophy might be meant to indicate that philosophy has no proper traffic with such myths, being one and all not arrived at through reason.[13] Hence while there is no direct evidence that this was Boethius's view, he may provide a clue through his literary model, which he would expect his readers to catch. Yet even if this is Boethius's view, it cannot be the whole story. If it were, Lady Philosophy should tell the Prisoner either to become a student of theology, or that philosophy has failed him and he should have faith. She does neither of these things, continuing instead to address

[12] See *De fide catholica* 204.234–243, where Boethius calls the doctrine of the Afterlife the "foundation of our religion." The evidence of the *Anecdoton Holderii* disproves the old nineteenth-century hypothesis that Boethius was not a Christian (in part due to his non-acceptance of the Afterlife Solution): see Alain Galonnier, *Boèce: Opuscula sacra I, Capita dogmatica (Traités II, III, IV)* (Leuven: Peeters, 2007), 380–409.

[13] This line of reasoning is given by Magee, "The Good and Morality," 194–5.

the Problem of Desert, precisely as though the Afterlife Solution had been refuted, not merely dismissed or set aside.

Boethius has another reason for not accepting the Afterlife Solution. His second reason is philosophical in nature, but takes some careful reading of his text. When Lady Philosophy states part of her preferred solution to the Problem of Desert early on, sketching her strategy for answering it, she alludes to the Afterlife Solution as follows (4.4.14):[14]

> Nor am I now, [in answering the Problem of Desert], working away at a point that might occur to just anyone, namely that decadent behavior is corrected by retribution and led back to the right way by fear of punishment, being also an example to the rest to avoid what is blameworthy. Instead, I think that there is a *different* way in which the wicked are unhappy when they are not punished, yet no regard at all is given to any form of correction or to setting an example.

Lady Philosophy is clear here that she is not laboring (*molior*) the Afterlife Solution, with its covert appeal to self-interest. It is true that people are motivated by fear of punishment, but that point, which "might occur to just anyone" (note the trace of contempt), is no part of a philosophically adequate solution. There is instead a different way (*alio quodam modo*) to address the Problem of Desert—a philosophical approach that allows us to explain the genuine, if not apparent, unhappiness of the wicked, without any appeal to punishment or its deterrent effects, or analogously reward and its motivational effects. That is to say, Boethius is at pains to set the Afterlife Solution aside in favor of a different strategy, one that resolves the Problem of Desert despite the fact (*tametsi*) that it pays "no regard at all" to the elements of the Afterlife Solution. The point at issue here is subtle. The philosophical *problem* with the Afterlife Solution lies precisely in its appeal to reward and punishment, as well as in its further appeal to their exemplary and deterrent effects. Boethius's objection is not that the Afterlife Solution makes false claims about the Afterlife. It does not. As noted at the start of the preceding paragraph, Boethius (though perhaps not Lady Philosophy) recognizes the existence of the traditional Afterlife with its delights for the good and griefs for the wicked. Nor is Boethius's objection that the motivational and deterrent effects that these goods and griefs have are psychological rather than philosophical grounds. Undoubtedly they are psychological, but motives for behavior can be reasons as well as causes, and there is no sign that Boethius thinks that people are not motivated by

[14] Neque id nunc molior quod cuiuis ueniat in mentem, corrigi ultione prauos mores et ad rectum supplicii terrore deduci, caeteris quoque exemplum esse culpanda fugiendi; sed alio quodam modo infeliciores esse improbos arbitror impunitos, tametsi nulla ratio correctionis, nullus respectus habeatur exempli.

reward and punishment. Rather, Boethius objects to any philosophical appeal to the goods and evils of the Afterlife,[15] such as is made in the Afterlife Solution, as morally irrelevant to our present status, and *ipso facto* rejects the Afterlife Solution—indeed, it is no 'solution' at all in Boethius's eyes, for, as he tells us, the view that goods in the Afterlife somehow cancel or mitigate suffering in this life is mistaken. More precisely, Boethius objects to the notion that there is a moral calculus, some possible 'payment' for undeserved agonies that makes them morally acceptable. The key idea behind the Afterlife Solution is that future deserved goods and evils can somehow morally balance present undeserved evils and goods, that is, that these (present and future) goods and evils are commensurable. Boethius rejects that claim. But since their presentness or futurity makes no difference to their status as goods or evils,[16] as neither does their deservedness or undeservedness, Boethius is in fact rejecting the claim that goods and evils are commensurable *tout court*. Boethius is an 'anti-commensurabilist.'

Unfortunately, Boethius gives no further reasons in the *Consolation of Philosophy* in support of his anti-commensurabilism. Since the balancing of goods and evils underlies not only the Afterlife Solution but also modern consequentialist moral theories, it is especially frustrating that he says no more. We can, however, suggest two lines of argument about why the Afterlife Solution, though mistaken, seems initially appealing. Each supports a version of anti-commensurabilism and could have been what Boethius had in mind. It should be borne in mind, however, that while these two lines of argument are not historically anachronistic, they are speculative.

First, there is a distinction that needs to be drawn between two situations that might otherwise be confused.[17] It ought not to be that you suffer some evil. *A fortiori*, it ought not to be that you suffer some evil and then receive some good. But given that you suffer some evil, it is better that you then receive some good rather than not. The fact that the state of affairs in which you receive some later good is better than the state of affairs in which you

[15] I take the unrestricted claim "*any* philosophical appeal" from the way in which Boethius phrases his rejection: no regard at all (*nulla ratio* and *nullus respectus*) is given to the constituents of the Afterlife Solution.

[16] Boethius's position therefore does not turn in any interesting way on there being an Afterlife; he simply rejects the idea that some goods or evils can counterbalance other goods or evils, whether this life is taken together with the Afterlife or taken instead on its own. Deserved goods in the Afterlife do not counterbalance undeserved evils in this life, and likewise later deserved goods in my life do not counterbalance earlier undeserved evils in my life. Boethius's position is thus of wider philosophical interest than the context in which it was developed might suggest.

[17] See David Lewis, "Semantic Analyses for Dyadic Deontic Logic," in S. Stenlund (ed.), *Logical Theory and Semantic Analysis* (Dordrecht: D. Reidel, 1974), 1–15.

do not might lead you to think that a sufficient good could make that state of affairs as good as, if not better than, the state of affairs in which you do not suffer the evil in the first place. However, the two cases are logically different. The latter only has the value that it has conditionally, namely given that you suffer some harm, whereas in the former you do not suffer harm at all. The evil-plus-sufficient-good state of affairs can only be compared to the absolute case if the good is enough (whatever that may mean) to "cancel" the evil—that is, if we assume that the goods and evils are somehow commensurable. Such an assumption is not forced on us by logic; we are not inconsistent if we hold the three claims enunciated at the beginning. They do not provide grounds for accepting commensurability. We can maintain that one ought not to suffer an evil, and admit that given that one suffers evil it is better to then receive good rather than not, without accepting the commensurability of the goods and evils involved, or thinking that the latter situation might somehow be the same as the initial situation. The reason for rejecting commensurability here is the same as that suggested in Boethius's anti-commensurabilism. If someone suffers an undeserved evil (say), and suffering an undeserved evil is morally objectionable, then any morally objectionable features there are to suffering undeserved evil, whatever they may be, are not changed by receiving goods, even deserved goods.

Second, the persistent attraction of the Afterlife Solution may come from confusing it with the situation in which someone contracts to suffer some otherwise undeserved evil for a later good. Here the consent involved in the contractual agreement does cancel the undeservedness of the evil suffered. (We do not consent to the travails of this life for the sake of rewards in the Afterlife, but put that aside.) It might be thought that consent must therefore track the commensurability of the goods and evils involved. Hence the goods and evils must be commensurable in themselves. But this is not so. It is one thing for me to break your leg and then pay your medical bills with something extra for your inconvenience; it is quite another thing for us to agree beforehand that if I pay your medical bills with something extra for your inconvenience I am permitted to break your leg. In the latter case there is no wrongdoing, and hence you suffer no evil (certainly no undeserved evil); your consent gives me permission to break your leg, as indeed it would even if you offered me nothing in return for doing so. But the former case is quite different. It is wrong for me to break your leg, and *a fortiori* wrong for me to break your leg and then pay your medical bills with something extra for your inconvenience; paying your medical bills and a little extra does not make it any less wrong for me to break your leg in the first place, which is an undeserved evil you suffer. This is true even if you would have agreed to the bargain had it been offered to you in advance. The fact that you would have agreed to have your leg broken had you been given the offer (no matter what the offer might have involved) does not cancel the wrongdoing in my breaking your leg without first obtaining your consent. Thus consent does not track commensurability but instead bestows permission, making what is otherwise morally unacceptable acceptable.

The fundamental point in both lines of argument is that suffering undeserved evil cannot be made right through some form of compensation. The later bestowal of goods does not take away the fact that suffering an undeserved evil is wrong; equally, the later bestowal of evils does not take away the fact that enjoying undeserved goods is wrong. It may be a better state of affairs all around when those who suffer undeserved evils receive goods and those who enjoy undeserved goods suffer evils, but this does not affect the moral wrongness of suffering undeserved evils or enjoying undeserved goods. This is why Boethius rejects the Afterlife solution. Lady Philosophy wants a solution in which "no thought is given" to future goods or evils because they are simply irrelevant to the moral wrongness that makes the Problem of Desert a pressing philosophical problem in the first place.[18] Boethius sets himself the much harder task of solving the Problem of Desert while foregoing any appeal to pie-in-the-sky-when-you-die.

Instead of the Afterlife Solution, Boethius adopts what we can call the *Socratic Solution* to the Problem of Desert, so-called because he derives it from the positions taken by Socrates in Plato's *Gorgias*.[19] In a nutshell, the Socratic Solution defends the following thesis:

[S] Each person gets exactly what he or she deserves.

[18] At least one of Boethius's scholastic commentators seems to have gotten his point exactly. Around 1380, Pierre d'Ailly raises a doubt in Q. 1 art. 6: "Supposing that there were no postmortem happiness or reward, should human happiness then be placed in goods that are subject to fortune or in virtuous actions?" (Chappuis 162*). He argues that while it "seems to many" that without reward or punishment in the Afterlife human happiness would consist in sensuous pleasures, virtue, as the proper exercise of human capacities, would still constitute human happiness (163*). The Afterlife is irrelevant.

[19] Boethius likely knew the *Gorgias* directly, but he also knew the tradition of Neoplatonic commentary on the *Gorgias*, which undoubtedly influenced his reading. The positions he discusses are likely Socratic and not Platonic in origin, though all attributions to Socrates are tenuous; we can at least say that the positions taken by Socrates in the *Gorgias* resemble those found in the Speech of the Laws in the *Crito*. His views doubtless are indebted to Stoic ethics (and its understanding of Socrates) as well, both in its own right and as absorbed by the Neoplatonic tradition. Gruber, *Kommentar*, is the starting-point for scholarly study of these philosophical influences on the *Consolation of Philosophy*.

Since no one meets with an undeserved fortune, there is no problem with the distribution of desert; everyone gets what he or she deserves, contrary to appearances, and hence no Problem of Desert to solve—the rug has been pulled out from beneath it. Now the Socratic Solution might seem to be no more than a philosophical sleight-of-hand, a cheap trick to make the problems we have been concerned with vanish. It is not. A solution to the Problem of Desert will show us either why people do not get what they deserve, or why they do. Given Boethius's acceptance of Divine Providence, he needs to explain how it is people do all get what they deserve. Both the Afterlife Solution and the Socratic Solution deny that there is any traction to the Problem of Desert, in exactly the same manner. The Afterlife Solution proposes that each person gets what he or she deserves, though only in the long run. The Socratic Solution proposes that each person gets what he or she deserves, though appearances are deceptive. In each case we deny any mismatch between people's deserts and their fortunes. Part of the immediate appeal of the Afterlife Solution is that it gives full recognition to undeserved fortune in this life, which it buys at the price of trading away present fortune for future just deserts. As we have seen, Boethius rejects any such trade-off as a philosophical confusion. The price of the Socratic Solution, of course, is that there seem to be genuine instances in this life of undeserved fortune, which Boethius must now show are one and all merely apparent.

The bulk of Book 4 of the *Consolation of Philosophy* is devoted to arguing for the Socratic Solution in a variety of ways. Boethius takes [S] to follow from four subordinate theses:

[S1] The good are powerful (and hence able to attain their ends), whereas the wicked are powerless (and hence unable to attain their ends).

Lady Philosophy offers four arguments for [S1] in 4.2.

[S2] Virtue is its own reward, and vice is its own punishment.

As an anti-commensurabilist, Boethius rejects the trade-off among goods and evils characteristic of consequentialist moral theories. By contrast, he emphasizes the intrinsic value of goodness. The virtuous have genuine happiness through their possession of the Supreme Good, and the vicious fail to get what they want and are beset by debilities, not strictly in control of themselves. These are constitutive features of virtue and vice, which are therefore not merely instrumental to these results but analytically tied to them. Now since the good deserve to be happy and the wicked deserve to be unhappy, we are close to being able to derive [S]. Boethius does so by endorsing two further 'Socratic' theses (which are especially clear in 4.4):

[S3] The only benefit or harm that matters is moral improvement or worsening.
[S4] Only you can morally improve or worsen yourself.

In combination with [S2], these two theses allow us to conclude that each person gets what he or she deserves (4.3). The good get genuine happiness, and their condition cannot be worsened by the wicked; the wicked fail to get what they really want, and are 'punished' by worldly success—which allows them to persist in their genuine unhappiness, victims of their own ignorance, self-delusions, and desires. All that matters is one's moral condition, after all, and on the moral scales—not the scale of worldly success—the virtuous win and the wicked lose. Hence each person gets exactly what he or she deserves, as the Socratic Solution maintains, and the Problem of Desert has been resolved.

Rather than follow Boethius through the twists and turns of his arguments for [S1]–[S4], we can take a shortcut to understand why he opts for the Socratic Solution, based on the considerations discussed in fleshing out his rejection of the Afterlife Solution. If there is no commensurability among goods and evils, then no amount of goods or evils can affect the wrongful moral status of suffering an undeserved evil or enjoying an undeserved good. But if nothing can affect their moral status, their wrongfulness cannot be ameliorated. Yet even a single instance of undeserved fortune is enough to pose the Problem of Desert. Hence there cannot be even a single instance of such wrongfulness. But since people clearly have the fortunes they have, their fortunes must in every case be deserved rather than undeserved—which is what the Socratic Solution maintains.

To understand why Boethius opts for the Socratic Solution is not to make it plausible, to be sure, and much of what Boethius says in Book 4 tries to put the best face on it. His personal situation gives him credibility; to maintain that imprisonment and imminent execution is exactly what he deserves—here the character and the author merge—earns the *Consolation of Philosophy* a hearing it would not otherwise merit. Yet philosophers and theologians have not generally followed Boethius in adopting the Socratic Solution. This is not because they misunderstood him. Quite the contrary; the Latin commentary tradition on the *Consolation of Philosophy* in the Middle Ages seems to have understood Boethius very well, better than the modern tradition. Witness one of the most popular mediæval commentators, the Dominican friar Nicholas Trevet (1265–1334), who gives a concise and lucid summary of the whole work in his Preface (8–9):[20]

[20] Tractat enim in opere isto de consolatione miseri qui propter amissionem temporalium deicitur in merorem putando per hoc quod non equa meritis praemia reddantur.

In this work, Boethius deals with the consolation of someone miserable who, depressed over the loss of temporal goods, is thrown into grief, thinking on this account that he was not given proper reward for his deserts. Boethius shows that the contrary view holds, proving that in accordance with infallible divine judgment genuine rewards are given to the good and penalties due to the wicked, which anyone who is suffering persecution can be consoled by when he calls up its memory.

Boethius's subject, Trevet correctly declares, is the Problem of Desert: the Prisoner is miserable because he believes that he does not deserve his fortune; Boethius proves that the contrary view is correct, namely that people do get exactly what they deserve—the Socratic Solution—and remembering that people get exactly what they deserve provides consolation to those suffering adverse fortune. Nicholas does not seem upset by Boethius's rejection of the Afterlife Solution; if anything, he gives the impression that Boethius quite rightly rejects it. This impression is borne out even when we descend to details, though of course there are many differences among the commentators. William of Conches (1080–*ca.*1150), for instance, does not blink at Lady Philosophy's brusque dismissal of the Afterlife Solution at 4.4.22; the only remark he offers is minimal (240.48–51): "Since Lady Philosophy had said that the penalty for evils is ended with death, so that someone with a depraved mind not think that there will be no punishments after death, Boethius asks Lady Philosophy whether that is the case." Nicholas Trevet repeats William's comment in his discussion of 4.4.22, and cleverly proposes that Lady Philosophy is worried about a potential difficulty (576): since it has been argued that the wicked are happier if punished than not, would not punishment in the Afterlife make sinners happier than they are in this life, contrary to intent? Trevet's answer, that the sinners in Hell are worse off because they recognize their errors but are unable to redeem themselves, is ingenious if not textual. Likewise, where William offers no comment at all on the suggestion in 4.4.14 that the Afterlife is irrelevant to the Problem of Desert, Trevet, in contrast, declares that Lady Philosophy meant that there is *another*, not a "different," way in which people get what they deserve: in addition to whatever rewards and punishments the Afterlife may hold, people also get what they deserve in this life.[21] Despite individual

Contrarium cuius manifestat Boethius ostendo secundum iudicium diuinum infallibile uera praemia bonis malisque poenas debitas reseruari, quod quicumque persecutionem patiens cum ad memoriam reduxerit consolari poterit.

[21] Trevet on 4.4.14 (573): Sed praeter istas [causas] est tertia de qua subdit SED ALIO QUODAM MODO, scilicet a praedictis ARBITROR INFELICIORES ESSE IMPROBOS IMPUNITOS TAMETSI, id est quamuis, NULLA RATIO CORRECTIONIS NULLUS RESPECTUS EXEMPLI

differences, the commentators find Boethius's Socratic Solution to be acceptable and to provide the consolation sought by the Prisoner in his distress. In some respects, this should not be a surprise. The mediæval commentator took his job to be explaining the text, not differing with it. Even someone such as Pierre d'Ailly, whose *quaestiones* are far removed from low-level glossing or *explication du texte*, is clearly in sympathy with Boethius. If we went no further than the commentary tradition, we might think that mediæval readers, unlike modern ones, found Boethius's solution to the Problem of Desert unproblematic, and indeed took consolation in it.

Not all readers of Boethius wrote commentaries, though. Freed from the conventions that held the commentator to explain his text systematically, other mediæval authors could voice their disagreement with Boethius and the Socratic Solution. Consider the case of Jean Gerson (1363–1429), Chancellor of the University of Paris and an influential clergyman. At one point, after the Council of Constance, he was exiled from France by the Duke of Burgundy; in his humiliation he wrote his own *Consolation of Theology*, a prosimetric work in four books for which he was given the honorific title of *Doctor consolatorius*. His work is a dialogue between Volucer and Monicus, and right at the beginning Gerson invokes Boethius and spells out his dissatisfaction with him (1.2 188):

MONICUS: You have rightly praised theology, Volucer, but in getting consolation against the vicissitudes of chance, against the vanity of worldly happiness, why is the dialogue of Boethius and Lady Philosophy not enough? It is elegantly written, lucid, and distinguished, maintaining the most profound and true views.

VOLUCER: Do not be surprised, Monicus, if theology is put before philosophy. For as grace is more excellent than nature, as the mistress to her handmaid, as the teacher to the student, as eternity to time, as understanding to mere calculation, as things which are not seen to things which are seen, so too theology is more excellent than philosophy... Let us commence with theology beginning with the Word from the Supreme Being, with which Lady Philosophy ended her consolation in Boethius.

The next-to-last sentence in the *Consolation of Philosophy* is an exhortation (5.6.47): "Pour out your humble prayers to Heaven!" Philosophy, it appears, can only offer cold comfort; theology is needed to provide the ultimate solace from the ultimate source, God Himself—a loving and caring God, not "the God of the philosophers." As Volucer goes on to

HABEATUR. Deinde cum dicit et quis, inquam, prosequitur Philosophia istum modum tertium alium a praedictis. Et primo quaerit Boethius quis sit iste modus...

say, "theology begins its consolation with a journey from the point at which philosophy gives out" (1.2 188). Nor can philosophy reach all the way to God's judgments (190). In the end, Volucer offers his own prayer, meant to parallel the closing exhortation of Lady Philosophy (4.5 244):

> We raise our eyes to Heaven and declare: God is the Father of mercies and of all consolation, in Whose mercy we must hope, conforming ourselves to His will, from Whom comes the virtue of patience and in Whom is serenity of conscience.

Consolation is a divine gift; philosophy cannot provide it, because God's loving mercies are beyond the province of mere reason.

Gerson's view that consolation is properly a matter of religious belief rather than reasoned argumentation seems to have won out by the end of the Middle Ages. Sir Thomas More (1478–1535), like Boethius, was a devout Catholic who was imprisoned under sentence of death by a ruler who was also a Christian but of a different persuasion. At the beginning of his 1534 work *Dialoge of Comfort Agaynst Trybulacion* 1.1, written in direct emulation of Boethius during his imprisonment while awaiting his eventual execution, More writes (10.15–24):

> Howbeit in very dede, for any thyng that euer I red in [the old morall philosophers], I neuer could yet fynd, that euer these naturall resons, were able to give sufficient comfort of them selfe for they neuer strech so ferre, but that they leve vntouchid for lak of necessarye knolege, that speciall poynt, which is not onely the chief comfort of all but without which also, all other comfortes are nothyng: that is to wit the referrying the fynall end of their comfort unto God, & to repute & take for the speciall cause of comfort, that by the pacient suffraunce of their tribulacion, they shall attayne His favour & for their payne receve reward at His hand in Heven.

According to More, consolation comes from God alone, since by suffering patiently people hope to receive rewards after death. As with Gerson, philosophy does not stretch so far as to provide consolation, since philosophers *qua* philosophers do not have access to this all-important truth. Thus we return to the Afterlife Solution to the Problem of Desert.

But should we? I'd like to close with a plea for Boethius's Socratic Solution, on the basis of some modern considerations. What matters, more than anything else, is what matters morally. Hence the only sense of harm that (morally) matters is 'moral harm,' that is, morally worsening or bettering someone. Mere physical pain, imprisonment, and the like do not matter, because they do not matter morally—they are outside one's control, and being a victim of circumstance is no moral failing. That, I take it, is the point of the Socratic Solution. Put this way, I find it very plausible. Of course I would rather not be imprisoned, tortured, executed; but those things are not up to me, and therefore are not moral matters, which means they do not really matter at all. We get what we morally deserve, because what we morally deserve is entirely up to us. Perhaps this is cold comfort, not the "consolation" Boethius hoped to provide. His brand of cognitive therapy seems no match for the hot emotions one feels in being victimized, even while recognizing, intellectually, that it does not matter, since it does not matter morally. Yet this is odd. Were not people just as prone to anger, to resentment, to feelings of revenge in Antiquity and the Middle Ages? Perhaps, in the end, it is a modern failing—not a mediæval one.

The University of Toronto

BIBLIOGRAPHY

Boethius, Anicius Manlius Severinus. *Boethius: De consolatione philosophiae, opuscula theologica*, ed. C. Moreschini (Munich: K. G. Saur, 2000).

Chadwick, Henry. *Boethius: The Consolations of Music, Logic, Theology, and Philosophy* (Cambridge: Cambridge University Press, 1981).

Galonnier, Alain. *Boèce: Opuscula sacra I, Capita dogmatica* (Traités II, III, IV) (Leuven: Peeters, 2007).

Gruber, Joachim. *Kommentar zu Boethius: De consolatione philosophiae*, 2nd edn. (Berlin: Walter de Gruyter, 2006).

Jean Gerson. *De consolatione theologiae*, in *Jean Gerson: Oeuvres complètes 9: L'oeuvre doctrinale, op. 449* (Paris: Desclée et Cie, 1973), 185–245.

King, Peter. "Boethius: The First of the Scholastics," *Carmina philosophiae* 16 (2007), 23–50.

Lewis, David. "Semantic Analyses for Dyadic Deontic Logic," in S. Stenlund (ed.), *Logical Theory and Semantic Analysis* (Dordrecht: D. Reidel, 1974), 1–15.

Magee, John. "The Good and Morality: *Consolatio* 24," in J. Marenbon (ed.), *The Cambridge Companion to Boethius* (Cambridge: Cambridge University Press, 2009), 181–206.

Marenbon, John (ed.). *The Cambridge Companion to Boethius* (Cambridge: Cambridge University Press, 2009).

More, Thomas. *A Dialoge of Comfort Agaynst Trybulacion* [1534], in L. Martz and F. Manley (eds.), *The Complete Works of St. Thomas More*, vol. 12 (New Haven: Yale University Press, 1976).

Nicholas Trevet. *Expositio super Boethio De consolatione*, part. ed. Edmund Silk (unpublished partial draft manuscript, among the editor's papers held at Yale University, n.d.).

Pierre d'Ailly [Petrus de Aliaco]. *Le traité de Pierre d'Ailly sur la consolation de Boèce, Qu. 1*, ed. Marguerite Chappuis, Bochumer Studien zur Philosophie 20 (Amsterdam: B. R. Grüner, 1993).

Relihan, Joel. *The Prisoner's Philosophy: Life and Death in Boethius's "Consolation"* (Notre Dame: University of Notre Dame Press, 2007).

Tränkle, Hermann. "Ist die *Philosophie Consolatio* des Boethius zum vorgesehened Abschluss gelangt?" *Vigiliae christianae* 31 (1977), 148–56.

William of Conches. *Guillelmi de Conchis Glosae super Boetium*, ed. L. Nauta, *Corpus christianorum continuatio mediaevalis* 158 (Turnhout: Brepols, 1999).

Genuine Agency, Somehow Shared? The Holy Spirit and Other Gifts

Marilyn McCord Adams

1. PRESENTING PROBLEMS

Medieval philosophical theology is firm: the world as we know it results from the exercise of genuine agency, both Divine and human. Genuine Divine agency creates and sustains, is the source of the being and the well-being of everything else. But creatures also exercise genuine agency. The reason is that creatures come in Aristotelian natural kinds. Aristotle argued against Plato that the nature of a substance individual X had to exist *in* X and not separately from X (the way the Platonic form was supposed to exist separately from Socrates). Every substance nature includes and/or gives rise to formal functional principles that explain the individual substance's functions. Thus, an action A belongs to a subject X, only if a formal functional principle of A-ing exists in X.

As simple, the Divine essence is identical with Its formal functional principles of thinking and willing. Creatable natures either include formal functional principles in their substantial form, or emanate necessary accidents that are formal functional principles to act and be acted upon in certain ways. However great created functional powers may be, they can do nothing without Divine concurrence. In general concurrence, God is the first cause who acts by understanding and willing, while the creature (say fire) is a secondary cause that acts through its own form (through the formal active principle included in or necessarily consequent upon its nature) together with God to produce the effect.

For present purposes, three points are important. First, medieval Aristotelians did not view this as a competitive situation. In general concurrence, genuine Divine agency does not compete with genuine created agency. Rather, they insisted, genuine Divine agency and genuine created agency play different roles and collaborate to produce the effect.[1] Second, God creates, sustains, and concurs with any created agent whatever—cows and stones as much as humans and angels,[2] Lucifer as much as Gabriel, Judas as much as Peter and Paul.[3] Nothing other than God could be or do anything apart from genuine Divine agency. Third, Augustinian Trinitarian theology insisted that—whatever may be true within the Godhead—Divine persons express "one action, one will *ad extra*." Because all three persons of the Trinity share numerically the same Divine essence, and the essential formal functional principles of understanding and willing are identical with the Divine essence, they share numerically the same thoughts and numerically the same volitions regarding creatures. The acts of creating, sustaining, and concurring belong no more to one Divine person than to another.

By contrast, in his controversy with Pelagius, Augustine did put genuine Divine agency and genuine human agency into competition. Pelagius evidently restricted God's role in salvation to the grace of creating human beings with free will and giving the law to reveal Divine commands. Human beings were free to obey and win heaven or disobey and go to hell. Augustine countered that God should get more credit. Augustine's strategy was to enlarge the role of genuine Divine agency by shrinking the role of genuine created agency. Human nature—he contended—had been damaged by the fall, so that we suffer under ignorance (of Divine norms) and difficulty (in willing what we believe to be right). At first he affirmed, then later denied that it was within our power to have faith that believes and asks God's help. In the middle of his controversy with Pelagius, Augustine declared that legal conformity to Divine commands is of no value unless it proceeds from a whole-hearted love of God—something not within our power to produce. Towards the end of the debate, Augustine insisted that our wills are more in God's power than in our own. Augustine's more extreme statements and subsequent—perhaps even more radical—interpretations, called into question whether God's plan of salvation left any room for genuine merely human agency at all. Call this the "Genuine Agency Problem."

Medievals inherited this problem frame. Their goal was a solution that made room for both genuine Divine and genuine human agency. They

[1] Their confident assessment was problematized in the modern classical period by Malebranche. For a contemporary evaluation, see Alfred J. Freddoso, in his "Medieval Aristotelianism and the Case against Secondary Causation in Nature," in T. V. Morris (ed.), *Divine and Human Action: Essays in the Metaphysics of Theism* (Ithaca: Cornell University Press, 1988), 74–118.

[2] Peter Lombard, *Sententiae* I, d.17, c.5, sec. 4, 147.

[3] Peter Lombard, *Sententiae* I, d.17, c.5, sec. 4, 147.

fixed on a promising premise: if we are to be worthy of Divine acceptance and able to perform meritorious acts, God must make us holy. They thought of two ways that God might do this: viz., through what God does as an efficient cause, and/or through a special kind of presence by which God indwells the elect and so turns them into sacred space.

The Bible speaks of both. On the one hand, the elect enjoy a distinctive participation in Divine action: "God is at work in you, both to will and to work for his good pleasure" (Philippians 2:13). Again, St. Paul declares, "I worked . . . though it was not I, but the grace of God which is with me" (I Corinthians 15:10); or, more comprehensively, "it is no longer I who live, but Christ who lives in me" (Galatians 2:20). On the other hand, the Paraclete, indeed the whole Trinity will indwell believers in Jesus (John 14:23–24) with the result that they become God's temples (I Cor 3:16–17; 6:19); Christ indwells believers' hearts by faith (Ephesians 3:17). The Bible also talks of "missions" and "gifts": the Father will send the Counselor (John 16:7; cf. Ephesians 1:17); and "The love of God has been poured into our hearts by the Holy Spirit Who has been given to us" (Romans 5:5).

In itself, indwelling seemed not to be an efficient-causal connection and so looked like a way for God to make humans holy without compromising their genuine agency. But biblical language raised two further problems. First, biblical indwelling must be something different from Divine omnipresence,[4] because Godhead is metaphysically present to each and every creature—non-rational as well as rational, reprobate as well as predestinate—while God indwells only rational creatures and only some of them at that! How can selective indwelling be metaphysically possible for an omnipresent, necessarily concurrent Creator and Sustainer? What can this relation be? Call this the "Special Connection Problem."

Second, not only do Bible verses imply that God is specially connected to some creatures and not others; they seem to divide the Trinity by implying that one Divine person indwells as opposed to the others: *Christ* indwells believers' hearts by faith; *the Holy Spirit* has been given to us. How is it metaphysically possible for one Divine person to be involved in created being and doing when the other Divine persons are not? Call this the "Divided Trinity Problem."

Peter Lombard's *Sentences* launch thirteenth- and fourteenth-century treatments of these problems. His answer to the Special Connection Problem made the Divided Trinity and Genuine Agency Problems seem

[4] Peter Lombard, *Sententiae* I, d.17, c. 5, sec. 4, 147. See Aquinas, *Summa theologica* I, q.8, a.2, c; q.8, a.3, c.; q.8, a.4, c.

more acute. Bonaventure, Aquinas, and Scotus are most focused on the Genuine Agency Problem and use their solutions to it as a basis for dealing with the other two.

2. LOMBARD'S PROBLEM: THE GIFT OF THE HOLY SPIRIT?

a. Construing the authorities

In his *Sentences*, Peter Lombard squarely confronts Romans 5:5—"the love of God has been poured into our hearts through the Holy Spirit that has been given to us"—and raises the question, "is this gift the Holy Spirit Itself or some other" merely created "gift that the Holy Spirit gives?" Eminent authorities seem to disagree: Ambrose and Augustine say "the Holy Spirit Itself," while Bede insists, not the Holy Spirit Itself, but a gift of grace.[5] In Book I, distinction 17, Lombard sides with Ambrose and Augustine and forwards two theses:

[T1] the Holy Spirit is the love of the Father and the Son by which they love one another and us;

[T2] "the Holy Spirit is [a] the love or charity by which we love God and neighbor"—[b] "the charity... that makes us love God and neighbor."[6]

Lombard insists, the Holy Spirit is not given to us so that we might *exist*, but so that we might be *holy*.[7] Through that gift, not only the Holy Spirit but the whole Trinity indwells us.[8]

In Lombard's circle, [T1] was uncontroversial, but [T2] was startling and provocative. Lombard declares, the Holy Spirit is *no mere cause* of that charity by which we love God and neighbor. The Holy Spirit *is* the charity by which we love God and neighbor.[9] Lombard is emphatic: the charity by which the Father and the Son love each other, and the charity by which we love God and neighbor are not two charities or two loves, but one![10]

5 Peter Lombard, *Sententiae* I, d.14, c.2, secs. 1 & 4, 128.
6 Peter Lombard, *Sententiae* I, d.17, c.1, sec. 2, 142, 145–6.
7 Peter Lombard, *Sententiae* I, d.18, c.4, sec. 3, 157.
8 Peter Lombard, *Sententiae* I, d.17, c.4, sec. 2, 145–6.
9 Peter Lombard, *Sententiae* I, d.17, c.3, 144.
10 Peter Lombard, *Sententiae* I, d.17, c.6, sec. 4, 149–50.

b. No genuine agency?

Immediately, the Genuine Agency Problem raises its head. The Father and the Son are not supposed to be the only lovers in this picture. We, too, are supposed to be lovers of God and neighbor. If *we* act to love God and neighbor, then there must be some motion or affection in our own souls by which we are moved and affected to love God. But the Holy Spirit is not a motion or action in our soul. To say so would be to confuse the Creator with the creature![11] Again, the ignorance and difficulty into which we have fallen require repair in the form of faith, hope, and charity. These are in us through the Holy Spirit, as gifts of the Holy Spirit. But the Holy Spirit is not said to be the faith by which we believe or the hope by which we hope. So why suppose that the Holy Spirit is the charity by which we love?[12]

Lombard's reply acknowledges that the *acts* of believing, hoping, and loving are *in* the soul as in a receiving subject. (This is a minimum condition of genuine human agency.) Nevertheless, it is the Holy Spirit Who works acts of believing, hoping, and loving in the soul. But the Holy Spirit does so in different ways. Whereas the Holy Spirit produces acts of faith and hope in us by means of virtues of faith and hope infused into us, the Holy Spirit works acts of love by Itself alone and not by means of any virtue—infused or otherwise—in us.[13] The Holy Spirit is *not the act* by which we love God and neighbor. But whereas habits in the soul make the soul's actions more prompt, delightful, and expeditious, Lombard wants to say that—when it comes to producing acts in us of loving God and neighbor—the charity that the Holy Spirit *is* takes the place of any infused habit that the objectors suppose the soul to have and so—according to (T2b)—"makes us love God and neighbor."

c. Divided Trinity, special connections

If the Holy Spirit Itself is the gift, what does it mean to say that a Divine person is *given?* Juggling scriptural proof-texts to distinguish being sent from being given, Lombard explains that the Holy Spirit is *eternally* given insofar as it proceeds from the Father and the Son: the Holy Spirit is the love they give to each other. But the *temporal* donation of the Holy Spirit to creatures is something wrought by the whole Trinity. Thus, the Holy Spirit can be said to give Itself to us, just as much as the Father and the Son give

[11] Peter Lombard, *Sententiae* I, d.17, c.6, sec. 6, 150–1.
[12] Peter Lombard, *Sententiae* I, d.17, c.6, sec. 5, 150; c.8, 151.
[13] Peter Lombard, *Sententiae* I, d.17, cc.8–9, 151–2.

the Holy Spirit to us (one action, one will *ad extra*).[14] Likewise, it is necessary to distinguish eternal from temporal missions. The Son and the Holy Spirit are eternally sent, insofar as each proceeds from a Divine person: the Son is begotten by the Father, while the Holy Spirit proceeds from the Father and the Son. Within the Godhead, only two—the Father and the Son—are eternal senders, and only two—the Son and the Holy Spirit—are eternally sent.

Lombard stipulates, only those Divine persons can be said to be temporally sent that are also eternally sent. Each of the Son and the Holy Spirit is temporally sent into creatures, both visibly and invisibly. The Son is sent visibly in the Incarnation when He assumes a human nature, but invisibly "when He transfers Himself into the souls of the pious in such a way as to be perceived or known by them."[15] The Holy Spirit is sent invisibly when It is the charity by which we love God and neighbor and when It illumines the minds of the faithful.[16] The Holy Spirit is sent visibly when attention is called to Its invisible mission by a visible sign such as the descending dove at Jesus' baptism or the tongues of flame at Pentecost.[17] Lombard underscores a difference between the visible mission of the Son and that of the Holy Spirit: viz., the Son is united with a human nature in hypostatic union and so becomes human, but the Holy Spirit is not united with the dove or dove-appearance in such a way as to become a dove or dove-appearance. Neither is the Son hypostatically united with the saints to whom He is invisibly sent the way the Word is made flesh in Mary's womb and becomes human.[18]

3. ADDITIONAL HYPOSTATIC UNIONS?

a. Attempted clarifications

Lombard's treatment is bold and suggestive, but it is not metaphysically precise. In his *Commentary on the Sentences*, Bonaventure mentions an "ancient" interpretation that understands Lombard to be positing a relation of hypostatic union between the Holy Spirit and the human wills of the elect who receive this gift. Just as the whole Trinity brings it about that the Son alone is united to the flesh formed in Mary's womb, so the whole Trinity brings it about that the Holy Spirit alone is united to the created

[14] Peter Lombard, *Sententiae* I, d.15, c.1, secs. 2–4, 131–2.
[15] Peter Lombard, *Sententiae* I, d.15, c.7, 135–6; d.16, c.1, sec. 1, 138.
[16] Peter Lombard, *Sententiae* I, d.16, c.1, sec. 1, 138.
[17] Peter Lombard, *Sententiae* I, d.16, c.1, secs. 1–2, 138.
[18] Peter Lombard, *Sententiae* I, d.16, c.1, secs. 2–5, 138–40.

will. To be sure, there are disanalogies. Theological consensus has it that God the Son has assumed one and only one human nature: the Incarnation of the Son is *unique*. But—on this hypothesis—the Holy Spirit would be hypostatically united to many created wills at once, indeed to the wills of all who at any given time are acceptable to God. Moreover, theological consensus had it that once God the Son assumes His human nature, He will never lay it aside: the Incarnation of the Word is *permanent*. Natures do not change with respect to their essential constitution: what it is to be human is eternally the same. By contrast, created will-power is essentially "convertible." It would be unseemly for the Holy Spirit to remain hypostatically united to a created will if that created will turned against God. So Its hypostatic union to created wills would be temporary and episodic.[19]

Hypostatic union would seem to solve the Special Connection and Divided Trinity Problems: hypostatic union is the special connection not shared by all three persons, but all three Divine persons act together to send one Divine person into personal union with a creature. Hypostatic union seems to promise a way out of the Genuine Agency Problem as well. For X to be a genuine *agent*-subject with respect to A-ing, it is not enough for X to be the receiving subject of A-ing. In addition, the formal principle of A-ing has to exist in and be operative in X when X becomes the receiving-subject of A-ing. (T2b) seems problematic because it seems to imply that our souls are merely receiving subjects of acts of loving God and neighbor, because the charity which is their formal functional principle (the active principle that makes those acts of love exist in us) exists in something else—viz., the Holy Spirit Itself! But hypostatic union means that the person in whom the two natures are united acts (and/or suffers) through formal functional principles in both of its natures. God the Son acts through His Divine nature to sustain and govern the cosmos and through His human nature to take a walk, to touch blind men and bleeding women, to break bread and eat fish. Because both natures are *His* natures, statements such as 'This man created the heavens and the earth' and 'God suffered and died on the cross' turn out true. Likewise, if the Holy Spirit were to assume the created will, the Holy Spirit would be acting through Its own created will-power to produce acts of loving God and neighbor. The Holy Spirit would be the person that produces the act, but—on the hypostatic-union hypothesis—that would not mean that the created will was not genuinely active, because the Holy Spirit would be understood to produce those acts by exercising Its own created will-power.

[19] Bonaventure, *Sent.* I, d.17, p. 1, a. u, q. 1; Quaracchi I.294.

b. Queries and quandaries

This appeal to hypostatic union is ingenious, resourceful, and shows an instinct for theoretical economy. Hypostatic union is an explanatory posit already added to the array of available metaphysical connections to explain the Incarnation of God the Son. Why not use it again to explain the special connection between the Holy Spirit and those to whom It has been sent as a gift? Why not explain the Holy Spirit's indwelling St. Paul's heart in terms of the Holy Spirit's becoming hypostatically united to St. Paul's will?

Certainly, there are some issues to be thought through. First, there is a further striking disanalogy. In the Incarnation, God the Son assumes the *whole* human nature, complete with body and soul, with all of its active and passive causal powers. But the present hypostatic-union hypothesis has the Holy Spirit assuming, not the whole human nature, but the human will, one of the soul's powers. Medievals disagreed about the relation between the intellectual soul and its essential powers. Some (e.g., Aquinas) argued that the soul's essential powers were necessary accidents that emanated from the substantial form,[20] while others (e.g., Scotus[21] and Ockham[22]) maintained that intellect and will were really the same as the intellectual soul itself. Either way, for the Holy Spirit to assume a human will, would be for It to assume a *part* of a human nature.

Perhaps adherents of the hypostatic-union hypothesis would not have found this disanalogy defeating. After all, they were already committed to the notion that when Jesus died, His human body and soul ceased to be united to each other, but each and both remained separately united to God the Son.[23] In the interval between death and resurrection, God the Son was separately united to parts of a human nature. Why would it be worse to say that the Holy Spirit assumes only the human will (whether a necessary accident or the intellectual soul) in the first place?

There is a second difficulty. The Genuine Agency Problem is not focused on whether the Holy Spirit can cause or even be the remote agent-subject of a human act of will, but on whether and how that act of love can belong to the human being (e.g., to St. Paul) at the same time. On the hypostatic-union hypothesis, that would be the case only if the same

[20] Aquinas, *Summa theologica* I, q.54, a.3, c; q.77, a.1, c.

[21] Scotus, *Op.Ox.* II, d.16, q.7, nn.15–19; Wad VI.2.770–3.

[22] Ockham, *Quaest. in II Sent.*, q.20; OTh V.435–440.

[23] See Scotus, *Ordinatio* III, d.2, q.2, n.95; Vat IX.159; III, d.16, qq.1–2, n.39; Vat IX.549–550. Likewise, Ockham, *Quaest. in III Sent.*, q.1; OTh VI.21–23; *Quodlibeta* II, q.10; OTh IX.160.

individual will-power could belong both to the Holy Spirit and to St. Paul at one and the same time. If it did, then the special connection between the Holy Spirit and St. Paul would consist in the fact that the same individual will-power is hypostatically united to the Holy Spirit *and* is either St. Paul's soul or a necessary accident emanating from and inhering in St. Paul's soul. The result would be that numerically the same soul power—by virtue of two different metaphysical relations of union—could belong to two persons at once. If human will-power is a necessary accident, then it is united to the substance of St. Paul by virtue of being an accident that inheres in his soul. If human will-power is really the same as the intellectual soul, then it is united to St. Paul by virtue of being really the same as the soul that is an essential part of the individual human being that St. Paul is.

If the will did belong to two supposits, each of the supposits could be denominated from its acts (e.g., the Holy Spirit could be said to will and St. Paul could be said to will). But much depends on how the Holy Spirit uses that created will to produce those acts. If, by (T2b), the Holy Spirit *makes* the human will love God and neighbor, that suggests that the Holy Spirit uses Its Divine will to cause an act of loving God and neighbor in Its human will. Such activity could still count as self-determination for the Holy Spirit, because *ex hypothesi* both wills belong to It: Its Divine will would be controlling Its human will, the way a human being exercises self-control by using will-power to curb sensory appetites. But even if the Holy Spirit acted freely in Its human will-act, how could St. Paul also be said to will freely? Whether or not the Holy Spirit is hypostatically united to St. Paul's will would make no difference: if the Divine will is the total efficient cause of the human will-act, the resultant act of loving God and neighbor would not be free for St. Paul, and the Genuine Agency Problem would not have been solved after all.

If the Holy Spirit did not go beyond general concurrence, however, if the human will-acts of loving God and neighbor were relevantly produced by the active power of the human will itself, then both the Holy Spirit and St. Paul would be denominated from the human will's active power and from its freely produced acts. That way, both agents could be said to act freely, and the Genuine Agency Problem would be solved. This is because the Holy Spirit's co-action by virtue of "co-owning" St. Paul's will would not by itself include any extra efficient causal input.

Third, some—Scotus, for one—would have challenged the notion that numerically the same individual nature or part-nature could belong to an individual creature and to a Divine person at one and the same time. For Scotus the default is that an individual substance nature self-supposits: it *is* its own supposit. That is, it does not depend on another as its subject, but subsists in itself. Individual substance natures have a natural aptitude to self-supposit, but they do not necessarily self-supposit. By Divine power, they can be assumed by a really distinct other—i.e., an "alien" supposit—on which they would depend as their subjects. Self-suppositers are independent (i.e., do not depend on another as on a subject), while alien-supposited natures are dependent. Scotus concludes that it would not be metaphysically possible for numerically the same individual nature to be self-supposited and alien-supposited at one and the same time. If what goes for wholes goes for parts, then no human soul could be part of a self-suppositing nature (e.g., St. Paul's) and be "alien" supposited by a Divine person (e.g., the Holy Spirit) at one and the same time.[24]

Had he considered it, Ockham might have given a different answer. Not only does he concede the metaphysical possibility that numerically the same human nature be assumed by all three Divine persons at once; he allows that—by Divine power—numerically the same intellectual soul could be united as the dominant substantial form of three human beings (e.g., Sts. Peter, James, and John) at once.[25] Since, for Ockham, will-power is really the same as the intellectual soul, the three human beings would share numerically the same will-power and be denominated by numerically the same will-acts. Analogously, Ockham might claim that numerically the same intellectual soul could be simultaneously united to make something one *per se* with an individual human composite and assumed by a Divine person. Ockham would have insisted that, strictly speaking, only individual substance natures can be supposited, and that even broadly speaking only individual substance natures and/or their parts can be assumed. The Holy Spirit could not, strictly or broadly speaking, *assume* a quality. But Ockham might not deny that there was some other analogous way of being united with a quality (as opposed to a substance or a substance-part) by which the Holy Spirit could own it.[26]

[24] For a discussion of Scotus' understanding of self-suppositing, alien-suppositing, and hypostatic union, see my "What's Metaphysically Special about Supposits?" *Proceedings of the Aristotelian Society* Supplementary Volume 79 (2005), 15–52. See also my *Christ and Horrors: The Coherence of Christology* (Cambridge: Cambridge University Press, 2006), ch. 5, 123–8.

[25] *Quaestiones variae*, q.6, a.vii; OTh VIII.239–40.

[26] For Ockham's treatment of self-suppositing, alien-suppositing, and hypostatic union, see my "Relations, Subsistence, and Inherence, or Was Ockham a Nestorian in Christology?" *Noûs* 16 (1982), 62–75; "The Metaphysics of the Incarnation in Some Fourteenth Century Franciscans," in *Essays Honoring Allan B. Wolter* (St. Bonaventure, NY: Franciscan Institute Publications, 1985), 21–57; and "What's Metaphysically Special about Supposits?".

c. Infused habits after all?

Having brought up the hypostatic-union hypothesis in the first place, Bonaventure simply dismisses it. Lombard cannot consistently hold it, while denying any infused habit of charity in the soul. Bonaventure explains that the capacity for hypostatic union is supernatural. That means that no creatable nature includes within it any natural passive capacity to be so united, because *natural* capacities can be actualized by merely natural causes. Therefore, if any creature is capable of hypostatic union, it must be made such by a supernatural infused habit that expands its passive capacities beyond what is natural and disposes it for hypostatic union.[27] Thus, Bonaventure concludes against Lombard, hypostatic union would presuppose infused charity in the soul.[28]

Bonaventure himself does not believe that Lombard held the hypostatic-union hypothesis, however. Rather, Lombard recognized that "that by which we love God" can be understood three ways. The whole Trinity is an *efficient cause* by which we love God and neighbor. The Holy Spirit, Who is that love by which Father and Son love each other and us, is the *exemplar cause* of our love for God and neighbor. And an affection or motion in our soul (i.e., the act) is the *formal cause* of our love for God and neighbor.[29]

Bonaventure's own verdict is that these claims are true so far as they go and imply no division of the Trinity or confusion of creature's with the creator's action.[30] Any defects lie not in what they affirm, but in what they leave out. The Genuine Agency Problem weighs with Bonaventure. The charity by which we love God must be a virtue in us, because not only does God cooperate with us, but "*we cooperate with God. We are his helpers.*" Because our wills are "convertible" in the sense of being powers for opposite actions, they need a regulator to dispose them to will what God wills them to will. Divine omnipresence does not suffice. The created will has to receive some influence from Divine presence. What enables us to cooperate with God is an infused habit of charity, which is a likeness of Divine love (= the Holy Spirit) and disposes the will to will what is good and godly.[31] A habit of infused charity is needed to perfect the soul by distinguishing it from others (marking those who are accepted

[27] Bonaventure, *Sent.* I, d.17, p. 1, a. u, q. 1; Quaracchi I.294.
[28] Bonaventure, *Sent.* I, d.17, p. 1, a.u, q.1; Quaracchi I.294.
[29] Bonaventure, *Sent.* I, d.17, p. 1, a. u, q. 1; Quaracchi I.294.
[30] Bonaventure, *Sent.* I, d.17, p. 1, a. u, q. 1; Quaracchi I.295–6.
[31] Bonaventure, *Sent.* I, d.17, p. 1, a. u, q. 1; Quaracchi I.295.

by God from those who are not), by ordering and disposing it for eternal life.[32]

Looking forward to the life to come, Bonaventure endorses the tag that "like is known by like." Deiformity is required for beatific vision and enjoyment. To fit fallen humans for heaven requires nothing less than the re-creation or the re-formation of them. But re-formation requires a form, in particular an informing habit that restructures the soul towards greater Godlikeness.[33]

4. AQUINAS: INFUSED QUALITIES AS THE FOUNDATIONS OF SPECIAL CONNECTIONS

a. The necessity of infused habits

Aquinas agrees with Bonaventure: the Holy Spirit is given to us to make us holy. To make us holy, is to perfect us. But Divine omnipresence and concurrence will not be enough to perfect *us*. What perfects a creature is an inherent form,[34] and God is not and cannot be an inherent form.[35] Aquinas gives detailed development to the views he shares with Bonaventure. Like Bonaventure, Aquinas' elaboration of the contention—that perfecting forms in us are needed—can be subsumed under the rubric of three sorts of cause.

i. Final causality. For Aquinas, creation actualizes a creatable nature's potency for actual being (*esse*). The nature's inward principles of motion serve to define and to orient the creature to its natural end. Natural active and natural passive powers are matched: there is no natural passive power that cannot be actualized by a natural active power, and natural active powers can actualize only *natural* passive powers. Voluntary agents are further perfected for voluntary actions—so that they can not only perform them but do so promptly and delightfully—by habits of which the corresponding acts are an efficient cause.[36] For example, acts of choosing coffee engender a coffee-choosing habit; choices to act in the face of danger, the virtue of courage. Habits do not causally determine the will (they are at

[32] Bonaventure, *Sent.* I, d.17, p. 1, a. u, q. 1; Quaracchi I.294.

[33] Bonaventure, *Sent.* I, d.17, p. 1, a. u, q. 1; Quaracchi I.295.

[34] Aquinas, *Sent.* I.17.1.1.ad 1um.1288; *De caritate*, a.1, ad 13em.

[35] Aquinas, *Sent.* I.17.1.1.c.1287; *De caritate*, a. 1, ad 8, 13, 14, 18. *Summa Theologica* I, q.3, a.8, c. & ad 2um.

[36] Aquinas, *Sent.* I.17.1.3.c.1313.

most partial causes of the will's act), but they make it easier for the will to act in accordance with them.

"Re-creation" endows the creature, not with natural, but with supernatural being (*esse*) and orders it to its supernatural end. None of human nature's inward principles of motion orders it to beatific vision and enjoyment of the Divine essence, or to loving God as a source of intimate companionship and happiness, as opposed to loving God as the first cause of the natural order. Aquinas emphasizes, human nature furnishes us with no passive powers to receive acts of beatific vision and enjoyment. Neither is there to be found anywhere in creation the natural active power to produce them in us.[37] What we need is the addition of supernatural inward principles of motion: supernatural passive powers to receive supernatural acts, and supernatural active powers to cooperate in producing them. If habits are what perfect a voluntary agent, and active and passive causal tendencies are what internally order a thing to its end, supernatural infused habits are required. Once again, Aquinas emphasizes: human nature includes neither the passive power to receive such supernatural habits (they are not "educible from the potency of the matter"), nor active power to cooperate in producing them. It is Divine power that infuses them,[38] and when it does so, it thereby raises us up to "super-nature," endows us with supernatural being (*esse*) and orders us to our supernatural end.

ii. Exemplar causality. To be suited for our supernatural end, we must be made more "deiform," more godlike. In Aquinas' mind, the supernaturally infused habits, not only dispose us to greater functional similarity, they do so by virtue of being godlikenesses themselves. Not only the soul, but the soul's powers must be elevated. Because Aquinas understands the soul to emanate its essential powers as really distinct necessary accidents, he reckons that the supernaturally infused perfecting habits must be many, including graced-making grace in the soul, the theological virtues—faith, hope, and charity—in the soul's powers, and infused wisdom in the intellect. Graced-making grace is the foundation. Sometimes he says that it likens the soul to the Divine essence and so disposes the soul to beatific vision and enjoyment,[39] but other times to God the Son's personal property of filiation thereby fitting us to be adoptive daughters and sons.[40] Infused wisdom, which enlightens the intellect and prompts love, likens us

[37] Aquinas, *Sent.* I.17.1.3.c.1313.

[38] Aquinas, *Sent.* I.17.2.5.ad 3um.1404.

[39] Aquinas, *Summa theologica* I, q.43, a.5, ad 2um & ad 3um.

[40] Aquinas, *Sent.* I, d.16, q.3, c. 1255.

to the Divine Word.[41] Infused charity likens us to the Holy Spirit Who is the love by which Father and Son love one another.[42]

iii. Efficient causality. On Aquinas' reading, Lombard would not have been tempted by the—to Aquinas' mind—ridiculous notion that *the act* of love that we experience is the Holy Spirit Itself![43] What makes Lombard's view untenable is the Genuine Agency Problem. On Aquinas' reading of (T2b), Lombard holds that the Holy Spirit is *the* efficient cause of our act of loving God and neighbor, so that the only formal active principle involved in producing the act is located in the Holy Spirit. The created will would be a merely receiving subject of that act. Aquinas draws out the untoward consequences in four arguments.

First, unless the act of love proceeds from a formal active principle within us, the act will not be voluntary. By definition, both natural and voluntary actions proceed from inward principles of motion. External causes can act alone to produce motions or changes in both rational and non-rational creatures. But not even God can make such motions or changes count as natural or voluntary, respectively, because omnipotence does not include the pseudo-power to make contradictories true simultaneously. When the archer shoots the arrow upwards, the arrow's upward motion is violent, not natural. When something external is the total efficient cause of a rational creature's act, the act is not voluntary but coerced.[44]

Second, on Lombard's view, no merely human being would act according to its own form in loving God and neighbor. But agents that do not act according to their own form, but only insofar as they are moved by another, are only *instrumental* agents (e.g., like the saw moved by the carpenter). If the human will were only an instrumental agent of the Holy Spirit, then it would not be within the power of the human being whether or not to love God and neighbor (any more than it is within the power of the saw whether or not actually to cut this piece of wood). If the act were not voluntary, it would not be meritorious either.

Third, habits are what enable a power to act promptly and delightfully. But on Lombard's view, there is no habit of charity in the human will to incline it to love God and neighbor. Aquinas concludes that if Lombard were right, the human will would be unable to perform such acts promptly and delightfully.[45]

[41] Aquinas, *Summa theologica* I, q.43, a.5, ad 2um & ad 3um; see also *Sent.* I.15.4.1. c.1146; I.15.5.1.2.1193.

[42] Aquinas, *Summa theologica* I, q.43, a.5, ad 2um & ad 3um; see also *Sent.* I.15.4. c.1146; I.15.5.1.2.1193; I.17.1.c & ad 2um.1287 & 1289.

[43] Aquinas, *Sent.* I.17.1.1.c.1287; *De caritate*, a.1, c.

[44] Aquinas, *De caritate*, a.1, c.

[45] Aquinas, *De caritate*, a.1, c.

Fourth, being meritorious is a perfection of an act. But function (*operatio*) pertains to the supposit. So far as necessity and contingency and perfection are concerned, the function follows the conditions of the proximate cause (in this case, the human being) and not the first cause (God). Hence, there is no perfection in an action unless there is perfection in the proximate functional power from which it proceeds. Functional power is perfected by a habit. Aquinas infers that there is no perfection in an action unless there is a habit infused into the functional power of the agent-supposit from which it proceeds. Just as the political virtues (e.g., justice) make their possessor good and in consequence render her/his acts good; so the habit of charity perfects the will of the human being to make him/her the object of Divine favor and in consequence makes his/her free acts in accordance with right reason and/or Divine commands meritorious. If—as Lombard maintains—there were no habit of charity perfecting the human will, no human acts would be meritorious.[46]

Aquinas' own conclusion is that we must be able to perform the act of loving God and neighbor *through our own form.* Since none of our natural forms is the formal active principle through which such an act can be produced, what we need is a supernaturally infused habit of charity to serve as the formal principle of an act of love. God is the *efficient* cause, but the supernaturally infused habit of charity is the *formal* cause of the human being's being graced.[47] The habit received into the agent-supposit's functional power actualizes its potency to be in a state of first act with respect to charity or meritorious action. The habit is a partial efficient cause of the agent-supposit's moving from first to second act with respect to charity or meritorious action.[48] Presumably, since Aquinas thinks the act of loving God and neighbor is voluntary, created will-power is also a partial efficient cause. Where, then, does the Holy Spirit come in? Aquinas' answer is significant: "the Holy Spirit, Who is uncreated charity, is in the human being that has created charity, moving the soul to an act of love, the way God moves all things to the actions to which they are inclined by their own forms."[49] In other words, the Holy Spirit acts—along with the Father and the Son—by general concurrence!

To the objection that it denigrates Divine power to suggest that it has to act through the intermediary of a habit of charity in producing an act of love in the creature, Aquinas protests that exactly the opposite is the case.

[46] Aquinas, *Sent.* I.17.1.1.c.1287??.

[47] Aquinas, *Sent.* I.17.1.1.ad 5um.1292.

[48] Aquinas, *Sent.* I.17.1.1.ad 1um & 3um & 6um.1288 & 1290 & 1293; I.17.1.2.ad 3um.1305.

[49] Aquinas, *De caritate*, a.1, c.

The habit of charity is a formal cause of meritorious action. But it is a sign that an agent is stronger rather than weaker that it can produce formal active principles in other things, all the stronger the more perfect the produced formal active principles are. Thus, it would be impressive if God were to act alone to produce all of the effects here below. But it is even more impressive that Divine power has acted to introduce formal active principles into creatures and collaborated with them to produce said effects.[50]

b. Special connections

For Aquinas, supernaturally infused habits are required to make the elect holy. But Divine indwelling and missions still play a role. Aquinas advances two accounts of special connections, both of which make the latter to depend upon the former.

i. The "Metaphysical" Account: The first tackles both the Special Connection and Divided Trinity Problems at once. Aquinas is clear. The whole Trinity is the efficient cause of these infused habits: "one action, one will *ad extra*" holds where creation and preservation are concerned. But while—according to Aquinas—the Trinity are in everything by essence, presence, and power,[51] the further special connections of indwelling and mission arise because these particular infused habits ground primitive non-mutual relations between the creature into whom they have been infused and Godhead as a whole or one Divine person in particular.[52] Since not every created effect is the foundation of such relations, indwelling and mission constitute "special connections" of God to some creatures rather than others and of the creature to one Divine person as opposed to the others. On this account, the infused habits are prior in the order of explanation to the special connections (the relations of indwelling and mission).[53]

In general, Aquinas reaches for the category of non-mutual relations when he tries to explain how an eternal, absolutely simple, and immutable God can be newly related to temporary and transient creatures.[54] God becomes the creator of X, when the creature X comes into existence, but nothing real (no *res*) in God is said to change thereby. Aquinas' analysis is

[50] Aquinas, *De caritate*, a.1, ad 13–14em.

[51] Aquinas, *Summa theologica* I, q.8, a.3, c.

[52] Aquinas, *Sent.* I.14.1.1.ad 2um.1023; I.14.1.2.c & ad 1um & ad 3um.1034–5 & 1037; I.14.2.1.1.c & ad 2um.1051 & 1053.

[53] Aquinas, *Sent.* I.14.2.2.c & ad 2um.1065 & 1067.

[54] For a detailed treatment of Aquinas on relations, see Mark G. Henninger, *Relations: Medieval Theories 1250–1325* (Oxford: Clarendon Press, 1989), ch. 2, 13–39.

that the relations creator/creature are non-mutual: the created thing is the foundation of a real relation of created dependence. Because God is the term of that real relation of created dependence (i.e., X depends on God), God is said to bear a relation of reason to the creature (i.e., God is the creator of X). Again, when God the Son assumes a particular human nature into hypostatic union, nothing real (no *res*) changes in God the Son. Rather the human nature is the foundation of a real relation of being assumed, a relation of which God the Son is the term. And because of this, God the Son is said to bear a relation of reason to the assumed human nature (i.e., God assumes it). Likewise here: neither Godhead nor any Divine person undergoes any real change (any change of *res*) when It indwells or is sent to a creature. Rather the supernatural habit newly infused into the creature (e.g., graced-making grace into St. Paul's soul, wisdom into his intellect, charity into his will) is the foundation of a primitive real relation of being indwelt or being that to whom someone is sent. Insofar as the Trinity/the Divine person is the term of such a relation, It bears a relation of reason to that creature (e.g., God indwells St. Paul, the Holy Spirit is sent to St. Paul).

Thus, when Aquinas appeals to the category of non-mutual relations, and posits special primitive relations to connect Godhead with some creatures and creatures with one Divine person and not another, he is re-using old strategies already deployed in his analyses of creation- and assumption relations. All the same, indwelling and mission (and their co-relations) are *not the same* primitive relations as assuming (and being assumed). Like Bonaventure, Aquinas is clear that the Holy Spirit does not join Itself in hypostatic union to the creature's will.[55] By contrast with the hypostatic-union hypothesis, Aquinas sees indwelling and mission as additional primitive relations, different from the assumption relation.

Not every creature can be the foundation of a real relation of *being indwelt* or of *being the one to whom a Divine person is specially sent*; only supernatural habits that God alone has the active power to produce in souls, can. Moreover, not every supernatural habit grounds such relations. Aquinas identifies graced-making grace infused into the soul as the foundation of a real relation of being indwelt, of which the whole Trinity is the term. That is, when St. Paul's soul is infused with graced-making grace, the whole Trinity indwell or make their home with him. Again, God the Son is sent in the flesh to teach us many things. But it is infused wisdom or knowledge of God that makes the soul one to whom God the Son is specially sent. That is, when St. Paul's mind is infused with knowledge of God, God the Son is

[55] Aquinas, *Sent.* I.17.1.1.c.1287.

sent to him and indwells "the inner man." Likewise, supernaturally infused charity grounds the real relation of being one to whom the Holy Spirit has been specially sent and given. That is, when St. Paul's will is infused with the supernatural habit of charity, the Holy Spirit is specially sent and given to him. Since these habits would be not only "above and beyond" but contrary to the essential principles of non-rational creatures, Aquinas infers that Godhead and individual Divine persons can have these special connections to rational creatures only.[56]

What makes it the case that the infusion of these habits (as opposed to others) gives rise to real relations of being indwelt and being sent to? Aquinas may think that graced-making grace, infused wisdom or knowledge of God, and infused charity fill these roles because they are special godlikenesses: graced-making grace, of Godhead; infused knowledge or wisdom, of the Son's personal property as Word; infused charity, of the Holy Spirit's personal property as the love between the Father and the Son.[57] If so, Aquinas could explain that it is simply the nature of these infused habits—when posited—to ground such real relations, just as it is the nature of whiteness—when two white things are posited—to ground mutual real relations of similarity. Even so, this rationale is incomplete, because, for a creature, to be is to be somehow godlike. The question rises again: what is so distinctive about these godlikenesses—viz., the infused habits of graced-making grace, supernatural wisdom or knowledge of God, and charity—that they ground special connections, when other godlikenesses do not? Perhaps in the end Aquinas will have to say that this is primitive, a necessary consequence of what these special habits (by contrast with those habits) are.

The real relation of dependence on God as Creator necessarily stays with a creature throughout its existence. The real relations of being indwelt by the Trinity or of being one to whom a Divine person is sent, pertain to a creature only when it acquires and so long as it has the infused habits. They are lost by mortal sin and restored by penance and absolution. In some moods, Aquinas would say that these real relations stay with a human being from the beginning and throughout its supernatural being (*esse*). Moreover, both infused wisdom and infused charity come in degrees, and so *ante-mortem* can be augmented. Aquinas connects the sending of the Son and Holy Spirit into a creature, with a new condition in that creature—viz., its fresh reception of infused habits.[58] Will it be right to speak of a new

[56] Aquinas, *Sent.* I.15.4.1.ad 3um.1149.

[57] Aquinas, *Sent.* I.15.4.1.c.1146; I.15.5.1.2.1193. *Summa theologica* I, q.43, a.5, ad 2um & ad 3um.

[58] Aquinas, *Sent.* I.15.1.1.c.1088; I.15.3.1.c & ad 3um.1124 & 1127; I.15.4.2.c.1155.

mission of the Son or the Holy Spirit every time infused wisdom or infused charity is augmented? Aquinas' answer is negative. It will be right to speak of a new mission of the Son or the Holy Spirit into a creature only where the increase is such as to enable or issue in some new function: e.g., prophecy, miracle-working, or the ability to turn all temptation aside.[59] In the blessed in heaven, there is no augmentation, but there are still new revelations by which the recipient is able to know God in a new way and so to love God under a different aspect.[60]

Here, Aquinas follows rough theological consensus, but fails to give metaphysical satisfaction. Metaphysically, relations depend on their foundations. Indeed, for Aquinas, real relations are really the same as their foundations. Even if R1 and R2 are relations of the same species, they will be numerically distinct if their foundations F1 and F2 are really distinct. Metaphysically, the question should be, does augmenting the degree of infused wisdom or charity change the identity of the foundation in such a way as to require a numerically distinct relation of mission or indwelling?

ii. The Intentional Access Account: In *Summa Theologica* I, q.43, a.3, Aquinas distinguishes God's general omnipresence in creatures from "a special way" in which God exists in rational creatures as the intentional object of their knowledge and love. When God exists in the knower as what is known and in the lover as what is loved, God is said "not only to exist in but to dwell in rational creatures as in His temple." Such indwelling is nevertheless grounded on infused habits. Here Aquinas identifies graced-making grace as what confers on rational creatures "the power of enjoying"—of knowing and loving—"the Divine persons";[61] likewise, infused wisdom as what enlightens the intellect, and infused charity as what inflames affection. Infused wisdom grounds the sending of the Son, and infused charity the sending of the Holy Spirit.[62]

Here Aquinas' focus is on our ultimate end, which is beatific vision and enjoyment of Godhead. Creatures bear many relations to God by metaphysical necessity, and will do so for eternity. But in describing the union for which we are supernaturally destined, Aquinas' attention is not on these, but on cognitive and affective access. Aquinas holds that the natural capacities of the human mind equip it only to understand the quiddities of material things. His own view is that we have no natural capacity for intuitive awareness of immaterial beings with the possible exception of our

[59] Aquinas, *Sent.* I.15.1.2.1192.
[60] Aquinas, *Sent.* I.15.5.1.3.c & ad 1um.1195 & 1197.
[61] Aquinas, *Summa theologica* I, q.43, a.3, c.
[62] Aquinas, *Summa theologica* I, q.43, a.5, ad 2um & ad 3um.

own souls and mental acts. Even though God is omnipresent, our natural cognitive limitations keep the Divine essence behind the veil. Likewise, if nature builds in appetitive inclinations to love God above all as the source and end of natural good,[63] it includes none to love God above all *as an object* of happiness or social companionship.[64] The union for which we are headed is not the metaphysical relation of hypostatic union, but the union of intuitive vision and enjoyment of the Godhead. The metaphysical changes required to make this possible are precisely the supernaturally infused habits which expand our cognitive scope and affective range. The goal is an indwelling and mutual abiding, which consists in overflowing delight in the experienced presence of the Beloved, a shared joy in knowing and being known.

Aquinas leaves this account sketchy. After all, he has identified the infused forms that re-create and restructure the soul as *habits*, not acts. Aquinas joins many in holding that—apart from the human soul of Christ and a few saints—the elect do not enter into beatific vision and enjoyment before death. If the special way that God is in rational creatures is as an intentional object of acts, it would seem that Divine indwelling in the elect as in His temple is an eschatological hope to be realized only beyond the grave. Perhaps, however, Aquinas thinks that Divine indwelling begins with infused habits that target beatific vision and enjoyment. Alternatively, he could say that Divine indwelling comes with acts of love of God above all as an object of happiness and social companionship—will-acts that are based on cognitive acts that fall short of beatific vision. If so, those who use their infused wisdom and infused charity to perform such acts might get an anticipatory version of the mutual abiding for which the elect are destined in the life to come.

Seemingly, Aquinas identifies the "special way" in which things exist in (or indwell) rational creatures quite generically in terms of their being the intentional object of acts of knowledge and/or love. Such an understanding will certainly allow for God to exist in us *ante mortem*. Unfortunately, the criterion is so permissive as to allow anything and everything else we think of and love to indwell us, too.

Aquinas' metaphysical account and his intentional access account are logically independent of one another, but they are also logically compatible. Although he does not say so explicitly, he may intend the intentional access account to supplement the metaphysical account. One difference between my knowledge and love of the chocolate ice cream I am eating and my

[63] Aquinas, *Summa theologica* I–II, q.109, a.3, c & ad 1um.

[64] Aquinas, *Summa theologica* I–II, q.109, a.3, ad 1um.

knowledge and love of God, is that my habit of loving chocolate ice cream does not bear a real relation of being-indwelt-by to chocolate ice cream the way my infused habit of charity is supposed to bear a real relation of being-indwelt-by to the Holy Spirit.

5. SCOTUS ON THE ROLE AND RELEVANCE OF INFUSED HABITS

Bonaventure and Aquinas emphasize: the correct counter to Pelagius is not that the Holy Spirit *is* or is the total efficient cause of our love-act, but that God perfects the soul with inward functional principles, which they identify with infused habits. Scotus accepts theological consensus that supernaturally infused habits are needed to make us holy, or, more precisely, to make us worthy of Divine acceptance and our acts meritorious. But Scotus seeks further clarification. Exactly what role—compatible with genuine human agency—could such habits play? Granted that virtues are habits, can there be habits or formal active principles of moral goodness and merit, in particular? Scotus reviews four answers to the first question, rejecting two while finding the other two defensible.

a. Henry of Ghent: supernatural causes for supernatural effects!

In his *Quodlibet* IV, q.10, Henry of Ghent distinguishes acquired from infused habits. Acquired virtues presuppose the being (*esse*) of the nature along with the functional principles that it essentially includes and/or that are essentially consequent upon it. What acquired virtues do is to perfect that nature and its functional principles. The nature is the functional principle of the act. Acquired virtue only affects *the way* the act is done (e.g., promptly and delightfully, expeditiously). By contrast, supernatural virtues do not presuppose but constitute the soul in supernatural being (*esse*) and redound to the soul's powers to make their acts meritorious. Henry concludes that supernatural virtue is *the* principle of supernatural action. The theological virtues thus confer both supernatural being (*esse*) and supernatural functioning.[65]

[65] Henry of Ghent, *Quodlibet* IV, q.10, fol. 100G–101L; summarized in Scotus, *Lectura* I, d.17, p.1, q.u, nn.32–37; Vat XVII.194; *Lectura* II, d.26, q.u, nn.7–8; Vat XIX.194; *Ordinatio* I, d.17, p.1, q.2, n.21; Vat V.146.

b. Scotus' critique of Henry's opinion

Scotus counters that it is the metaphysical role of habits to perfect powers. But a power is the principle by which—simply and primarily—a thing is able to act. In declaring the supernatural habit the *only* active principle in the production of the meritorious act, Henry turns the habit into the power itself![66] If the supernaturally infused habit of charity *is* the power to produce the act, then it no more perfects created will-power in which it inheres than heat (which is itself the power to produce heat) perfects the wood in which it inheres. Heat is not a necessary accident of wood (the way—Aquinas would say—it is a necessary accident of fire), but is only produced in the wood by an external cause. Consequently, when the heat acts on its own to produce heat in surrounding objects, the act may be said to be "shared" with the wood insofar as the wood is the receiving-subject in which the heat inheres. But the heating-action does not pertain to the wood properly speaking because the wood qua wood does nothing to produce heat.

Scotus raises the standards for genuine agency. In order for X to count as the agent-subject of A-ing, not only is it not enough for the *act* of A-ing to exist in X as in a subject; it is not enough for a *habit* that is an active principle of A-ing to exist in X as in a subject. It is further required either [a] that the habit in question be a natural perfection of X (the way heat is a natural perfection of fire) or [b] that some active principle included in or naturally consequent upon the nature of X be active in the production of A. Supernaturally infused habits are *ex hypothesi* not natural perfections of human beings. Consequently, if infused charity in St. Paul were the sole active principle producing in St. Paul an act of loving God and neighbor, that act would only be shared with St. Paul the way heating-action is shared with the wood. St. Paul would not be its agent-subject properly speaking.[67]

Scotus drives this point home with the further observation that if—among the formal active principles existing in St. Paul—supernaturally infused charity were the only active principle involved in the production of the love-act, then supernaturally infused charity could produce that act even if it existed on its own, separate from any and every subject, the way Avicenna admits that heat could produce heat even if it existed separately from fire or wood.[68] Moreover, habits are natural causes that—barring

[66] Scotus, *Lectura* I, d.17, p.1, q.u, n.46; Vat XVII.197–198; *Ordinatio* I, d.17, p.1, q.2, n.22; Vat V.147.

[67] Scotus, *Lectura* I, d.17, p.1, q.u, nn.47 & 49; Vat XVII.198; *Ordinatio* I, d.17, p.1, q.2, n.23; Vat. V.147.

[68] Scotus, *Ordinatio* I, d.17, p.1, q.u, n.23; Vat V.147–8.

obstructions—act to the limit of their powers. If charity were the sole active principle in the production of the love-act, the love-act would be produced naturally and so would not be free,[69] nor would it be imputable to St. Paul, because it would not be within his power to control whether or not the habit produced the act.[70]

Conversely, if supernaturally infused charity did give the will supernatural being (*esse*) and action (*agere*), then that charity would so dominate the will that it could never sin mortally, so long as the charity existed in it.[71]

c. Godfrey of Fontaines: two causes, two effects?

The moral of Scotus' critique of Henry is that the love-act will not be free and imputable to St. Paul unless—whatever other active principles may be at work—his will-power is one of those active principles and his will-power retains control over whether to act or not. Godfrey of Fontaines agrees with this conclusion. In *Quodlibet* XI, q.4, he maintains—*contra* Henry—that acquired and infused virtues are related to acts the same way: the act has its substance from the power and its intensity from the habit. For Godfrey, the labor of love-act production is divided between two causes—will-power and supernaturally infused charity—that produce quasi-two different effects: the substance of the act and the intensity of the act, respectively. The power informed by the habit is the formal active principle of the intense act.[72]

d. Scotus' rejection of Godfrey's position

Godfrey justifies invoking two causes by distinguishing quasi-two effects. Scotus finds Godfrey's position philosophically confused, because the intensity of an act is not distinct from the substance of an act in any way that would allow the two causes to divide and conquer.[73] What causes the substance, causes the intensity: the infinite will, an act of infinite intensity; finite wills, acts of finite intensity. Nor is there any degree of intensity in a will-act that so lies outside the scope of will-power as a species as to require

[69] Scotus, *Lectura* I, d.17, p.1, q.u, nn.48–9; Vat XVII.198; *Ordinatio* I, d.17, p.1, q.2, n.24; Vat V.148.

[70] Scotus, *Ordinatio* I, d.17, p.1, q.2, n.26; Vat V.149.

[71] Scotus, *Lectura* I, d.17, p.1, q.u, n.50; Vat XVII.199; *Ordinatio* I, d.17, p.1, q.2, n.25; Vat V.149.

[72] Godfrey of Fontaines, *Quodlibet* XI, q.4; PhB V.22–24. Scotus, *Lectura* I, d.17, p.1, q.u, n.51; Vat XVII.199; *Ordinatio* I, d.17, p.1, q.2, n.27; Vat V.149–150.

[73] Scotus, *Lectura* I, d.17, p.1, q.u, n.52; XVII.199; *Ordinatio* I, d.17, p.1, q.2, n.28; Vat V.150.

a supernaturally infused habit as a co-cause. Will-power as such ranges over acts of any and all finite degrees up to and including a will-act of infinite degree. Inhering habits might perfect finite will-power to enable it to cause acts of higher intensity. But Godfrey misdivides the labor when he says that the habit causes the intensity and will-power the substance.[74] If he were right, while the habit was infused, all of the will's acts would have the same intensity, because the habit—as a natural cause—would always act to the limit of its power![75]

Henry of Ghent and Godfrey of Fontaines both recognize the supernaturally infused habit of charity as an *active* principle in the production of the love-act. Scotus judges both accounts untenable, Henry's because it assigns created will-power no active role, and Godfrey's because it gives the supernaturally infused habit the wrong role. Scotus recognizes two other positions, both of which he deems defensible and which differ over whether the habit is an active or a merely passive disposing principle in love-act production.[76]

e. Partial causes of a single effect?

Accepting what is good and rejecting what is allegedly mistaken in Godfrey, the third approach holds that will-power and the infused habit of charity are two partial causes that make essentially one total cause of a single effect (the love-act). These two partial causes are of different orders (unlike the two sailors dragging the ship). Neither depends on the other for its causality (just as mother and father, the intellect and its object each have their causal powers independently of the other). A given finite will-power could act alone to produce a less perfect love-act, but the infused charity perfects that finite will-power so that together they produce a more perfect love-act. Of the two, will-power is the principal cause—it is that by which the agent can have a will-act—and the habit is the secondary or perfecting cause—it is that by which the agent can have a more perfect act than its will can produce all by itself.[77] Nevertheless, there is no degree of a created will-act that requires a supra-natural cause; any and all degrees fall within the

[74] Scotus, *Lectura* I, d.17, p.1, q.u, nn.54–55; Vat XVII.200; *Ordinatio* I, d.17, p.1, q.2, n.31; Vat V.151–2.

[75] Scotus, *Lectura* I, d.17, p.1, q.u, n.53; Vat XVII.200; *Ordinatio* I, d.17, p.1, q.2, nn.29–30; Vat V.150–1.

[76] Scotus, *Ordinatio* I, d.17, p.1, q.2, n.53; Vat V.160.

[77] Scotus, *Lectura* I, d.17, p.1, q.u, nn.75–6, 79, 83, 85–7; Vat XVII.205–9; *Ordinatio* I, d.17, p.1, q.2, nn.32–40; Vat V.152–6.

scope of will-power as such.[78] By contrast, the habit, no matter what its degree, would not be sufficient to produce the will-act.[79]

f. Infused habits as passive dispositions?

If Aquinas and Bonaventure read Lombard to say that the Holy Spirit alone is the efficient cause of the love-act, and if Henry of Ghent holds that the infused habit does all of the work, the fourth approach seizes the other extreme to say that efficient causality belongs to created will-power, while the infused habit is not an active principle at all, but only a passive disposing principle that inclines the power to its function. Scotus cites the following methodological principles in its favor:

[P1] causality should not be attributed unless it is evident in the nature of things;
[P2] perfect causality should not be denied to a cause unless there is an obvious imperfection in its causality.[80]

There would be a reason to deny perfect causality to will-power, if there were some feature of the will-act for which will-power could not account. Now habits are usually posited to explain the agent's ability to function easily, delightfully, expeditiously, and promptly. The fourth position does not deny that habits are needed to explain such modalities. Rather it insists that all of them have to do with the suitability of the action to the power *insofar as it is a passive receiver of the action and not insofar as it is an active producer of the action.* Consequently, it concludes that the habits in question are passive disposing principles that make the power more receptive to its function.[81]

When all is said and done, Scotus opts for the third approach—that will-power and infused habits are efficient partial causes of the will-act of loving God above all (see sec. 5.e above). But before he can work out the details, Scotus needs to attend to the second question: can there be formal active principles of moral goodness or merit in particular?

g. Habits as active causes of moral goodness or merit?

"Yes" might seem to be the obvious answer. Aristotelian action theory dictates that an agent can do (be an efficient cause of) acts of type A only

[78] Scotus, *Ordinatio* I, d.17, p.1, q.2, nn.79–80; Vat V.178–9.
[79] Scotus, *Ordinatio* I, d.17, p.1, q.2, n.85; Vat V.181.
[80] Scotus, *Ordinatio* I, d.17, p.1, q.2, n.47; Vat V.158.
[81] Scotus, *Ordinatio* I, d.17, p.1, q.2, nn.48–50, 87–91; Vat V.158–9, 181–4.

if it has within it a formal active principle of A-ing. Scotus agrees: Aristotle's *Ethics* can be read as implying that moral virtues are active principles.[82] Likewise, theological consensus dictates that the infused habit of charity is necessary for an agent and its act to be accepted by God as worthy of eternal life. Doesn't it follow that moral virtues are formal active principles of acting morally, and infused charity a formal active principle of earning merit?[83]

Technically, Scotus thinks, the answer is "no." The bottom line for Scotus is that both moral goodness and merit signify relations to norms: in the former case, conformity to right reason;[84] in the latter, to Divine statutory policies for accepting acts accompanied by infused charity as worthy of eternal life.[85] Moreover, these relations (like the relation of similarity between two white things) are internal relations, in Scotus' sense that—given the existence of the relata—they cannot but obtain.[86] Consequently, the existence of such relations does not require any further efficient causal explanation over and above what is involved in the production of their relata. Scotus concludes, we do not have to suppose that the habits are or contain formal active principles that explain the moral goodness or the merit of the acts. If heat heats, it is a formal principle of heating. If the will loves, there is a formal active principle of loving in the will. A habit of charity, whether acquired or infused, may even be—as Henry, Godfrey, and the third opinion claim—a formal active principle *of loving*. What there is not, according to Scotus, is a formal active principle *of moral goodness* or a formal active principle *of meriting*.

Scotus makes two further points. First, if what right reason dictates is what it is prior to and independently of anyone's will, the statutes regarding Divine acceptance and merit are instances of positive law whose existence and contents do depend on the will of God, the ruling legislator. No creature is intrinsically—by the very nature of what it is—worthy of eternal life, because it is a finite good. Finite goods provide the Divine will with a reason to love them, but the reason is always defeasible.[87] Only infinite goodness (i.e., the Divine essence Itself) constitutes a reason for loving that cannot be trumped. That there are any statutes relating humans to eternal

[82] Scotus, *Ordinatio* I, d.17, p.1, q.2, nn.57–9; Vat V.161–2.
[83] Scotus, *Ordinatio* I, d.17, p.1, q.2, nn.121–2; Vat V.198–9.
[84] Scotus, *Ordinatio* I, d.17, p.1, q.2, nn.60–2, 94–98; Vat V.163–4, 184–9.
[85] Scotus, *Ordinatio* I, d.17, p.1, q.2, nn.142–5; Vat V.208–9.
[86] For an analysis of Scotus' theory of relations, see my *William Ockham* (Notre Dame, IN: University of Notre Dame Press, 1989), ch. 7, 217–59. See also Henninger, *Relations*, ch. 5, 68–97.
[87] Scotus, *Ordinatio* I, d.17, p.1, q.2, n.149; Vat V.210–11.

destinies, and that they are what they are, is a product of God's free and contingent volition.[88]

Second, Scotus observes, infused virtues are not merely ornamental; they exert efficient causal power to incline the will. Scotus holds that moral virtues[89] and infused habits[90] are highly suitable to the rational soul. Because he understands beauty to be constituted by suitability relations, Scotus compares virtues to ornaments that contribute to making the soul beautiful and furnish a reason, albeit defeasible, for Divine acceptance. Nevertheless, Scotus denies that mere ornamentation is sufficient to make the soul's acts meritorious. Even souls with infused charity perform indifferent acts (e.g., willing to stroke one's beard) and commit venial sins.[91] Scotus rejects the view that infused charity is merely ornamental, insisting that it inclines the will, whether by being a formal active principle (as the third view holds) or a passive receptive principle (as the fourth view contends).[92]

With these explanations in hand, Scotus lays out his own position. Following the third view (sec. 5.e above), Scotus maintains that will-power is the principal, while infused charity is a secondary efficient cause of the love-acts.[93] Scotus seems to limit God's efficient causal contribution to producing the quality that the love-act is, to infusing the habit and general concurrence.[94] By contrast, *God* is the principal cause of any act's counting as meritorious, because God is the One Who lays down positive laws ordering acts and agents to eternal destinies.[95] When it comes to the criteria that God has chosen for counting an act meritorious and so ordering it to an eternal reward, both infused charity in the soul and the free exercise of will-power according to the dictates of right reason, are still involved. But the priorities are reversed: where God's reasons for Divine acceptance are concerned, infused charity is the principal reason and the exercise of free choice the secondary reason.[96] Scotus emphasizes, God would not have to make infused charity a necessary condition for Divine acceptance and merit. God could have established other policies. Scripture

[88] Scotus, *Ordinatio* I, d.17, p.1, q.1, n.144–5; Vat V.208–9.

[89] Scotus, *Ordinatio* I, d.17, p.1, q.2, n.62; Vat V.163–4.

[90] Scotus, *Ordinatio* I, d.17, p.1, q.2, n.131; Vat V.203.

[91] Scotus, *Lectura* I, d.17, p.1, q.u, nn.58–60; Vat XVII.201; *Ordinatio* I, d.17, p.1, q.2, n.132; Vat.204.

[92] Scotus, *Ordinatio* I, d.17, p.1, q.2, nn.133–5; Vat V.204–5.

[93] Scotus, *Ordinatio* I, d.17, p.1, q.2, n.151; Vat V.211.

[94] Scotus, *Ordinatio* I, d.17, p.1, q.2, n.191; Vat V.229.

[95] Scotus, *Ordinatio* I, d.17, p.1, q.2, n.146; Vat V.209.

[96] Scotus, *Ordinatio* I, d.17, p.1, q.2, nn.152–7; Vat V.211–14.

and the sayings of the saints persuade him that this is God's actual policy, however.[97]

Thus, for Scotus, whether or not a love-act is produced, and whether or not a will acts in accord with conscience, remains, always or for the most part, within the will's power. But whether or not the soul has infused charity, and whether or not any of its acts count as meritorious, are not within the will's power but depend rather on free and contingent Divine policies. Scotus finds this division of labor acceptable, however, because merit and eternal destinies should, in the last analysis, be up to God.

h. Reinterpreting Lombard

Bonaventure and Aquinas agree: Lombard did not hold that the Holy Spirit is *the act* by which we love God and neighbor, but rather that the Holy Spirit is *the efficient cause* that acts immediately—without the cooperation of any infused habit—to produce that love-act in us. Scotus rejects their interpretation. Scotus' Lombard *does* think an infused habit is involved in the production of the love-act and of meritorious acts generally, although—Aquinas and Bonaventure are right to think—it is not an infused habit in the will. Rather, in *Sentences* I, d.37, Lombard recognizes a supernatural habit of grace, which is infused into the souls of the regenerate to make them tabernacles of the Holy Spirit. To borrow Aquinas' language, it is infused grace in the soul rather than charity in the will that is the foundation of the relation of being indwelt of which the Holy Spirit is the term. Because grace is infused into the soul rather than the will, it can function as the root of the other virtues of faith and hope infused into the soul's powers. The latter don't ground relations of being indwelt, because—unlike grace—faith and hope involve imperfections (a lack of certainty and a lack of possession) and so will not be retained after death.[98] The disanalogy between the way the Holy Spirit produces acts of faith and hope in us on the one hand, and love-acts in us on the other, is not that the Holy Spirit acts by means of habits in producing the former but without any habit in producing the latter. Rather Scotus' Lombard does not recognize infused charity as a really distinct habit from infused grace and the soul.

[97] Scotus, *Ordinatio* I, d.17, p.1, q.2, nn.160 & 164; Vat V.215 & 217.

[98] Scotus, *Lectura* I, d.17, p.1, q.u, nn.32–7; Vat XVII.194; *Ordinatio* I, d. 17, p.1, q.1, nn.167–71; Vat V.218.

Accordingly, he thinks that the Holy Spirit acts together with infused grace and the soul's will-power to produce the act.[99] Scotus analyzes the position he attributes to Lombard into a sequence of instants of nature:

n1: grace or charity is infused into the soul and the Holy Spirit thereby indwells;

n2: grace infuses faith and hope (and no other habit) into the soul's powers;

n3: the Holy Spirit elicits an act of faith by means of the habit of faith and an act of hope by means of the habit of hope;

n4: by means of grace in the soul and the Holy Spirit that indwells, the will elicits an act of love.[100]

Likewise, for meritorious acts generally: the Holy Spirit sanctifies the grace-infused soul by indwelling it. And by means of infused grace and the indwelling Holy Spirit, the will elicits a meritorious act.[101]

i. Special connections and divided Trinity?

Scotus seems not to deal *ex professo* with the Special Connection and Divided Trinity Problems. It is literally in passing, in his discussion of Lombard, that Scotus hints at his answers to them. Scotus explains that according to Lombard, it is "by means of grace and the indwelling of the whole Trinity, which is appropriated to the Spirit," that "the will elicits a meritorious act."[102] Evidently, Scotus is attributing to Lombard the view that, properly speaking, it is not only the Holy Spirit but the whole Trinity that indwells the grace-infused human being. Just as the whole Trinity acts in concert to infuse virtues, so, properly speaking, the whole Trinity indwells by means of the root-virtue that They infuse. It is only "by courtesy" that such indwelling as belongs to the whole is "appropriated" to the Holy Spirit, the better to accommodate the language of Scripture. Strictly speaking, there is no divided action, but the Trinity as a whole may be said to foster a special connection to some creatures and not others (in this case, to the elect and not the damned)!

[99] Scotus, *Lectura* I, d.17, p.1, q.u, n.39; Vat XVII.195; *Ordinatio* I, d.17, p.1, q.1, nn.169–70; Vat V.218–19.

[100] Scotus, *Lectura* I, d.17, p.1, q.u, n.38; Vat XVII.194–5.

[101] Scotus, *Lectura* I, d.17, p.1, q.u, n.41; Vat XVII.196–7.

[102] Scotus, *Lectura* I, d.17, p.1, q.u, n.41; Vat XVII.196–7.

6. OCKHAM'S REVISIONS

a. Elevating agent and action

The Holy Spirit is given to make us holy, not only to repair our nature of any damage taken as a consequence of Adam's fall, but to elevate us and our acts, to make us worthy of eternal life. Aquinas and Henry of Ghent want to explain such elevation by appeal to infused supernatural habits. They take these habits to exceed nature twice over: we have no natural passive power to receive them, and no creature has or is active causal power to produce them. These habits, they think, give us supernatural being (*esse*), re-order us to our supernatural end, and constitute formal active causal principles that perfect our acts by making them meritorious.

Scotus and Ockham agree that special Divine action is required to elevate rational creatures to worthiness of eternal life, of beatific vision and enjoyment of God. But not even God can fit us for our supernatural end simply by infusing habits, and that for two reasons. First, Scotus thinks it is metaphysically incoherent to imagine that any power could make us receive habits which we have no natural passive power to receive. Not even God could augment the receptive power of the intellect so that it could be the subject of color![103] Second, whether or not such habits are naturally producible or receivable, they will in any event be created qualities. Creatures are only finite goods; what they essentially are constitutes at most a defeasible reason for producing them. No creature is by its very nature intrinsically worthy of Divine acceptance. Infusing finitely many finite accidents into a finite substance could not raise any rational creature to such a level of natural excellence as to make it naturally entitled to eternal life.[104]

Ockham agrees with Scotus that the meritorious act of loving God above all has to have the creature's own will for its chief formal active principle.[105] So far as Aristotelian method is concerned, Ockham also joins Scotus in contending that neither experience nor demonstrative reason would lead us to posit infused habits to explain the human acts we witness. Infused habits are not required to account for the action or its intentional direction.

[103] For an extensive discussion of Scotus' insistence that the soul must have a *natural* passive power to receive any accidents that it receives and his critique of Aquinas, see Allan B. Wolter, "Duns Scotus on the Natural Desire for the Supernatural," reprinted in *The Philosophical Theology of John Duns Scotus* (Ithaca and London: Cornell University Press, 1990), ch. 6, 125–47.

[104] Ockham, *Quaest. in I Sent.* d.17; OTh III.452–3, 455–6.

[105] Ockham, *Quaest. in I Sent.* d.17, q.1; OTh III.470, 473–4.

Unadorned will-power is itself power to love God above all and for God's own sake, and power to will what right reason dictates because right reason dictates it. Infused habits are not required to account for the intensity of the action. There is no level of intensity of will-acts that falls outside the scope of will-power as such. Nor are infused habits needed to account for the manner of an action (that it is performed promptly, delightfully, expeditiously, etc.). Acquired habits would do just as well.[106]

Where meritorious acts are concerned, Divine action is not required to be or (by infusing habits) to supply extra efficient causality for the production of the act over and above that involved in general concurrence. Rather Divine action is needed to accept the created agent and/or its act as worthy of eternal life. Divine ordinance is what sets the norms that make such created actions count as meritorious. Like Scotus, Ockham emphasizes that the criteria for Divine acceptance and merit are a product of God's free and contingent volition. God could have made free choice in accordance with right reason and/or Divine commands sufficient for worthiness of eternal life. Metaphysically, there neither is nor could be any necessary connection between the inherence of an infused habit before death and the soul's continued existence after death, much less the perpetual existence in the soul of acts of beatific vision and enjoyment. If—as the Saints say—God also demands infused habits in the agent, that is a function of Divine free choice and it was within Divine power to choose otherwise.[107]

b. Twisting Lombard's wax nose

Ockham notes the controversy over how to construe Lombard, when in *Sentences* I, d.17, he seems to deny infused charity, but in *Sentences* II, d.27, he appears to posit infused grace in the soul. If others try to harmonize by bringing Lombard closer to the common opinion, Ockham counters by turning Lombard into an Ockhamist. What if, when Lombard claims that the Holy Spirit is the charity that makes us love God and neighbor, he means that charity without which no one can be accepted by God or do anything meritorious—viz., God's will to accept? Taken that way, "charity" principally signifies the Divine will and connotes someone worthy of

[106] Ockham, *Quest. in III Sent.* q.9, a.1; OTh VI.279–80; *Quaestiones variae*, q.6, a.8; OTh VIII.246–7.

[107] Ockham, *Quaest. in I Sent.* d.17, q.1; OTh III.445, 452–5; I, d.17, q.2; OTh III.471–2; *Quaestiones variae*, q.1; OTh VIII.21. For an extensive discussion of Ockham's position and his interactions with opponents such as Peter Aureol, Walter Chatton, and John Lutterell, see my *William Ockham*, ch. 30, 1257–97. See also Rega Wood, "Ockham's Repudiation of Pelagianism," in P.V. Spade (ed.), *The Cambridge Companion to Ockham* (Cambridge: Cambridge University Press, 1999), 350–73.

eternal life. What if "love God and neighbor" is short for "love God and neighbor meritoriously"? Lombard's meaning would then be this: God's will-act of Divine acceptance is the charity that makes our will-act of loving God and neighbor meritorious. No Genuine Agency Problem arises on this interpretation, because Divine charity does not keep created wills from being efficient causes of their will-acts, but rather counts them as worthy of eternal life. Nor would Lombard have to deny the further gift of an infused habit that inclines us to the love of God. What he would be claiming is that the infused habit is not of itself what makes its possessor worthy of Divine acceptance or his/her acts meritorious, because the infused habits without the charity that the Holy Spirit *is*—viz., the Divine will to accept—will not suffice to make the agent or its acts acceptable.[108]

c. Special connections, divided Trinity?

When it comes to theological statements about the procession, the sending, and the giving of Divine persons, Ockham finds the issue more verbal than substantive. All agree that the following are to be maintained:

[1] each and every Divine person is an efficient and final cause of each and every creature;

[2] two Divine persons—the Son and the Holy Spirit—eternally proceed, and two Divine persons—the Father and the Son—eternally produce;

[3] each and every Divine person can cause a special gift in a rational creature—not only gifts given to those already graced, but also a gift that makes the creature graced;

[4] only the Son and no other Divine person is incarnate;

[5] each and every Divine person can be provided to do whatever a rational creature reasonably requests.[109]

His predecessors have offered different ways of accommodating wording found in the Scriptures and the sayings of the Saints to express these claims. In some cases, they have advanced philosophically unacceptable theories to explain the semantics. Ockham agrees with Bonaventure, Aquinas, and Scotus: no hypostatic union is involved in the Holy Spirit's proceeding, being sent or given to elect rational creatures; only God the Son is sent via hypostatic union into human being.[110] Nor is the Holy Spirit's proceeding,

[108] Ockham, *Quaest. in I Sent.* d.17, q.3, c; OTh III.476–7.
[109] Ockham, *Quaest. in I Sent.* d.14, q.1; OTh III.425.
[110] Ockham, *Quaest. in I Sent.* d.14, q.1; OTh III.425.

being sent or given to elect rational creatures to be accounted for in terms of any doctrine of non-mutual relations (such as Aquinas espouses), a doctrine which Ockham regards as philosophically incoherent. Ockham contends that a relation of reason's obtaining between X and Y depends upon some intellect's comparing and thus relating them, and is thus a being of reason. By contrast, that X and Y are really related, pertains to X and Y prior to and independently of any activity of the intellect relating them. The Holy Spirit really proceeds, not only eternally but temporally. The Holy Spirit is really sent and is really given. And—*pace* Aquinas—it cannot *really* proceed, be *really* sent or given because of any being of reason![111] Nevertheless, the fact that the Holy Spirit and the rational creature are really related, means neither that the real relation is a thing really distinct from its relata,[112] nor that the real relation must be founded on any infused habit in the creature. The Holy Spirit is really given to a creature, the way one friend offers himself to another to do what the other reasonably asks, to be used and enjoyed as the other wishes. But this can happen whether or not any other gifts, in the form of infused habits, are given to that rational creature as well.[113]

Given [5] above, however, there seems to be no metaphysical basis for saying that it is the Holy Spirit that is given as opposed to the Father and the Son. The Saints' way of speaking singles out the Holy Spirit and assigns It this function "by appropriation." In fact, the Saints say that the Holy Spirit is given when graced-making grace or charity is infused. Ockham observes, this is primarily conventional usage. They might just as well have said that the Holy Spirit is given when wisdom or faith are infused. But they did not.[114]

So far as missions are concerned, Ockham endorses the following nominal definition:

[Def 1] 'Divine person X is invisibly sent to creature Y' entails '[i] Divine person X eternally proceeds from Divine person Z and [ii] some new effect H is produced in the soul of Y and [iii] H manifests the fact that X eternally proceeds from Z.'

On this analysis, [i] means that only the Son and the Holy Spirit is eligible to be sent. The Father cannot be sent, because the Father does not eternally proceed from another Divine person. If the Holy Spirit or other Divine

111 Ockham, *Quaest. in I Sent.* d.14, q.1; OTh III.426–7; d.15, q.u; OTh III.435. See also I, d.30, q.5; OTh IV.394.

112 Ockham makes this explicit for procession in *Quaest. in I Sent.* d.14, q.1; OTh III.428.

113 Ockham, *Quaest. in I Sent.*, d.14, q.1; OTh III.431.

114 Ockham, *Quaest. in I Sent.* d.14, q.2; OTh III.431–2.

persons could be *given* to a creature apart from any other gifts, [iii] means that no Divine person is *sent* to a creature apart from the infusion of some habit that manifests the eternal mission of the Divine person in question.[115] By contrast,

[Def 2] 'Divine person X is visibly sent to a creature Y' entails [iv] X is invisibly sent to Y, and [v] some visible sign accompanies the invisible sending and manifests it.[116]

Ockham notes that visible appearances occurred under the old covenant without any invisible mission, because the Holy Spirit is given only after the resurrection and ascension of Christ.[117] Moreover, the visible appearances are not always simultaneous with the invisible appearances that they manifest: e.g., the human soul of Christ was full of grace from the beginning, but the invisible mission of the Holy Spirit to him was manifested later by the descent of the dove.[118] As to the question whether the visible signs were a real dove and real fire or only dove- and fire-appearances, Ockham is sure only that it was whichever God wanted. Nevertheless, Ockham inclines to think that it was a real dove and real fire![119]

7. SURVEYING THE SOLUTIONS

All of our authors agree: Pelagius was wrong, because—over and above creating, sustaining, and general concurrence; over and above publishing the ten commandments—God acts to make the elect holy. God makes the elect holy by "extras" that God efficiently causes and by indwelling their souls.

a. Genuine agency

Bonaventure and Aquinas read Lombard as making the Divine will the total efficient cause of the created will-act of loving God above all. Bonaventure, Aquinas, and Henry of Ghent all agree: for the act of willing A to belong to X, it is not enough for X to have a formal passive principle for receiving an act of willing A. There must also exist in X a formal active principle for willing A. What human beings need to be the genuine agents of meritorious acts, is not for the Divine persons to be the total efficient

115 Ockham, *Quaest. in I Sent.* d.15, q.u; OTh III.435.
116 Ockham, *Quaest. in I Sent.* d.16, q.u; OTh III.437–8.
117 Ockham, *Quaest. in I Sent.* d.16, q.u; OTh III.439.
118 Ockham, *Quest. in I Sent.* d.16, q.u; OTh III.438.
119 Ockham, *Quaest. in I Sent.* d.16, q.u; OTh III.439.

cause of such acts, but for the Divine persons to endow the soul with more and better formal active principles. The "extras" produced by genuine Divine agency are supernatural habits infused into human souls. Henry of Ghent tries for balance. Genuine Divine agency is predominant because the Divine persons are the sole cause of the supernatural infused habits, and because infused charity is the only formal active principle in St. Paul's soul involved in producing the will-act of loving God above all. Nevertheless, the will-act belongs to St. Paul, because St. Paul is its receiving subject and because the formal active principle involved in producing it (the infused habit) is *in* him! Aquinas strikes a different balance, maintaining that the infused habit and St. Paul's will-power are each and both efficient partial causes of his will-act to love God above all.

Scotus' standards for genuine agency are higher. He maintains that for an act of willing A to belong to X, it is not enough for X to be the passive receiving subject of formal active principles for willing A. For an act of willing A to belong to X, the operant formal active principles must be *naturally suited* to X, either because they are included in X's nature or naturally suited to perfect it. Supernaturally infused habits—as Bonaventure, Aquinas, and Henry of Ghent conceive of them—are not naturally suited to creatures. So making X a passive receiving subject of them does not help secure genuine agency for X.

Scotus and Ockham contend that for an act of willing A to belong to X, X's own will-power must be at least an efficient partial cause of it. They also maintain human will-power is sufficient to account any observed human will-acts, no matter what their intensity. No extra formal active principles need to be infused into X to enable X to be a genuine agent in loving God above all or in willing to do whatever right reason dictates because right reason dictates it. On the contrary, Scotus worries that supernatural infused habits might interfere with X's genuine agency by causally determining the will-act. Scotus flirts with demoting supernaturally infused habits to passive disposing conditions before he finally concedes that such habits are partial active causes of will-acts.

Scotus and Ockham agree. Human beings do not need God's help to produce will-acts to love God above all or to do whatever right reason dictates because right reason dictates it. The "extras" genuine Divine agency is needed to produce are Divine policies for counting human actions and agents worthy of Divine acceptance. The principal obstacle to human worthiness is not damage but finitude. Even supernaturally infused functional habits cannot solve this problem, because they also are finite, indeed less metaphysically excellent than the human soul itself.

b. Special connection, divided Trinity

Biblical language—that the Son and/or the Holy Spirit are sent, that the Holy Spirit is given, that one or all of the Divine persons indwell believers—can be construed in ways that are metaphysically "heavy" and in ways that are metaphysically "light." Going metaphysically "heavy" preserves the original intuition that indwelling is in itself a non-causal connection between God—whether the Trinity as a whole, or the Son or the Holy Spirit alone—and the human person. Hypostatic union of the Holy Spirit with the created will-power in itself leaves open what the Divine will may have or have not done to determine created will-acts. Likewise, Aquinas' suggestion that there are primitive relations whose foundations are infused habits and whose terms are either the Trinity as a whole or one Divine person apart from the others—could be combined either with Henry of Ghent's contention—that infused habits are the only active principles in producing the will-act of loving God above all—or with Aquinas' more modest claim—that infused habits and human will-power collaborate as partial active causes. Going metaphysically "heavy" also preserves the notion that indwelling is something more than the inherence of supernaturally infused habits.

Metaphysically "light" interpretations (such as Scotus and Ockham sponsor) come with fewer philosophical difficulties. The Trinity are specially connected to the elect, because They cause special benefits to exist in the elect: in this cradle-to-grave life, the theological virtues and many other habits to make them more godlike; in the world to come, infused habits plus permanent acts of seeing and enjoying God. To say that the Trinity or the Son or the Holy Spirit indwells, or that the Son or Holy Spirit is sent or given to St. Paul could be reduced to references to intra-deical Divine productions and to the existence of one or another infused habit in St. Paul's soul. Thus, "the Son is sent to St. Paul" would turn out to mean something like "the Father eternally begets the Son and the Trinity cause a supernatural habit of wisdom in St. Paul's soul," while "the Holy Spirit is given to St. Paul" would mean something like "the Father and the Son breathe the Holy Spirit and the Trinity cause a supernatural habit of charity to exist in St. Paul's soul." Likewise, "the Son indwells St. Paul" would mean "the Trinity cause a supernatural habit of wisdom in St. Paul's soul," while "the Holy Spirit indwells St. Paul" would mean "the Trinity cause a supernatural habit of charity in St. Paul's soul." Talk of one Divine person being given or sent without the others is explained away as "appropriation" or as a theologically conventional manner of speaking. On such reductions, "sending," "giving," and "indwelling" do turn out to be causal notions: there is the intra-deical causality by which the Father produces the Son, and the Father and Son produce the Holy Spirit; and there is the extra-deical causality by which the Trinity as a whole infuses supernatural habits into the elect. Nevertheless, on such reductions, sending, giving, and indwelling would not signal any Divine further interference in genuine human agency over and above the infusion of the supernatural habits themselves.

University of North Carolina, Chapel Hill

BIBLIOGRAPHY

Adams, Marilyn McCord. "Relations, Subsistence, and Inherence, or Was Ockham a Nestorian in Christology?" *Noûs* 16 (1982), 62–75.

—— "The Metaphysics of the Incarnation in Some Fourteenth Century Franciscans," in *Essays Honoring Allan B. Wolter* (St. Bonaventure, NY: Franciscan Institute Publications, 1985), 21–57.

—— *William Ockham* (Notre Dame, IN: University of Notre Dame Press, 1989).

—— "What's Metaphysically Special about Supposits?" *Proceedings of the Aristotelian Society* Supplementary Volume 79 (2005), 15–52.

—— *Christ and Horrors: The Coherence of Christology* (Cambridge: Cambridge University Press, 2006).

Bonaventure, *Commentaria in quatuor libros Sententiarum Magistri Petri Lombardi*, in the Fathers of the College of St. Bonaventure (eds), *Opera Omnia* (Quaracchi: Typographia Collegii S. Bonaventure, 1882–1902), vols. I–IV.

Cross, Richard. *The Metaphysics of the Incarnation: Thomas Aquinas to Duns Scotus* (Oxford: Oxford University Press, 2002).

Freddoso, Alfred J. "Medieval Aristotelianism and the Case against Secondary Causation in Nature," in T. V. Morris (ed.), *Divine and Human Action: Essays in the Metaphysics of Theism* (Ithaca: Cornell University Press, 1988), 74–118.

Godfrey of Fontaines. *Quodlibeta*, ed. M. De Wulf, J. Hoffmans, and O. Lottin, *Les Philosophes Belges* (Louvain: Institut Supérieur de Philosophie de l'Université, 1914–1935), vols. I–V.

Henninger, Mark G. *Relations: Medieval Theories 1250–1325* (Oxford: Clarendon Press, 1989).

Henry of Ghent. *Quodlibeta* (Paris, 1518; repr. Louvain: Bibliothèque S.J., 1961).

John Duns Scotus. *Opera omnia*, ed. C. Balic et al. (Vatican City: Typis Polyglottis Vaticanis, 1950–) [= Vat].

—— *Opera omnia*, ed. L. Wadding (Lyon, 1639; repr. Hildesheim: Georg Olms Verlagsbuchhandlung, 1968) [= Wad].

Peter Lombard. *Sententiae in IV libris distinctae*, ed. the Fathers of the College of St. Bonaventure (Rome: Grottaferrata, 1971).

Thomas Aquinas. *Scriptum super Sententiis. Corpus Thomisticum* http://www.corpusthomisticum.org/iopera.html.

Thomas Aquinas. *De caritate* in *Quaestiones disputatae ad fidem optimarum editionum* (Paris: P. Lethielleux, 1884), vol. II.

—— *Summa theologica* (Matriti: Biblioteca de Autores Cristianos, 1955–8).

William Ockham. *Opera theologica*, ed. G. Gál et al. (St. Bonaventure, NY: Franciscan Institute Publications, 1967–86), vols. I–X [= OTh].

Wolter, Allan B. "Duns Scotus on the Natural Desire for the Supernatural," reprinted in *The Philosophical Theology of John Duns Scotus* (Ithaca: Cornell University Press, 1990), 125–47.

Wood, Rega. "Ockham's Repudiation of Pelagianism," in P. V. Spade (ed.), *The Cambridge Companion to Ockham* (Cambridge: Cambridge University Press, 1999), 350–73.

What Lucifer Wanted: Anselm, Aquinas, and Scotus on the Object of the First Evil Choice

Giorgio Pini

1. THE LUCIFER PROBLEM

Suppose that God created the world entirely good and that evil made its first appearance through the free choice of one of God's creatures—say, Lucifer.[1] These two claims, which constitute the core of a long-standing way to explain why there is evil in a God-created world, have sometimes been thought to be inconsistent. Here is how a prominent critic of this tradition, John Hick, describes the problem:

> The basic and inevitable criticism is that the idea of an unqualifiedly good creature committing sin is self-contradictory and unintelligible. If the angels are finitely perfect, then even though they are in some important sense free to sin they will never in fact do so. If they do sin we can only infer that they were not flawless—in which case their Maker must share the responsibility for their fall and the intended theodicy fails.[2]

[1] The claim that evil was introduced into the world by a rebel angel called "Lucifer" is based on an idiosyncratic interpretation of a few biblical passages, first and foremost among which is Isaiah 14:12–14. See Neil Forsyth, *The Old Enemy: Satan and the Combat Myth* (Princeton: Princeton University Press, 1987), 134–9. Whereas most details of Lucifer's story will not be relevant to what follows, the two aspects to be retained are that God created Lucifer entirely good and that Lucifer's evil choice was unprecedented. For an excellent treatment of the main philosophical difficulties connected with the first evil choice, see Scott MacDonald, "Primal Sin," in G. B. Matthews (ed.), *The Augustinian Tradition* (Berkeley: University of California Press, 1998), 110–39.

[2] John Hick, *Evil and the God of Love* (New York: Harper & Row, 1966), 68–9. As Hick notices, this criticism is already found in Schleiermacher.

The claim is that, even though it is possible for an entirely or unqualifiedly good agent to be *able* to make an evil choice, actually making an evil choice is incompatible with being entirely or unqualifiedly good. The tacit piece of reasoning behind this claim is presumably that rational agents make evil choices only if they have a motive; but agents have a motive to do evil only if they are not entirely or unqualifiedly good, for it is assumed that to be motivated to do evil and to be entirely or unqualifiedly good are incompatible features. So if God created Lucifer entirely good, Lucifer had no motive to do evil and thus was not the sort of agent who would make an evil choice. By contrast, if Lucifer did make an evil choice, then he had a motive to do evil and thus it is not the case that God created Lucifer entirely good.

Striking as this argument is, one may object to the key assumption that to be motivated to do evil and to be entirely good are incompatible features. For it is not uncommon for morally good agents both to be motivated to make evil choices and actually to make evil choices. For example, they may not know that their choices are evil or they may believe that they are going to get something good out of what they would otherwise not choose. This objection, however, misses the point. For moral goodness is only one component of Lucifer's overall goodness. The claim that God created Lucifer entirely good can be plausibly taken to entail that Lucifer was not only morally good, but also *intellectually flawless* and *supremely happy*, i.e. as happy as he could be. Because Lucifer was supremely happy, he had no reason to change his condition. Because Lucifer was intellectually flawless, he had no wrong belief about what was good for him—specifically, he did not have the wrong belief that he could be happier than he was. Therefore, Lucifer knew that he had no reason to change his condition. But Lucifer did choose to change his condition in some respect (e.g. by getting something that he did not have). Accordingly, his choice appears to be irrational. Now only agents who are flawed in some respect make irrational choices. Therefore, if Lucifer's choice was irrational, Lucifer was not created entirely good and his choice was not the first occurrence of evil, contrary to what has been assumed.

So Hick's criticism turns out to be potentially devastating for traditional attempts to explain the presence of evil in the world as the result of a created agent's free choice. However, it is not accurate to claim, as Hick did immediately before the passage I have quoted, that the belief that evil was introduced by the fall of the angels was historically successful only because the thinkers who embraced it were "content to refrain from examining it."[3] In fact, that belief has been subjected to intense scrutiny at least from Augustine

[3] Hick, *Evil and the God of Love*, 68.

onwards. Several medieval thinkers tried to solve the difficulty Hick mentions by considering what the object or goal of the first evil choice might have been. What did Lucifer want (and presumably fail) to achieve? Their hope was to identify an object such that a flawless agent might have plausibly and rationally wanted to attain it through a choice that should nevertheless be described as evil.

In the growing literature about medieval views on Lucifer's fall, surprisingly little attention has been paid to the object of his choice. I have decided to focus on the views of three great medieval thinkers, i.e. Anselm, Thomas Aquinas, and John Duns Scotus, in order to identify some of the basic moves in this debate. As will emerge from what follows, there is a major divide between Anselm and Aquinas, on the one hand, and, on the other hand, Scotus. While both Anselm and Aquinas held that the first occurrence of evil could be explained only if God did not create Lucifer as supremely happy, Scotus held a view that did not commit him to that claim.

Those three authors' treatments of Lucifer's choice turn out to be of special philosophical interest in two different areas. First, from the point of view of moral psychology, Anselm, Aquinas, and Scotus inquired whether flawless rational agents can make evil choices without giving up their rationality. This is arguably one of the deepest problems concerning evildoing. Second, from the point of view of the philosophy of religion, those thinkers inquired whether God could have created the world in such a way that an evil choice, even though possible, would have been less attractive than it actually was—perhaps so unattractive that no rational agent would have actually made it. This is arguably one of the most challenging questions that a theodicy based on the notion of free will has to answer.

In what follows, I first consider Anselm's claim that Lucifer's choice did not exceed the limits of what was naturally possible for him. According to Anselm, Lucifer chose to obtain something that he could have obtained through the exercise of his natural capacities. Then, I turn to Aquinas's view that Lucifer chose something beyond what was naturally possible for him, i.e. something that he could have obtained only through God's supernatural intervention. Finally, I present Scotus's view that the object of the first evil choice might have exceeded the limits of what is logically possible. Specifically, Lucifer may have wished to be God's equal. In some way, it would be hard to think of an act of rebellion more radical than a wish not for an alternative state of affairs but for something literally inconceivable and unactualizable. Scotus's suggestion is that, in a completely good world created by a supremely good God, evil could not have occurred unless one had considered what lay beyond the realm of what is logically possible.

2. ANSELM: WILLING MORE HAPPINESS

In a short and dense exchange between student and teacher in Anselm's dialogue *On the fall of the devil*, the student rejects the teacher's suggestion that what Lucifer wanted was to be "inordinately like God."[4] The student's argument is based on the premise that God is such that nothing like him can be thought. In other words, God is necessarily unique. The student further assumes that only somebody slow-witted could know what God is without knowing that he is necessarily unique. Lucifer, however, was not slow-witted (*ita obtunsae mentis*). Thus, since Lucifer must have known what God is (something that even an unbeliever knows, according to Anselm), he must also have known that God is necessarily unique. But a choice to be like God presupposes the belief that it is possible to be like God. And having that belief in turn entails having the belief that God is not necessarily unique. Therefore, Lucifer could not have wanted to be like God.[5]

The teacher accepts the student's argument. He explains that the claim that Lucifer wanted to be like God should not be interpreted as meaning that Lucifer wanted to be "completely equal to God." Rather, Lucifer wanted something that God did not want him to want. Accordingly, Lucifer wanted something by his own will, without subjecting his will to God's will—he wanted what he wanted independently of whether God approved of his willing it or not. Now the teacher goes on to notice that it is God's prerogative to will something by his own will without subjecting his will to a superior will, for no will is superior to God's will. The implicit conclusion is that Lucifer wanted to be like God only in a qualified sense—not because the object of his pursuit was to be like God but because, by willing what he willed, he did not subject his will to God's will. But this qualified equality with God was not the target of Lucifer's choice. Rather, it was a by-product of his willing something that God did not want him to will.[6]

[4] The traditional claim that Lucifer wanted to be God's equal was based on Isaiah 14:14: "I will ascend above the height of the clouds, I will be like the most High." See also Ezekiel 18:1–9 and the similar promise made by the serpent to Adam and Eve in Genesis 3:5, "you shall be as Gods." (I quote from the King James Version.)

[5] Anselm, *De casu diaboli* 4 (ed. Schmitt, 241). For a slightly different interpretation of this passage, see Marilyn McCord Adams, "St. Anselm on Evil: De casu Diaboli," *Documenti e studi sulla tradizione filosofica medievale* 3 (1992), 429–30.

[6] Anselm, *De casu diaboli* 4 (ed. Schmitt, 242). For a recent treatment of Anselm's account of Lucifer's fall, see Peter King, "Scotus's Rejection of Anselm: The Two-Wills Theory," in L. Honnefelder et al. (eds.), *John Duns Scotus 1308–2008: Investigations into His Philosophy* (Münster: Aschendorff, 2011), 359–65; and King, "Angelic Sin in Augustine and Anselm," in T. Hoffmann (ed.), *A Companion to Angels in Medieval Philosophy* (Leiden: Brill, 2012), 273–81.

What, then, did Lucifer want? The teacher admits, somewhat disappointingly, that he does not know. But teacher and student agree that the mysterious object of Lucifer's choice must have satisfied four requirements. First, it must have been something advantageous for Lucifer, because it is assumed that rational agents only want what they believe is either just (i.e. something that God wants them to will) or advantageous for them. But it is impossible to make an evil choice by willing something just, because evil is nothing else than injustice, i.e. willing something against God's will. Therefore, Lucifer must have willed something advantageous. Second, it must have been something that Lucifer was able to attain, presumably because rational agents do not intend to achieve something they know they cannot get. Third, it must have been something that Lucifer did not receive when he was created, because he had received all he had from God and so he could not have made an evil choice by willing what he already had. Fourth and finally, the object of Lucifer's choice must have been something that God would have given to Lucifer if Lucifer had refrained from willing it.[7] Accordingly, in the rest of the dialogue, Anselm refers to the object of the first evil choice merely as "something more (*illud plus*) that God did not want to give them [i.e. the angels] yet."[8]

So Anselm can account for the possibility of the first evil choice only by positing that God did not create Lucifer and the other angels supremely happy. The reason Anselm gives for God's decision is that he wanted the angels to deserve supreme happiness by their own merit, i.e. by not willing what God wanted them not to will. But Lucifer chose to be happier. Even though that choice was rational, it was nevertheless evil, because it was in conflict with God's will.

There are two problematic aspects in Anselm's view. First, there is something troubling in the claim that God decided to create his creatures less happy than they could naturally be. According to Anselm, God set a limit to the happiness his creatures enjoyed at the moment of their creation in order to allow them to prove themselves. Anselm's God is a tempting God, who put his creatures to a test. Second, the claim that Lucifer's choice to be happier was entirely natural but nonetheless evil is also worrisome. The reason why Lucifer's choice was evil is not that it did not fit with Lucifer's nature or needs but only that God did not want Lucifer to decide to be happier at that moment. Even though the responsibility for making an evil choice remains with Lucifer, that choice perfectly matched Lucifer's nature. Not only did God put his creatures to a test, he also did nothing to make the test easier.

7 Anselm, *De casu diaboli* 6 (ed. Schmitt, 241–3).
8 Anselm, *De casu diaboli* 6 (ed. Schmitt, 243).

3. AQUINAS: DELAYED BEATITUDE AND THE WILL TO BE BLESSED

Aquinas agrees with Anselm's two characteristic claims that Lucifer could not have willed to be unqualifiedly like God and that Lucifer and the other angels were not created supremely happy. But he gives new arguments in support of these claims. He also corrects Anselm in an important respect. According to Aquinas, it is not the case that Lucifer wanted something that he could have attained through the exercise of his natural capacities.[9]

Aquinas has two arguments to reject the view that Lucifer wanted to achieve equality with God "in an unqualified sense" or "absolutely." Both arguments are grounded on Lucifer's rationality.

First, Aquinas argues that for something to be equal to God involves a contradiction. Aquinas's demonstration can be reconstructed in this way. Suppose that it is possible for something to be equal to God. Then it is possible for the type "God" to be instantiated (at least) twice. But this is logically impossible. Aquinas's demonstration of the latter point is based on his characteristic view that God is subsisting existence itself (*ipsum esse subsistens*) and on the impossibility of there being two subsisting existences.[10] Aquinas further argues that Lucifer cannot have been ignorant of this, because of his purely intellectual nature and flawless condition before the fall. But one may assume that no rational agent tries to achieve what she knows to entail something impossible. Therefore, Lucifer could not have willed to be equal to God absolutely, i.e. to be a god.[11]

Second, Aquinas argues that, even if it were possible for somebody to become equal to God in an unqualified sense, that agent would lose her nature, i.e. she would not be the same sort of thing and, consequently, she would not be the same individual. But any agent desires her own good and does not care for the good that would happen to her (so to speak) if she were to become a different individual. Again, because of his intellectual

[9] I base my analysis on Aquinas's *Questions on evil.* See Aquinas, *Quaestiones disputatae de malo* (= *DM*) 16.3. For parallel treatments, see *Summa theologiae* (= *ST*) I, 63.3; *Scriptum super libros Sententiarum* 2.5.1.2. See Tobias Hoffmann, "Aquinas and Intellectual Determinism: The Test Case of Angelic Sin," *Archiv für Geschichte der Philosophie* 89 (2007), 122–56; and Hoffmann, "Theories of Angelic Sin from Aquinas to Ockham," in *A Companion to Angels*, 286–9. Specifically on the object of Lucifer's choice, see Edward J. Montano, *The Sin of Angels: Some Aspects of the Teaching of St. Thomas* (Washington: The Catholic University of America Press, 1955), 115–59.

[10] Here Aquinas is giving a condensed version of an argument he states in the *De ente et essentia* 4 (ed. Leonina 43: 376–7).

[11] *DM* 16.3 (ed. Leonina 23: 293b).

nature, Lucifer could not have missed this point. Therefore, Lucifer could not have willed to be equal to God in an unqualified sense.[12]

By a similar argument, Aquinas also concludes that Lucifer could not have desired not to be subject to God, because Lucifer knew that any creature is ontologically dependent on God and as a consequence a creature's not being subject to God entails its non-existence. But Lucifer could not will not to exist, because anybody who wills something wills something good *for herself*, and the satisfaction of that volition presupposes her existence.[13]

In these arguments, Aquinas presents Lucifer as a good metaphysician, well aware of subtle points concerning both his own identity and God's nature.

So what about the object of Lucifer's choice? It is here that Aquinas goes beyond Anselm. First, Aquinas claims that angels lacked nothing, for they were created perfect. In other words, Aquinas embraces the claim that Lucifer and the other angels were supremely happy at the moment of their creation. Second, however, Aquinas adds a qualification that puts him squarely back into Anselm's fold. For he distinguishes between the natural and supernatural orders. Even though the angels were perfect and had no potentiality with regard to the order of nature, they did have a potentiality for a supernatural good, which they could obtain only through God's aid. So Lucifer had no motive to make an evil choice concerning what he could achieve by his natural capacities, as he was perfectly happy in that respect. But Lucifer *could* have made an evil choice concerning something beyond what he could obtain by the exercise of his natural capacities, because in that respect he was *not* supremely happy.[14]

Even though it may look like an *ad hoc* move, the distinction between natural and supernatural orders and the corresponding distinction between a created agent's natural and supernatural goals are actually key aspects of Aquinas's thought. Suffice it to say that all rational creatures can reach a state of happiness by the exercise of their natural capacities. In addition to that, however, they also have a potentiality to experience a special kind of

[12] *DM* 16.3 (ed. Leonina 23: 293b–294a).

[13] *DM* 16.3 (ed. Leonina 23: 294a).

[14] *DM* 16.3 (ed. Leonina 23: 294a). See also *ST* I 62.1. On the angels' perfect happiness and impeccability in the natural order, see C. Courtès, "La peccabilité de l'ange chez saint Thomas," *Revue Thomiste* 53 (1953), 133–63. It should be mentioned that the issue of angels' impeccability is closely connected to the relationship between what is natural and what is supernatural, which is a very controversial theme among some Thomistic scholars. For some background, see S.-T. Bonino (ed.), *Surnaturel: A Controversy at the Heart of Twentieth-Century Thomistic Thought*, tr. R. Williams (Ave Maria: Sapientia Press, 2009).

intimacy with God, called the "beatific vision." Even though rational creatures have a potentiality for this supernatural experience, at the enjoyment of which all their actions are ultimately directed, they cannot actualize that potentiality by the exercise of their natural capacities. Their inability depends not on God's arbitrary decision but on the infinite gap between God and his creatures.[15]

Since ultimate happiness, even in the natural order, involves knowledge of God, at the moment of his creation an angel could achieve as much knowledge of God as he was naturally capable of. Specifically, he could know God by knowing himself as a faithful image of God.[16] But such knowledge of God is not the union and intimacy with God that is reached in the beatific vision. Such a union and intimacy with God can only be granted by God's grace. Although creatures *can* enjoy that union when God's grace is given, they *cannot* achieve that state by the exercise of their natural capacities. So the beatific vision is something possible for rational creatures but beyond what is *naturally* possible for them.

Now it is Aquinas's contention that angels could make an evil choice just because they were not blessed, for rational agents can make evil choices only in the pursuit of some good they do not yet have. The object of Lucifer's evil choice was precisely a missing good, i.e. the beatific vision. Lucifer simply wanted to be intimate with God, which he wasn't yet. The problem was not what Lucifer wanted, which was in itself good—actually, the supreme good a creature could enjoy. Rather, the problem was the *way* Lucifer wanted what he wanted. He wanted to achieve beatitude without God's help, i.e. not by grace. Thus, he wanted to see God by the exercise of his own natural capacities. Lucifer, however, never rebelled against his ontological dependence on God. Being a good metaphysician, he recognized that it would be impossible for him to exist if he did not depend on God:

> Therefore, the devil's first sin was that, to attain the supernatural happiness consisting of the complete vision of God, he did not elevate himself to God so as to desire with holy angels his ultimate perfection through God's grace. Rather, he wanted to attain his ultimate perfection by the power of his own nature without God bestowing grace, although not without God acting on his nature.[17] (Trans. Regan, 456)

[15] *ST* I 12.4.

[16] *ST* I 56.3.

[17] *DM* 16.3 (ed. Leonina 23: 394a). The English translation is from Thomas Aquinas, *On Evil*, translated by R. Regan, edited with an introduction and notes by B. Davies (Oxford: Oxford University Press, 2003).

I call this explanation of the origin of evil the "delayed beatitude model." An evil choice was a viable option for Lucifer only because his supernatural happiness (i.e. his union with God in the beatific vision) was delayed to a moment posterior to that of his creation.

It is worth stressing that Aquinas thought that the first occurrence of evil could not be explained by appealing to anything within the natural order. Rather, the appearance of evil can be explained only by considering the supernatural goal a rational creature can enjoy at God's discretion. In this way, Aquinas manages to preserve God's goodness. Unlike what is found in Anselm, God created Lucifer supremely happy, even though only with regard to the order of nature. Aquinas also manages to preserve Lucifer's rationality. Similarly to what Anselm had posited, he holds that Lucifer chose more happiness, i.e. supernatural happiness.

It is also worth stressing that, for Aquinas, God could not have created the world in such a way that Lucifer could have achieved the union with God by nature and not by grace. In other words, God did not arbitrarily subtract from the happiness that Lucifer could have naturally enjoyed. What Aquinas calls a divine rule, i.e. that Lucifer could achieve supernatural happiness only by grace and not by his own forces, is due to the unavoidable gap between God and the world, not to God's arbitrary decision. It is God's prerogative to enjoy beatitude naturally. All rational creatures need God's grace to reach that state, just because they are creatures.[18]

Since Lucifer wanted to achieve the union with God by his own forces, one can say that he wanted his own good inordinately and immoderately. This means that Lucifer wanted his own good in a way that was not commensurate to the limits of his nature.[19] Lucifer's *faux pas* was that, when he made his choice, he failed to consider the limits of his nature and his place in the world. According to Aquinas, this failure was cognitive but was not a genuine mistake. Lucifer did not entertain a wrong belief about his nature and his place in the world. Specifically, he did not think that he was able to be united with God without grace. Rather, Lucifer *failed to consider* that his nature was such that he could not be united with God without grace.[20] Thus, his cognitive failure, which preceded his evil choice,

[18] *ST* I 12.4 and 62.4. On the divine rule establishing that all creatures need grace in order to attain a state of supernatural happiness (i.e. the beatific vision) and on Lucifer's failure to subject himself to that rule, see *DM* 16.2 ad 1 (ed. Leonina 23: 289b); *DM* 16.2 ad 7 (ed. Leonina 23: 290b); *DM* 16.3 ad 1 (ed. Leonina 23: 294b). See Hoffmann, "Aquinas and Intellectual Determinism," 134.

[19] *DM* 16.2 ad 4 (ed. Leonina 23: 289b–290a).

[20] As Aquinas argues in *ST* I 12.4, this is not a revealed truth; rather, it can be known by natural reason.

was not that he had a wrong occurrent belief but that he failed to have a true occurrent belief about the limits of his nature and capacities.[21]

Aquinas is adamant that Lucifer's cognitive failure was not the sign of a natural flaw. By the exercise of his natural capacities, Lucifer *could* have had the right belief at the right time, i.e. he could have realized that he was unable to reach the union with God by the exercise of his natural capacities. That he did not form that belief was not in itself a fault. But it created the condition for a fault, namely the choice to pursue supernatural happiness by his own forces.[22]

In his account of Lucifer's choice, Aquinas avoids commitment to the two questionable points I noted in Anselm. First, God sets no arbitrary limit to the natural happiness enjoyed by his creatures. That the enjoyment of supernatural happiness is beyond what rational creatures can reach by their natural capacities does not depend on God's decision but on the gap between God and his creatures. Second, Lucifer's fault was not that he chose to be happier against God's will but that he did so without considering the limits of his nature (which even God could not have eliminated). That choice was an act of pride.

There is, however, a problematic point in Aquinas's account as well. It is true that God could not have created the world in such a way that an evil choice would have been impossible, because the gap between God and his creatures, on which the difference between natural and supernatural happiness depends, is a necessary characteristic of the world. Nevertheless, it seems that God could have created the world in such a way that an evil choice, although possible, would have never been made by a rational agent. For God could have made Lucifer enjoy the beatific vision from the very moment of his creation. If Lucifer had been supernaturally happy at the moment of his creation, he would have had no motive to make an evil choice. Lucifer's evil choice is explicable only if his beatitude was delayed. But God decided not to create Lucifer in a state of beatitude. So Lucifer could rationally make the evil choice to attain beatitude by his own forces. He did so, and evil entered the world. Aquinas justifies God's decision by stressing that beatitude was not owed to the angels from the moment of their creation, because it was not part of their natures but the goal at which their natures were aimed.[23] But the point of this claim is obscure. First, Aquinas himself admits that the beatific vision is the goal at which any rational creature's nature is ultimately directed. Undeniably, Lucifer

[21] *DM* 16.2 ad 4 (ed. Leonina 23: 290a).

[22] *DM* 1.3 (ed. Leonina 23: 16a). See Hoffmann, "Aquinas and Intellectual Determinism," 140–1.

[23] *ST* I 62.1.

was created naturally happy, but it is as if the rules of the game had been changed at the moment of his creation and a new goal was set for him—a goal distinct from that which he was naturally equipped to reach. Second, what is at issue is not so much what God, once he decided to create the world, owed to his creatures in order to make them naturally happy. Rather, what is at issue is whether God could have made things such that an evil choice would not have been made, independently of what he owed to his creatures out of strict justice. It is at best debatable whether Aquinas's remark that God owed nothing to his creatures does anything to justify the creation of a world where it is not just possible but even likely for a rational agent to make an evil choice. There is something disturbing in the thought that the world could have been such that no rational creature in their right mind would have made an evil choice, because they would have had no motive to do so, but God decided not to create the world in that way.

4. SCOTUS: A WISH FOR THE IMPOSSIBLE

Scotus's account of Lucifer's choice is characterized by great caution. Without committing himself to just one explanation of what Lucifer actually chose, Scotus nevertheless defends the view that the object of Lucifer's choice might have been to be God's equal. He defends this claim by arguing that the first occurrence of evil might have been a wish for something logically impossible. In that way, he sets the discussion over the first occurrence of evil on new grounds.

Similarly to what Anselm and Aquinas had held, Scotus thinks that the general object of Lucifer's choice was his own happiness.[24] Like Aquinas, Scotus thinks that Lucifer's choice was directed at his own *supreme* happiness. And again like Aquinas, Scotus holds that there is nothing evil

24 Strictly speaking, Scotus holds that Lucifer's choice for something that would make him happier is Lucifer's *second* volition. That act is preceded (logically but possibly even temporally) by Lucifer's act of loving himself excessively, i.e. as only God should be loved. While the first act is an act of love of friendship directed at himself, the second act is an act of love of desire directed at the enjoyment of happiness for himself (on the distinction between these two kinds of acts, see below). Here I will take into account only Lucifer's second act, directed at what would make him happier. Only the second act explains how the first act of self-love is excessive and therefore evil. See *Lectura* (= *Lect.*) 2.6.2, nn. 25–6 (ed. Vat. 18: 377); *Ordinatio* (= *Ord.*) 2.6.2, nn. 34–36 (ed. Vat. 8: 39–41); *Reportatio* (= *Rep.*) 2.6.2, nn. 4–5 (ed. Vat. 22: 618b–19b). In the absence of a critical edition, I make reference to the text of the second book of Scotus's *Reportatio* as printed in the Vivès edition. I have checked it against Tobias Hoffmann's transcription from mss. Oxford, Merton College, 61, and Oxford, Balliol College, 205. I thank Tobias Hoffmann for generously making his transcription available to me.

in the choice to be supremely happy. Such a choice was evil only because it was "immoderate," i.e. unchecked by the power Scotus attributes to the will to direct itself towards what it ought to will according to one's own nature.[25]

In his Parisian lectures on the *Sentences*, Scotus lists four possible ways Lucifer's choice may have been immoderate. First, Lucifer may have willed his happiness more intensely than it was fitting. In turn, this may have occurred in two ways, either by loving happiness for oneself more than for God (i.e. by willing to be happier than God) or by loving God as an object of use, i.e. because the union with God would make one happy, rather than as an object of fruition, i.e. because God is good in himself. Second, Lucifer may have willed to be happy more than it was fitting for his own nature. Third, Lucifer may have willed to achieve a state of supreme happiness earlier than he ought to do. Fourth, Lucifer may have willed to achieve a state of supreme happiness without having to deserve it.[26]

Of the four ways listed by Scotus, the third and the fourth presuppose the delayed beatitude model. If Lucifer wanted to be supremely happy too early, then he was not supremely happy at the moment of his choice. Similarly, if his choice was to achieve supreme happiness without deserving it, the assumption is that God wanted Lucifer to receive supreme happiness as a reward for his merits and so did not give it to him at the moment of his creation.[27] The first and the second way Lucifer's choice may have been

[25] Scotus takes over from Anselm the view that the will has two powers or inclinations, a first power directed at the agent's happiness (the *affectio commodi*) and a second power checking the will's exercise of its first power (the *affectio iustitiae*). See *Lect.* 2.6.2, n. 36 (ed. Vat. 18: 381); *Ord.* 2.6.2, nn. 49–51 (ed. Vat. 8: 48–51); *Rep.* 2.6.2, n. 9 (ed. Vivès: 621a–b). On Scotus's version of Anselm's doctrine of the two powers or inclinations of the will, see Thomas Williams, "The Unmitigated Scotus," *Archiv für Geschichte der Philosophie* 80 (1998), 162–81; Williams, "The Libertarian Foundations of Scotus's Moral Philosophy," *The Thomist* 62 (1998), 193–215; and most recently King, "Scotus's Rejection of Anselm," 365–77. For an overview of Scotus's position on angelic sin, see Tobias Hoffmann, "Duns Scotus's Action Theory in the Context of His Angelology," in *John Duns Scotus 1308–2008*, 403–20.

[26] Scotus, *Rep.* 2.6.2, n. 10 (ed. Vivès 22: 622b–623a). Neither in the *Lectura* nor in the *Ordinatio* does Scotus mention what in the *Reportatio* he gives as the second way. Moreover, in the *Lectura*, he subdivides the first way into two and expresses a preference for what in the *Reportatio* he lists as the second aspect of the first way. Finally, in the *Ordinatio* Scotus says that Lucifer's will to be happy may have been immoderate in still other ways that he does not care to mention. See *Lect.* 2.6.2, nn. 37–8 (ed. Vat. 18: 381–2); *Ord.* 2.6.2, nn. 52–3 (ed. Vat. 8: 51–2).

[27] Scotus accepts the distinction between natural and supernatural happiness, which is presupposed by the delayed beatitude model. See *Lect.* 2.4–5.1–2, n. 17 (ed. Vat. 18: 361); *Ord.* 2.4–5.1–2, n. 16 (ed. Vat. 8: 7). He also holds that God, as a matter of fact, did delay beatitude, even though he could have given it to his creatures at the moment of

immoderate, however, do not presuppose the delayed beatitude model. Suppose that Lucifer had enjoyed supernatural happiness since the moment of his creation. He could still have desired to be happier than God or have loved God in a utilitarian way. Similarly and even more interestingly, even if Lucifer had been as happy as he could be, he might have desired to be even happier, i.e. happier than it was fitting for his nature. In particular, Lucifer may have wished to be as happy as only God can be.[28] In those scenarios, God's decision to delay or not delay Lucifer's beatitude is irrelevant to explain his evil choice.

The possibility that Lucifer may have willed to be as happy as only God can be, which Scotus mentions as the second possible explanation of Lucifer's choice in his *Reportatio*, is particularly interesting, for it tallies with one of the most original aspects of Scotus's account of Lucifer's choice, namely his contention that Lucifer *could* have wanted to be God's equal, in direct opposition to what both Anselm and Aquinas had claimed.[29]

In all three versions of his commentary on the *Sentences*, Scotus devotes an entire question to argue that Lucifer could have wanted to be God's equal. Even though the basic elements of Scotus's position remain the same, it is possible to detect some evolution in the relative weight Scotus gives to one of two strategies he uses to defend his position. Scotus consistently holds that neither strategy, if taken by itself, is sufficient to explain every aspect of Lucifer's choice. But he changes his mind about which of the two strategies is fundamental and which adds some necessary but less important details to his solution.[30]

Scotus's first strategy is to argue that, if an agent wills to do something or to be in a certain state, it is not necessarily the case that that agent has a belief that she can actually do that thing or be in that state. Specifically, Lucifer may have been willing to be God's equal without having the false belief that he could be God's equal. Scotus's point is to show that Lucifer's evil choice does not entail any cognitive failure on his part.

their creation. See *Ord.* 2.4–5.1–2, n. 48 (ed. Vat. 8: 22). The controversial issue is whether God's decision to delay beatitude plays any role in explaining the origin of evil because it made room for Lucifer's evil choice, as Aquinas had maintained.

[28] Since happiness is the state of ultimate perfection of a certain essence, where all the capacities of that essence are exercised in the best way, it follows that the better a certain essence is, the happier it can be. So God is happier than any creature can ever be.

[29] The literal interpretation of the claim that Lucifer wanted to be "like God" had been commonly discarded after Anselm's criticism. Before Anselm, however, Isidore of Seville had endorsed the view that the devil thought he was God's equal and even God's superior. See Isidore's *Sentences* 1.10, in *Patrologia Latina* 83 (Paris: Vivès, 1862), 555b.

[30] Scotus, *Lect.* 2.6.1 (ed. Vat. 18: 371–4); *Ord.* 2.6.1 (ed. Vat. 8: 25–35); *Rep.* 2.6.1 (ed. Vivès 22: 614–17).

Scotus's argument is based on the traditional distinction between the so-called "love of friendship" (*amor amicitiae*) and "love of desire" (*amor concupiscentiae*). In Scotus's rendition, these two kinds of loves are two kinds of acts of the will. The act of loving something by love of friendship involves a two-place relation between the lover and the object of love. For example, parents may love their children by love of friendship. By contrast, the act of loving something by love of desire involves a three-place relation between the lover, the first object of love (*quod*), and the second object of love (*cui*), i.e. that for the sake of which the first object is loved or desired. For example, a parent may desire a good education (first object) for her children (second object).

Now Scotus holds that anything whatsoever can be the object of either act of the will as long as that thing is apprehended as good. This has two interesting consequences. First, somebody can be both the subject and the object of both acts of the will. For example, I can love myself by love of friendship and I can desire for myself something by love of desire. Second, in the case of an act of love of desire, no fit is required between the object of desire and that for the sake of which that thing is desired. The intellect must apprehend each of the two objects as good before the will connects those two objects by an act of love of desire, but it does not have to judge that there is a match between those two objects. Rather, it is the will's job to connect those two objects. The intellect does not have to follow suit. For example, if a parent loves her children by love of friendship and considers living forever a good thing, she may desire that her children live forever even though she does not have the false belief that living forever fits her children's nature.

Scotus uses this model to explain how Lucifer could have made a choice for the impossible, i.e. to be God's equal, without making any cognitive error. For Lucifer correctly cognized both himself and equality with God as good things. Accordingly, he could desire equality with God for himself. Since an act of love of desire does not require a corresponding complex act of the intellect judging that the two objects match each other, Lucifer did not have to form the belief that he could be God's equal. Only if Lucifer had formed that belief would he have made a mistake, because, while it is true that equality with God is something good and so a possible object of desire for a creature, the belief that a creature can be God's equal entails a contradiction.[31]

[31] *Ord.* 2.6.1, nn. 9–10 (ed. Vat. 8: 27–8). See also *Lect.* 2.6.1, n. 10 (ed. Vat. 18: 373); *Rep.* 2.6.1, n. 6 (ed. Vivès 22: 616a). In the *Reportatio*, Scotus calls the will a "comparative power" (*vis collativa*). My interpretation of this expressions is slightly different from the one proposed by Hoffmann. Hoffmann thinks that the claim that

Scotus's second strategy is to argue that for an agent to will to do something or to be in a certain state is actually *compatible* with that agent's having the belief that she cannot do that thing or be in that state. Specifically, Lucifer may have been willing to be God's equal while being fully aware that that was impossible. Scotus's argument is based on the distinction between two meanings of "choice" (*electio*). Let us call them "choice$_1$" and "choice$_2$". A choice$_1$ is any act of the will that follows the intellect's act of full apprehension, i.e. an act of the will that is carried out neither in a state of ignorance nor in a state of emotional perturbation. A choice$_2$ is a choice to *do* something, or, as Scotus says, an *efficacious* choice, i.e. an act of the will that follows the conclusion of a practical syllogism and as such is turned towards doing something. Even though Scotus does not say so explicitly, it seems that any choice$_2$ is also a choice$_1$. But Scotus is adamant that the reverse is not true. Not every choice that presupposes full apprehension is also a choice to do something. A choice$_1$ may be a mere wish.

Since practical syllogisms and deliberations are about things that agents believe to be able to achieve, only things that agents think are possible for them can be the objects of a choice$_2$. By contrast, the object of a choice$_1$ can be beyond the limits of what agents think they can attain. The object of a choice$_1$ can even be logically impossible. To have a wish for the impossible poses no threat to one's rationality as long as one judges the object of that wish to be impossible and as long as one does not decide to obtain it by a choice$_2$.[32]

Scotus calls a choice$_1$ that is not a choice$_2$ a "wish" (*velleitas*) or "conditional volition" (*velle sub condicione*) as opposed to a genuine choice or simple volition. The idea is that wishes should be interpreted as the consequents of conditionals of the form "If such-and-such were the case, I would want for *x* to occur," where the antecedent of that conditional may be either counter-factual or counter-possible. It is the nature of wishes that they can range not just beyond what is actual but even beyond what is logically possible.[33]

According to Scotus, wishes can be morally relevant. A mere wish can even be deemed worthy of the worst punishment or the best reward. In order for a volition to be morally good, it is both necessary *and* sufficient

the will is a collative nature entails that the will forms its own judgment. By contrast, I think that Scotus is calling attention to a class of volitional acts having two objects. I do not think that any "judgment of the will" is involved in those acts. See Hoffmann, "Duns Scotus's Action Theory," 408–12.

32 *Ord.* 2.6.1, n. 14 (ed. Vat. 8: 29). See also *Lect.* 2.6.2, n. 13 (ed. Vat. 18: 373–4); *Rep.* 2.6.1, n. 5 (ed. Vivès 22: 615b–16a).

33 *Rep.* 2.6.1, n. 5 (ed. Vivès 22: 615b).

that it is accompanied by the right circumstances, i.e. that it occurs to whom, when and how it ought to occur. But it is not necessary for that volition to be efficacious.[34] For example, my wish that all wars be ended is not a choice to do something but is nevertheless morally good (and perfectly rational).

Scotus applies this model to Lucifer's case. It would have been irrational of Lucifer to choose to be God's equal by a choice$_2$, i.e. to choose to become a god. But no threat is posed to Lucifer's rationality if he merely wished to be God's equal with full knowledge that to be God's equal is something good but impossible for any creature. But even though it involved no irrationality on Lucifer's part, that wish was nonetheless evil. Lucifer loved himself by love of friendship so much that he wished to be God's equal, even though such a love should be reserved only to God:

> With regard to the act of willing in the first way [i.e. as an efficacious volition], I say that the [evil] angel could not desire equality with God. In the second way [i.e. by a mere wish], he could, because he could love himself by as much love of friendship as that by which, according to right reason, he ought to have loved God. And nevertheless he could also have desired for himself as much good as he owed to God by love of desire, if one speaks of the act of the will that is called a "wish" (*velleitas*).[35] (Trans. mine)

So while the first strategy identifies a class of two-object volitions, the second strategy distinguishes between wishes and choices to do something. Throughout his career, Scotus is consistent in regarding each of these two strategies as necessary to account for Lucifer's choice. But in his first treatments he considers the first strategy as fundamental. Thus, the notion of two-object volitions is the core of Scotus's solution in the question devoted to this topic in the first version of his *Sentences* commentary, the *Lectura*, as well as in its revision, the *Ordinatio*.[36] In those two treatments, Scotus argues that Lucifer's choice was a two-object act of love of desire. Only when dealing with the objection that there is no choice about

[34] *Rep.* 2.6.1, n. 5 (ed. Vivès 22: 615b). For Aquinas's denial that Lucifer's choice can be a mere wish for the impossible because such a wish is not morally relevant, see *DM* 6.3 ad 9 (ed. Leonina 23, 294b–295a). It should be noticed that the Leonine text has Aquinas saying just the opposite, i.e. that a wish (*velleitas*) is not morally relevant. But the Leonine editors have deleted a *non* before *est voluntas* at 295, line 293. That deletion has no textual support, for the *non* is contained in the entire manuscript tradition, as evidenced in the critical apparatus and in the *Étude critique*, ed. Leonine 23, 58*. As a consequence, I think that the *non* should be reintegrated and the Leonine text should be corrected. On the notion of wishing and conditional willing in Aquinas, see Andrea Robiglio, *L'impossibile volere: Tommaso d'Aquino, i tomisti e la volontà* (Milan: Vita e Pensiero, 2002).

[35] *Rep.* 2.6.1, n. 5 (ed. Vivès 22: 615b–616b).

[36] *Lect.* 2.6.1, n. 10 (ed. Vat. 18: 373); *Ord.* 2.6.1, nn. 9–10 (ed. Vat. 8: 27–8).

impossible things does Scotus introduce the distinction between wishes and efficacious choices and argues that, within the broader class of two-object volitions, Lucifer's choice was a mere wish.[37] By contrast, in later treatments of this topic, it is the second strategy, based on the distinction between a mere wish and a choice to do something, that Scotus regards as fundamental. Thus, in an addition to his *Ordinatio*, he remarks that such a distinction can be the ground for the affirmative answer to the question whether Lucifer wanted to be God's equal.[38] And in his late Paris course on the *Sentences*, the so-called *Reportatio*, Scotus actually makes the distinction between wish and efficacious volition the core of his solution. He now holds that acts of the will are fundamentally divided into wishes and choices turned towards actions. Each of those broad classes can in turn have one or two objects, as Scotus explains when responding to some objections.[39]

I think that Scotus has good reasons for this shift in emphasis. The two-object character of a certain kind of volition is certainly an important tool to solve the problem of the first evil volition, but it works only if the distinction between wish and efficacious volition is presupposed. Suppose that Lucifer wanted to be God's equal by an efficacious choice, i.e. that he decided to become a god. The requirements for that choice being a two-object volition would be satisfied, but Lucifer would be the victim of a gross misapprehension, as he would believe that he could become God's equal. Only if the two-object volition is a mere wish is Lucifer's rationality preserved. The two-object structure of some acts of the will merely fleshes out the mechanics of Lucifer's wish.

Before considering the philosophical cash-out of Scotus's views on Lucifer's evil volition as a wish for the impossible, let me briefly consider Scotus's answers to Aquinas's two arguments that Lucifer, being a rational agent, could not have willed the impossible.[40]

Aquinas's first argument was based on the claims that for a creature to be God's equal includes a contradiction and that Lucifer could not will what is contradictory. Scotus grants that for a creature to be God's equal includes a contradiction. He also thinks that Lucifer knew perfectly well that that was the case. Nevertheless, Scotus trades on the claim that some acts of the will have two objects and that any two things can function as objects of those

[37] *Lect.* 2.6.1, n. 13 (ed. Vat. 18: 373–4); *Ord.* 2.6.1, nn. 14–15 (ed. Vat. 8: 29–30).

[38] *Ord.* 2.6.1, n. 16 (ed. Vat. 8: 30). As the Vatican editors note, the manuscripts make it clear that this paragraph must be considered as a later addition made by Scotus to the text of the *Ordinatio*.

[39] *Rep.* 2.6.1, nn. 5–6 (ed. Vivès 22: 615b–616a).

[40] Scotus takes into account four arguments against his position. Two of these arguments correspond to those Aquinas had given in *DM* 16.3 and *ST* I 63.3.

acts as long as each one of them is believed to be good. He also uses his distinction between mere wish and efficacious choice. It is sufficient for Lucifer to apprehend equality with God as good in order for him to be able to wish to be like God. The will connects its two objects, i.e. Lucifer's nature and God's equality, by an act of love of desire. That act is a wish that does not require any prior intellectual judgment that Lucifer can be equal to God.[41]

Aquinas's second argument was based on the view that for somebody to be God's equal implies the loss of her identity and thereby the end of her existence. Scotus mentions a simplified version of this argument, but his answer can be used to address Aquinas's more sophisticated version. Scotus proposes three ways to deal with this argument. First, he contends that it is possible for somebody to will her own non-existence, provided that that is not the main object of her volition but an unintended consequence of a prior volition. This is what happens any time somebody sins mortally, because when people sin mortally, they do not want to be subject to God, even though they can exist only if they are subject to God.[42] Second, Scotus contends that it is possible to will the antecedent without willing the consequent, as when somebody wants to have a few drinks but not to get a hangover.[43] Neither answer, however, is completely satisfactory if applied to Lucifer's case. For it may indeed be conceivable for human beings not to think about the consequences of their own actions. But a purely rational creature in ideal circumstances such as Lucifer should know better. In his *Reportatio*, however, Scotus proposes a third answer. Somebody may know that there is a necessary connection between antecedent and consequent and wish that that connection did not obtain. For example, I may know perfectly well that after having a few drinks I will get a hangover. However, I may wish that the connection between drinking and getting a hangover did not obtain. Lucifer was in that situation. He knew that, if *per impossibile* his wish to be like God had been granted, he would have ceased to exist, but he wished that the necessary connection between those two claims had not obtained. Again, Lucifer's rationality was not endangered because he was entertaining an impossible scenario with full knowledge that it was impossible.[44]

Scotus's Lucifer is in stark contrast to Aquinas's Lucifer. Aquinas's Lucifer wants to be in God's company. Scotus's Lucifer wishes to be God's equal. Aquinas's Lucifer is engaged in a genuine choice—he fails

[41] *Rep.* 2.6.1, n. 6 (ed. Vivès 22: 616a). See also *Ord.* 2.6.1, n. 17 (ed. Vat. 8: 31).
[42] *Ord.* 2.6.1, n. 20 (ed. Vat. 8: 33).
[43] *Ord.* 2.6.1, n. 21 (ed. Vat. 8: 33).
[44] *Rep.* 2.6.1, n. 7 (ed. Vivès 22: 616b).

to consider that he is not able to reach the union with God by his own forces and then chooses accordingly to reach that goal. Scotus's Lucifer is not engaged in any deliberation or genuine choice. He is a rebel only "in his mind," with full knowledge that what he wishes is impossible. Nevertheless, he still wishes it. There is something of a romantic dreamer in Scotus's Lucifer and there is something tragically futile in his choice.

What is possibly the most perplexing aspect of Scotus's account is that evil is introduced into the world through a mere wish. Both Anselm and Aquinas denied that that was the case. Anselm thought that Lucifer wanted something that he was actually able to attain. By contrast, Aquinas thought that Lucifer wanted something that he was not able to attain by the exercise of his natural capacities but that he could have obtained through God's help. Saying that Lucifer wanted something impossible would pose an unacceptable threat to his rationality, according to both Anselm and Aquinas. By contrast, Scotus manages to reconcile Lucifer's rationality with the claim that Lucifer wanted something impossible by arguing that Lucifer's act was a mere wish. But isn't it implausible to make what was possibly the most momentous act in the history of creation a mere wish? Wishes seem to be harmless. It is scary to think that evil may have been introduced into the world simply as the result of the wish for something known to be impossible.

With regard to this point, I would like to make two remarks. First, some wishes for the impossible *are* morally relevant and do tell much about the kind of persons we are. Think of some wishes about past events, such as the wishes associated with regrets or the lack thereof. Those wishes are morally relevant and some of them are not innocent. Just think about criminals' repentance or lack of repentance about their past crimes. Likewise, Lucifer's wish for something that did not merely go beyond what he could attain but even beyond any possible state of affairs that God could create looks like an act of radical rebellion. Even though Lucifer never had more than a mere wish and never took arms against God, that wish itself was as close as Lucifer could go to what may perhaps be described as an act of counter-creation—not merely the desire for an alternative order that God did not create but could have created, but the desire for something beyond the realm of what even God could have made.

Second, Scotus himself admits that Lucifer's wish, no matter how bad, may not have been unforgivable. He suggests that Lucifer may have made many successive choices that took him down a slippery-slope. Lucifer may have started with a wish to be equal to God, which was motivated by excessive self-love. If at that point he had repented, he would still have been forgiven. But he did not repent. Rather, he had another wish. Since he realized that there was no room for two gods, he wished that God did not exist. But to wish that God did not exist is an act of hatred against God. And that seems to be a rather serious fault, at least according to Scotus.[45]

Is there any further interest in Scotus's view on the first evil choice or should it be regarded as a curiosity? I would like to conclude by indicating at least two possible reasons why Scotus's position is worthy of serious consideration.

First, Scotus can explain the introduction of evil into the world without appealing to any supernatural event such as a supernatural union with God. The possibility of an evil choice follows from the existence of rational agents that are not God but may desire (quite rationally) to be like God. Specifically, Scotus does not need to postulate that rational creatures were not created supremely happy or that beatitude was delayed to account for the rationality of an evil choice.

Second, Scotus agrees with Aquinas that the possibility of an evil choice does not depend on a contingent decision made by God, such as the decision to create the angels less happy than they could have been with regard to their nature (as Anselm had contended). Rather, and again in agreement with Aquinas, Scotus thinks that the possibility of making an evil choice is an inevitable consequence of the gap between God and his creatures. Just as, according to Aquinas, no creature could be united with God by the exercise of their natural capacities, so, according to Scotus, no creature could be God's equal. Since this does not depend on God's arbitrary decision, God does not have any responsibility for the *possibility* of evil. But what about the *actual occurrence* of evil? Scotus's and Aquinas's accounts differ when one comes to consider whether God could have created the world in such a way that an evil choice, even though possible, would have been utterly unlikely. I have argued above that Aquinas held that nothing prevented God from giving beatitude to his creatures at the moment of their creation rather than later. Aquinas only stressed that, since God owes nothing to his creatures, God committed no injustice when he decided not to make his creatures blessed at the very moment of their creation. But it is compatible with Aquinas's account that God *could* have created the world in such a way that no one in their right mind would have made an evil choice. This is not the case for Scotus. According to Scotus's understanding of Lucifer's choice, there is no possible scenario where it would have been irrational and therefore less likely for Lucifer to wish to be God's equal. Given that both God and Lucifer exist, it is possible for Lucifer to have a wish to be God's equal, because God is necessarily better and happier than Lucifer. Thus, God could have

[45] *Ord.* 2.6.2, n. 78 (ed. Vat. 8: 65–6).

done nothing to make it less likely for Lucifer to have that wish. Actually, God seems to have already done all that could be done to make evil less likely. According to Scotus's hypothesis, Lucifer had to go beyond the realm of what is logically possible in order to introduce evil into the world. Since God's power extends over all that is possible, Lucifer found his realm and autonomy in the only area left to him—the impossible.[46]

Fordham University

BIBLIOGRAPHY

Adams, Marilyn McCord. "St. Anselm on Evil: De casu Diaboli," *Documenti e studi sulla tradizione filosofica medievale* 3 (1992), 429–30.

Anselm. *De casu diaboli*, in F. S. Schmitt (ed.), *Opera omnia* 1 (Edinburgh: Thomas Nelson and Sons, 1946).

Bonino, S. T. (ed.). *Surnaturel: A Controversy at the Heart of Twentieth-Century Thomistic Thought*, tr. R. Williams (Ave Maria: Sapientia Press, 2009).

Courtès, C. "La peccabilité de l'ange chez saint Thomas," *Revue Thomiste* 53 (1953), 133–63.

Forsyth, Neil. *The Old Enemy: Satan and the Combat Myth* (Princeton: Princeton University Press, 1987).

Hick, John. *Evil and the God of Love* (New York: Harper & Row, 1966).

Hoffmann, Tobias. "Aquinas and Intellectual Determinism: The Test Case of Angelic Sin," *Archiv für Geschichte der Philosophie* 89 (2007), 122–56.

—— "Duns Scotus's Action Theory in the Context of His Angelology," in L. Honnefelder et al. (eds.), *John Duns Scotus 1308–2008: Investigations into His Philosophy* (Münster: Aschendorff, 2011), 403–20.

—— "Theories of Angelic Sin from Aquinas to Ockham," in T. Hoffmann (ed.), *A Companion to Angels in Medieval Philosophy* (Leiden: Brill, 2012), 283–316.

Isidore. *Sentences*, in *Patrologia Latina* 83 (Paris: Vivès, 1862).

John Duns Scotus. *Opera omnia* (Paris: L. Vivès, 1891–95).

—— *Opera Omnia*, ed. C. Balić et al. (Vatican City: Typis Polyglottis Vaticanis, 1950–).

King, Peter. "Scotus's Rejection of Anselm: The Two-Wills Theory," in L. Honnefelder et al. (eds.), *John Duns Scotus 1308–2008: Investigations into His Philosophy* (Münster: Aschendorff, 2011), 359–78.

—— "Angelic Sin in Augustine and Anselm," in T. Hoffmann (ed.), *A Companion to Angels in Medieval Philosophy* (Leiden: Brill, 2012), 261–81.

[46] I am grateful to the participants in the 2012 Cornell Summer Colloquium in Medieval Philosophy and an anonymous referee for many useful comments that led me to revise earlier versions of this paper. I would also like to thank the audience of a Scotus conference held at Oxford in 2008, where I first tackled this topic.

MacDonald, Scott. "Primal Sin," in G. B. Matthews (ed.), *The Augustinian Tradition* (Berkeley: University of California Press, 1998), 110–39.

Montano, Edward J. *The Sin of Angels: Some Aspects of the Teaching of St. Thomas* (Washington: The Catholic University of America Press, 1955).

Robiglio, Andrea A. *L'impossibile volere: Tommaso d'Aquino, i tomisti e la volontà* (Milan: Vita e Pensiero, 2002).

Thomas Aquinas. *Opera omnia* (= ed. Leonina) (Rome: Commissio Leonina, 1882–).

—— *Scriptum super libros Sententiarum*, ed. P. Mandonnet (Paris: Lethielleux, 1929).

—— *Summa theologiae* (Cinisello Balsamo: Edizioni san Paolo, 1988).

—— *On Evil*, tr. R. Regan (Oxford: Oxford University Press, 2003).

Williams, Thomas. "The Libertarian Foundations of Scotus's Moral Philosophy," *The Thomist* 62 (1998), 193–215.

—— "The Unmitigated Scotus," *Archiv für Geschichte der Philosophie* 80 (1998), 162–81.

Some Twelfth-Century Reflections on Mereological Essentialism

Andrew Arlig

Peter Abelard held two views that imply a form of Mereological Essentialism: first, that a thing is nothing other than all its parts taken together, and second that no thing has more parts at one time than it does at another. Together, these theses entail that if a whole exists, then each part of that whole exists, and more importantly that if a part is taken away from the whole, the whole ceases to exist. In short, Abelard affirms a version of Mereological Essentialism.[1]

That Abelard held a version of Mereological Essentialism has long been recognized, and while some discussion will be needed here, the basic outlines of his theory have been well studied.[2] But what is less well understood is the context in which Abelard's views developed. Abelard did not develop his version of Mereological Essentialism in a vacuum. Like many of his contemporaries, Abelard studied Boethius's overviews of logic

[1] One qualification: In contemporary discussions Mereological Essentialism is sometimes construed as the essentialist thesis that if *P* is ever a part of *W*, in any possible world in which *W* exists, *P* exists and is a part of *W* (e.g. Roderick Chisholm, *Person and Object: A Metaphysical Study* (LaSalle, IL: Open Court, 1976), 145). Abelard's view is best construed as being a version of the claim that if *P* is ever a part of some whole *W* in this, the actual world, then *P* is a part of *W* at any time that *W* exists in this world (cf. Andrew Arlig, "Parts, Wholes and Identity," in J. Marenbon (ed.), *The Oxford Handbook of Medieval Philosophy* (Oxford: Oxford University Press, 2012), 455).

[2] See D. P. Henry, *Medieval Logic and Metaphysics: A Modern Introduction* (London: Hutchinson, 1972), 120–9; Henry, *Medieval Mereology*, Bochumer Studien zur Philosophie vol. 16 (Amsterdam: B. R. Grüner, 1991), 92–151; and Andrew Arlig, "Abelard's Assault on Everyday Objects," *American Catholic Philosophical Quarterly* 81 (2007), 209–27. But compare Christopher J. Martin, "The Logic of Growth: Twelfth-Century Nominalists and the Development of Theories of the Incarnation," *Medieval Philosophy and Theology* 7 (1998), 1–15, whose views will be discussed below.

and commentaries on Aristotle's Organon. As I will demonstrate, Boethius's terse remarks on part–whole dependence would have encouraged twelfth-century philosophers to reflect on a thesis like Mereological Essentialism. Boethius's mereological theses have been examined, but not altogether adequately.[3] Here I offer a new way of seeing precisely what Boethius claims and, more importantly, what he leaves underdetermined in his statements about part–whole dependence; it is a way that will help to frame both Abelard's theses about part–whole dependence and the responses that some of Abelard's contemporaries had to what they saw as a radically revisionist understanding of individual, complex things. That Mereological Essentialism was challenged by twelfth-century thinkers is no surprise. It is a remarkably severe thesis. Some of these twelfth-century challenges to Mereological Essentialism have been discussed before but, as I will show in what follows, not satisfactorily. In particular, I will show that the key texts are better understood if we take a conservative approach to the matters of attribution and the unity of the text.

This paper will proceed as follows. I will start by examining Boethius's suggestive, yet incomplete remarks about part–whole dependence and I will highlight several of the choices that were open to twelfth-century mereologists. I will then quickly survey Abelard's understanding of Mereological Essentialism in order to bring all readers up to speed, to relate Abelard's views to my new presentation of Boethius, and to address one challenge to the view that Abelard endorses Mereological Essentialism. Finally, I will present some of the more interesting challenges to Mereological Essentialism that were made by Abelard's contemporaries.

1. BOETHIUS ON THE PRIORITY OF PARTS

Twelfth-century philosophers were interested in parts and wholes for many of the same reasons that we still are. A complex thing is divisible into parts, and these parts seem to be related to the thing's individuality, identity, and conditions of persistence. But as is still true today, puzzles that turn out to be interesting for intrinsic reasons often get their impetus from something that is treated as an authority. In the Middle Ages, in particular, many interesting treatments of mereology were prompted by a close reading of a primary text. Aristotle's *Physics*, *On Generation and Corruption*,

[3] To date, the most detailed study is Andrew Arlig, *A Study in Early Medieval Mereology: Boethius, Abelard, and Pseudo-Joscelin* (Ph.D. dissertation, The Ohio State University, Columbus, OH, 2005), chapter 3.

Metaphysics, and *On the Soul*, for example, were works rich with mereological concepts and they invited generations of thinkers to undertake investigations (*quaestiones*) of parts, wholes, and their properties. None of these works were available for twelfth-century study. Instead, the primary sources of mereological concepts, principles, and puzzles were Boethius's *On Division* and his *On Topical Differences*—both fundamental parts of the twelfth-century curriculum—as well as his commentary on Cicero's *Topics*.

In *On Division*, Boethius itemizes the many ways in which one thing can be "divided" into other things. The three big modes of division are the division of a genus into its subordinate species, the division of a whole into its parts, and the division of an ambiguous word into its different senses. These modes are distinguished from one another by the nature of the things divided. One of the ways to distinguish between the division of a genus into its subordinate species and the division of a whole into its parts is that true parts are "prior in nature" to their whole.

Again, every genus is naturally prior to its own species, whereas a whole is posterior to its own parts. Some of the parts that put together the whole precede the completion of [the whole's] composition merely in nature, but others not only in account but also in time. From this it comes to be that we resolve a genus into posterior items and a whole into prior ones. And for this reason this is truly said: If the genus is destroyed, the species immediately disappears. If a species were destroyed, the genus could stand fast in its nature without destruction. The opposite holds in the case of the whole. For if a part of a whole perishes, the whole whose one part has been destroyed will not exist. But if the whole were to perish, the parts though scattered could persist. For example, if someone were to remove the roof from an intact house, the whole that was there will cease to be. But after the roof has been removed the walls and the foundation can stand fast.[4]

Boethius repeats this assertion about the priority of the part to its whole when he distinguishes the division of a whole from the division of an ambiguous word.[5] And an endorsement of the same principle is present in his commentary on Cicero's *Topics*.

A genus is always prior to its species, but a whole is found to be posterior to its parts. For unless the parts will have been, it is not possible to put together a whole. And due to this it comes to be that if a genus perishes, the species also perish. If a species disappears, the genus may remain. But in the case of the parts and the whole the opposite obtains. If any one part perishes, the whole necessarily disappears. But if the whole, which the parts compose, is dispersed the parts may remain once

[4] *De divisione* 879b–c (ed. Magee, 12–14). I am responsible for all translations from the Latin, although I have consulted and often benefited from existing translations, when available.

[5] *De divisione* 880a (ed. Magee, 14).

scattered. For instance, if a roof, walls, and a foundation of a house may be understood when placed in isolation from one another, then a house will not be—since the conjunction has been destroyed—yet the parts may remain.[6]

Notice that these remarks seem to hold for all parts and wholes, no matter what category of being these parts and wholes might belong to. But for medieval readers, the claim is taken to hold of only "integral" wholes, which are distinguished from "universal" wholes and "potential" wholes.[7] While medieval thinkers sometimes disagreed over the extension of the concept *integral whole* and the corresponding extension of *integral part*, almost all of them took things like houses to be clear instances of integral wholes.

Even when restricted to integral wholes, on a first pass Boethius's claim about the priority of the parts seems to be quite strong. Yet, there are some clues in the texts quoted above which suggest that Boethius's thesis might be more innocuous than it first appears. First, notice that Boethius routinely identifies the whole for which the parts are prior as "a whole whose part has been destroyed" or "the whole, which the parts compose." Perhaps, then, Boethius is only making the finnicky, yet innocent claim that the whole consisting of all the other parts *and X* depends upon *X*, and hence, if *X* were destroyed, *this* whole, the one that is *X* and all the rest, will perish. This last claim is only remarkable if coupled with the more contentious thesis that throughout its lifetime a particular thing must mereologically coincide—that is, share all its parts—with one and only one set of parts. Consider a house that has a specific door, *D*. Now suppose that I destroy *D* and replace it with another door. Does my house persist? A fairly common answer is that it does and that the house merely has a new door. This common answer relies on the assumption that a house need not coincide with the same specific set of parts throughout its history. If we can help ourselves to this assumption, then while it is true that the specific set of parts including *D*, which coincided with the house, no longer exists, the house nonetheless still exists. The house now coincides with a specific set of parts that does not include *D*.

A specific set of parts is a mereological sum. Hence, we might venture as a start that all Boethius means to say in the above quoted texts is that

[6] Ed. Orelli, 331.23–32.

[7] For the restriction to integral wholes, see e.g. Albert the Great, *In librum Boethii De divisione*, 31 f. The distinction between integral, universal, and potential wholes can be traced back to *On Division* 87d–888a (ed. Magee, 38). This clearly raises the question whether the part priority thesis stated at 879b–c was intended to be fully general, since if these were true for all three kinds of whole, numerous difficulties would arise (Arlig, *A Study in Early Medieval Mereology*, 84–113).

mereological sums are posterior to their parts; he does not mean to say that a particular house is posterior to its parts. But this formulation does not conform very well with the texts. Boethius does not talk about mereological sums—or the rough medieval equivalent, collections. His priority thesis is about houses. Hence, it appears that Boethius is asserting a form of Mereological Essentialism.

But perhaps there is a still way to capture the idea that while the house consisting of this part and all the others is dependent upon this part, the house is not dependent upon this part.

First, note that while houses might exist in virtue of a specific sum of parts, they require something more as well, namely, that these parts are arranged in a certain way. Boethius himself seems to be aware of this (see, especially, the passage from the commentary on Cicero), and it was an idea well appreciated even by Mereological Essentialists such as Abelard.

> For we will not find a crowd or a flock or a troop among animals dispersed over a great distance, but only among those congregated together. However, a ship or a house consists not only in a plurality or congregation of things, but in a definite composition of things. For one does not make a house or a boat when material is conjoined in any odd way, but only when the parts (*membra*) are unified by an appropriate composition.[8]

In addition to his requirement that a house have all its parts at every moment of its existence, Abelard makes it very clear that possessing the right structure (what he calls "composition") is an extra necessary condition for the house's persistence.

Thus, the items that are posterior to their parts are *arranged* sets of parts. With this idea in mind, let us now distinguish between the house consisting of all the other parts plus *D* and an everyday, particular, mereologically flexible house. Let us reserve phrases like "this house" and "a particular house" for everyday houses, and let us call the house consisting of all the other parts and *D* a *house-arranged mereological sum.* In general, let us distinguish between an instance of an F (or a particular F) and a mereological sum arranged so that it has the structure or form of an F, that is, an *F-arranged sum.* True, no philosopher whom we will examine—not Boethius, not any of the anonymous twelfth-century philosophers whom I will examine, and clearly not Abelard (as the previous quote shows)—explicitly talks about F-arranged mereological sums. However, I think it will be convenient to have this notion in our analytical toolbox if we wish to show that Boethius's dictum about part–whole priority is innocent. For

[8] Abelard, *Dialectica,* 431.31–36. See also Abelard, *Glossae super Praedicamenta,* 171.13–17, as well as *Dialectica,* 344.24–345.6 and 550.38–551.1.

the enemy of Mereological Essentialism should hope that particular houses and house-arranged sums are not the same. As Boethius has made plain, the persistence conditions of some F-arranged mereological sum are that it must consist of a specific set of parts and these parts must be arranged F-wise. If, as the Mereological Essentialist believes, an instance of an F (e.g. a house) *must* coincide with one and only one F-arranged mereological sum (because a house just *is* a specific house-arranged sum), then particular F's will have the same persistence conditions as F-arranged sums. But if one thinks that particular F's can coincide with more than one F-arranged sum over a lifetime, then the persistence conditions of particular F's diverge from F-arranged sums.

I grant that a house-arranged sum appears to have everything it takes to be a house. So, if one prefers, one could talk about short-lived, mereologically static houses and everyday, mereologically flexible houses.[9] This way of talking no doubt is more faithful to Boethius's words. And in fact, as I see it, Abelard will agree that a house-arranged sum is a house. Indeed, for Abelard, all houses just are house-arranged sums; there are no mereologically flexible houses. Nevertheless, I think it will be easier to distinguish house-arranged sums from particular houses than it will be to distinguish static houses from everyday houses. It is with the aim of avoiding possible confusion, that I urge the reader to humor me and to allow this bit of seemingly anachronistic technicality.

Suppose we think that Boethius is not espousing Mereological Essentialism and that he is signaling this by asserting that it is the whole of which some X is a part that is posterior to X. We might capture his part–whole priority thesis in this way:

Priority Thesis 1A: Mereological sums are posterior to their parts, since mereological sums are individuated by their parts. Moreover, since a house-arranged mereological sum is a mereological sum, if a specific mereological sum has been arranged as an F, then if a part of this F-arranged mereological sum is *removed*—that is, moved in such a way that the arrangement is compromised—then this F-arranged mereological sum is destroyed.

It is important that we distinguish this priority thesis from a related thesis:

Priority Thesis 1B: Since a house-arranged mereological sum is a mereological sum, if a part of this house-arranged mereological sum is *destroyed*, this house-arranged mereological sum is destroyed.

[9] Chisholm, more or less, does this in his discussion of the identity of a table through time (*Person and Object*, 97–104, esp. 98–9).

Boethius makes it clear in *On Division* that the destruction of the house occurs because the roof has been *removed*, or in the commentary on Cicero, because all the parts have been disjoined and *scattered*. In both cases, the parts are not necessarily *destroyed* when the conjunction and arrangement of the parts is compromised. In other words, Boethius's example of the house shows that the mere *removal* of a part can destroy the house. Clearly, the destruction of a part would count as a removal of the part. But a part's removal need not destroy the part. Hence, Priority Thesis 1A is stronger than 1B.

Thesis 1A is a fairly innocuous claim, since it is compatible with the notion that an individual house is the sort of thing that can coincide with more than one house-arranged mereological sum over the course of its history. In other words, Priority Thesis 1A is only an interesting, revisionary metaphysical thesis if it is combined with the more controversial thesis that an individual thing can have no parts at one time that it fails to have at another. As I announced in the introduction, Abelard will assert this more controversial thesis.

However, before we turn to Abelard, another notion suggested by Boethius's texts needs mention. Medieval readers of Boethius noticed that the parts that he picked were a roof, some walls, and a foundation. Boethius did not mention stones, nails, timbers, and so forth. Some medieval readers understood this to mean that Boethius's part–whole priority thesis extended only to what one might call primary, or "principal" parts. For example, here is what Albert the Great says.

> The contrary of this occurs in the disposition of a whole to its integral parts. For a whole will not be, but will perish and be destroyed, if one principal part of the whole, one that integrates the whole (*integrans totum*), perishes or is destroyed. But if a whole perishes and is destroyed, it does not follow on account of this that the principal parts that integrated the whole are substantially destroyed.[10]

In the case of a house, the parts that integrate, or make the whole complete, are the roof, the walls, and the foundation. A house lacking any of these is arguably an incomplete house. But a stone or a nail or a timber does not as such complete a house. A house can survive without having some one of these.

This seems to be a reasonable enough line of thought and it conforms rather well with a common understanding of houses. There is, however, a crucial ambiguity. Latin does not have definite and indefinite articles, which means that a claim such as "the existence of house implies the existence of roof, walls, and foundation" could mean, among other things:

[10] Albert the Great, *In librum Boethii De divisione*, 33.26–31.

1. The existence of *some* house implies the existence of some roof, some walls, and some foundation.
2. The existence of *this* house implies the existence of a roof (but not this one necessarily), some walls (but not necessarily these), and a foundation (but not necessarily this foundation).
3. The existence of this house implies the existence of *this* roof, *these* walls, and *this* foundation.

Claim (1) is the most defensible of the three precisely because it seems to be making a conceptual point about what it is to be a house. Claim (2) is also fairly innocuous, especially if we grant (1). If what it is to be a house is to be a thing consisting of a room, some walls, and a foundation, then if this house exists, there will be a roof, some walls, and a foundation. Claim (3) is the interesting reading, since it seems to invite us down the path toward Mereological Essentialism.

Both the notion of a principal part and the distinctions that we have just drawn about the priority of principal parts will be important later on. Hence, let us spell out two more theses that one could derive from Boethius's dicta.

Priority Thesis 2A: A whole is posterior to its principal parts, where this means that if this whole exists, there must be a roof, some walls, and a foundation.

Priority Thesis 2B: A whole is posterior to its principal parts, where this means that if this whole exists, this roof must exist and these walls must exist and this foundation must exist.

Both Priority Thesis 2A and 2B leave open the possibility that a determinate, individual house need not consist of a determinate stone plus all the rest. And, as we will see, this will be precisely the move that some twelfth-century thinkers will want to make.

With these possible readings of Boethius in place, we can now jump to the twelfth century. It would be wrong to suggest that Boethius *caused* any twelfth-century philosopher to endorse the view. It only takes a small amount of intellectual independence to see that parts might be crucial for determining identity and individuation. Moreover, as we have seen, Boethius's remarks do not have to be read as an endorsement of Mereological Essentialism—for anything other than F-arranged mereological sums, that is. Nevertheless, this overview should have made it apparent that a sensitive twelfth-century reader would have encountered a number of interpretive puzzles when he turned to Boethius's terse remarks about parts and wholes. And it is often in the context of reflections on Boethius's mereological ideas that one finds discussions of Mereological Essentialism.

2. ABELARD'S MEREOLOGICAL ESSENTIALISM

In several places in his writings, Abelard asserts that no thing (*res*) possesses more parts at one time than at another.[11] In the quotation to come, we will also see him assert that a thing is nothing other than its parts. These theses entail Mereological Essentialism, and not just for F-arranged sums but also particular F's. Abelard appears to be on record as endorsing precisely that:

> Therefore, anyone who attributes existence to this house thereby concedes the same to this little stone and all the other parts taken together, because this house is nothing other than this stone and all the additional parts taken together. Thus, when this house exists, it must be the case that this little stone and all the additional parts taken together [exist]. But if this collection of all [these parts] exists all at once, it necessarily follows that this little stone exists. For if this little stone is not, the collection of all [these parts]—that is, the [collection] of this little stone and the rest taken together—is not. Therefore, if this house is, this little stone is. Thus, if this little stone is not, this house is not.[12]

Obviously, Abelard is asserting something much stronger than either Priority Thesis 2A or Thesis 2B. This house not only must have these walls, these walls must consist of a specific set of stones.

Abelard's position is stronger than Thesis 2B despite his endorsement of the distinction between principal and secondary parts. Abelard thinks that there is a proper way to begin dividing a whole into its parts.[13] A house should not be first divided into halves and then halves of halves. Nor should one begin to divide a house by partitioning it stone by stone. Rather, one should begin the division of a whole by partitioning it with respect to those parts whose conjunction immediately brings about the completion of the whole. In the case of a house, the principal parts will be its roof, its walls, and its foundation. Thus, a "principal part" for Abelard is merely a part that is the result of the first, proper division of a whole.

Interestingly, Abelard defines his notion of principal parts in opposition to two other positions, the second of which he calls the "destructivist" position:

[11] See Abelard, *Glossae super Praedicamenta*, 300.20–1; Abelard, *Dialectica*, 423.29–30.

[12] Abelard, *Dialectica*, 550.9–17.

[13] See Abelard, *Dialectica*, 552.39–553.7. Abelard surely has in mind Boethius's remark that, "We resolve a book into verses, and these into words, and those again into syllables, and syllables into letters. Thus, it is the case that the letters, the syllables, the names, and the verses are seen to be some parts of the whole book, yet in another way they are taken to be not parts of the whole but parts of parts [of the whole]." (*On Division* 888a–b [ed. Magee, 40]).

Those who understand principalness in terms of destruction, say that only those [parts] that destroy the substance of a whole are principal, such as a head, which once cut off kills a man.[14]

Abelard thinks that the destructivist account of what it is to be a principal part will not work precisely because *every* part of a specific whole—not just the big parts or the first divisions of things—is necessary in order for the whole to exist.[15]

Houses and other artifacts, in Abelard's view, are discrete wholes.[16] But lest one think that he is restricting his claims about part–whole priority to discrete wholes, consider the fact that in his long discussion of destructivism, Abelard considers both a house and a human and he seems to conclude in the case of a human this:

Therefore, it must be that when even a hand is amputated this man, the one who existed previously, cannot remain.[17]

The only hesitation that Abelard expresses in his investigation is that perhaps not every partition of a man counts as a homicide:

But perhaps not every destruction of a man is called a homicide, but only that destruction which expels a soul from its seat. For a homicide is the killing of a man, and killing cannot occur without the expulsion of a soul.[18]

Now, one might read this as a very hasty rejection of the entire previous line of thought. But I think that Abelard is making a point similar to what he earlier says about houses:

[14] Abelard, *Dialectica*, 549.9–12. The first position is that principal parts are those parts of a whole that cannot be parts of a part of the whole (549.4–9). Abelard makes short work of this position by showing that any part can be considered to be a part of some part of the whole; all one has to do is start with a different first partition of the thing in question (549.21–34).

[15] Despite Abelard's attacks on destructivism, the position proved to be very popular in the twelfth century (and for that matter in later centuries). Consider, for example, *Introductiones Montane minores* (ed. De Rijk, 56.24–5), *Abbreviatio Montana* (ed. De Rijk, 87.34–35), and *Introductiones Montane maiores* 69vb. For the texts of the minor *Introductiones* and the *Abbreviatio*, see L. M. De Rijk, *Logica Modernorum: A Contribution to the History of Early Terminist Logic*, vol. II, part 2 (Assen: Van Gorcum, 1967). A critical edition of the greater *Introductiones* reportedly is forthcoming, but currently the text is in manuscript only (Bibliothèque Nationale (Paris) cod. lat.15141).

[16] Abelard, *Dialectica*, 419–20.

[17] Abelard, *Dialectica*, 552.32–3.

[18] Abelard, *Dialectica*, 552.34–7. It should be remembered that Abelard does not think that the soul is a form, let alone the form of the human body (*Glossae super Praedicamenta*, 212.37–213.5; cf. John Marenbon, *The Philosophy of Peter Abelard* (Cambridge: Cambridge University Press, 1997), 124–5).

We do [not] say that if this little stone is removed, that *a* house would not remain in the rest of the parts; rather, that *this* [house], namely, the one that is constituted out of this little stone and the additional parts, would not remain.[19]

If this stone is removed from the house, this house is destroyed; if this hand—or even this fingernail—is removed from this man, this man ceases to be.

Thus, Abelard's understanding of part–whole priority is quite general: it holds for all kinds of wholes, mere pluralities and aggregates, discrete as well as continuous wholes. The previous quotation provides sufficient evidence that Abelard has a position that is at least as strong as Priority Thesis 1B. Abelard is a little less forthright about what happens if a part is merely removed, but a careful examination of Abelard's discussions of mereological change will reveal that he is theoretically committed to something at least as strong as Priority Thesis 1A.[20] The question is whether he is committed to something even stronger. In some well-examined passages, Abelard asks whether strictly speaking any *res* can increase or decrease, if what it is to increase is for a thing to be made bigger by having something added to it and what it is to decrease is for a thing to be made smaller by removing something from it.[21] All that Abelard can conclude from these examinations is that no *res A* can have any *res B* added to it so that *A* increases and no *res A* can have any *res B* added to it so that *A* decreases: every mereologically simple *A* is *A* and only *A*, every complex *res* consisting of *A* and *B* always is *A* and *B* and only ever is *A* and *B*. But these *res* could be F-arranged mereological sums (or, again, if one prefers mereologically static, momentary F's), which leaves open the possibility that Abelard thought that a house or a man can coincide with more than one *res*.

Christopher Martin detects a commitment to something other than Mereological Essentialism in one of Abelard's "solutions" to the problem of increase.

However, perhaps [our difficulty] can easily be solved this way, namely, if we say that the thing that increases is that which, by means of the addition of something else, passes over into the sort of composite which does not retreat from its [sc. the

[19] Abelard *Dialectica*, 550.18–20. Without comment, but in my opinion correctly, D. P. Henry adds a "not" in line 18 of De Rijk's text (*Medieval Mereology*, 83).

[20] For more details, see Arlig, "Abelard's Assault on Everyday Objects," 211–17.

[21] Abelard, *Glossae super Praedicamenta*, 299–300; Abelard, *Dialectica*, 421–4. See Henry, *Medieval Logic and Metaphysics*, 120–9; Henry, *Medieval Mereology*, 116–39; Arlig, "Abelard's Assault on Everyday Objects."

prior thing's] nature or property.[22] For example, if some water is added to water, the water to which there has been an addition passes over into some composition that is also called water.[23]

Martin considers this to be Abelard's last word on increase,[24] and he takes this as evidence that some kinds of wholes can coincide with more than one mereological sum. But as I see it, all Abelard has done is to locate another way in which we can honor commonsense and say that "something" has increased or decreased.[25] The proposal in the passage quoted above is that, in a case where we add one bit *B* to another thing *A*, it is *A* that is said to be what has increased, provided that *A* is part of the second whole *A and B* and that both *A* and *A and B* have the same nature. However, it does not follow from this that the particular coinciding with *A and B is* the particular coinciding with *A*, and hence, it is hard to read this passage as asserting the claim that a particular can coincide with *A* and then coincide with *A and B*. Notice, as well, that the example that Abelard employs is a portion of homoiomerous stuff, viz. water, and homoiomeries are hard to individuate.

Abelard's summary of the lessons that he takes from the example of the "growing" portion of water makes it even more plain that we do not have here evidence of Abelard's disavowal of Mereological Essentialism.

[22] That which is said to increase is "quod per adiunctionem alterius *transit* in tale compositum quod a natura vel proprietate sua non recedit," which Martin renders as "which by the addition of something other *becomes* a composite that does not cease to have its nature or property" ("The Logic of Growth," 6, my emphasis). "Transforms into *x*" or "changes into *x*" is a perfectly acceptable rendering of "transit in *x*," but these translations imply that the prior composite is numerically identical to the posterior composite. Since I think that Abelard is not committed to this view, I prefer the ambiguity that one gets by rendering the verb in accord with its basic meaning.

[23] Abelard, *Glossae super Praedicamenta*, 299.30–4.

[24] Martin, "The Logic of Growth," 5–6. Martin assumes that the treatment of increase and decrease in the *Glossae super Praedicamenta* presents Abelard's final thoughts on this topic. Henry presents the treatment of increase in *Dialectica*, 421–4, as if it were Abelard's final word on the matter (Henry, *Medieval Mereology*, 122–39). Henry is perhaps working from De Rijk's contention that the *Dialectica* is later than the lectures on the *Categories*. Mews (Constant Mews, "On Dating the Works of Peter Abelard," *Archives d'histoire doctrinale et littéraire du Moyen Age* 52 (1985), 73–134) dates the *Categories* commentary later than the *Dialectica*, and his view is now more or less the standard one (see also Marenbon, *The Philosophy of Peter Abelard*, 40–3).

[25] In all of his treatments of the problem of increase, Abelard provides ways of interpreting the assertion that something gets bigger or smaller when bits and pieces are added or removed. For example, in his *Dialectica*, Abelard suggests that increase occurs when things that were once scattered are brought together into the same place (423.4–10).

Therefore, it is clear from what has been said that increase ought to be located more in that case where some composite by means of the addition of something passes over into something similar to it (*in consimile sibi*), than in the case where something's parts are merely multiplied.[26]

If Abelard meant to say that the particular coinciding with *A and B* is the same particular as that which coincides with *A*, he could have said so. But all he claims is that the particular coinciding with *A and B* is the same sort of thing as the particular coinciding with *A*. (And, indeed, it is not even clear that he is saying this much, since again, it is hard to individuate particulars in the case of portions of homoiomeries.) Thus I see no indication that for Abelard any particular can coincide with more than one F-arranged mereological sum.

I concede that we cannot entirely rule out the possibility that Abelard eventually arrived at the view that *some* particulars belonging to some natural kinds can coincide with more than one mereological sum. Abelard once distinguished between questions requiring that one provide a thing's nature ("what (*quid*) is X?") and questions demanding the name of a person ("who (*quis*) is X?").[27] Abelard's followers, the so-called Nominales, reportedly drew a distinction between, on the one hand, the *res* or substance that is such-and-so and, on the other, the person who is such-and-so, and while they are notorious for claiming that nothing grows (*nihil crescit*), they apparently asserted that one can say that Socrates or a man grows.[28] Thus, it is not entirely unreasonable to think that Abelard might have utilized such a distinction to show that while F-arranged mereological sums (his *res* or *essentia*) cannot gain or lose parts, persons can. But if Abelard did maintain such a view, we have no clear record of it, and hence, any speculation along these lines amounts to a case of reading back into Abelard a position that might have been held by some of his followers.

What Abelard *is* on record asserting is a position that at least *appears* to be an expression of the claim that if this stone is ever a part of this house, then if this stone is either destroyed or removed, this house ceases to exist. And this in itself was too revisionary a thesis for many twelfth-century

[26] Abelard, *Glossae super Praedicamenta*, 300.17–20. The case described in the second comparative clause is one where a collection of some *F*'s is increased by adding more things that are *F*—e.g. when my flock of sheep is "increased" by buying more sheep (300.4–16).

[27] Abelard, *Logica nostrorum petitioni sociorum*, 537.21–33. Compare Abelard, *Glossae super Porphyrium*, 35.33–36.3. For comment: Martin, "The Logic of Growth," 8.

[28] See for example texts 40b and 48d, pages 192 and 198 respectively in Yukio Iwakuma and Sten Ebbesen, "Logico-Theological Schools from the Second Half of the 12th Century: A List of Sources," *Vivarium* 30 (1992), 173–210. For analysis, see Martin "The Logic of Growth," 8–12.

thinkers. It is precisely this form of Mereological Essentialism that other schools in the twelfth century exerted so much energy to resist.

3. RESISTANCE TO MEREOLOGICAL ESSENTIALISM

The upshot of the previous section is that Abelard entertained and appeared to endorse Mereological Essentialism. Other twelfth-century philosophers took the threat of Mereological Essentialism seriously, and they considered a number of strategies for rejecting anything other than fairly toothless versions of the part–whole priority thesis. In this section, I will examine some of these strategies.

The key texts from which I will extract these strategies are anonymous fragments that have been passed down and now edited as one treatise, initially by Victor Cousin as the *Fragmentum Sangermanense*,[29] and more recently by Peter King as the *De generibus et speciebus*.[30] The *Fragmentum Sangermanense* is found in two manuscripts, Paris 13368 and Orléans 266.[31] King has made a convincing case that the Paris manuscript depends upon the Orléans. But if we turn to the Orléans manuscript and consider its nature, we can see that the *Fragmentum Sangermanense* is probably not one, integrated work by one author. Orléans 266 is an anthology of excerpts, often extracted without attribution, from distinct twelfth-century logical treatises. Minio-Paluello has summarized the contents of Orléans 266, and he sees not one treatise, but three excerpts:[32] The first excerpt, which corresponds to §§ 1–20 of the King edition (ed. Cousin, 507–10), Minio-Paluello identifies as "a problem on 'totum'." The second excerpt, corresponding to King's §§ 21–31 (ed. Cousin, 511–13), is described as "Problem 'de destructione Socratis'." The third excerpt, corresponding to King's §§ 32–fin. (ed. Cousin, 513–50),

[29] M. Victor Cousin (ed.), *Ouvrages inédits d'Abélard* (Paris: Imprimerie Royale, 1836), 507–50.

[30] King, *Peter Abailard and the Problem of Universals*, vol. 2, 143–85. King is currently producing a revised edition of this treatise, and he has generously shared a draft of this new version as well as a translation of the text. I do not know, however, whether he plans to continue to treat this text as one unit and to attribute this text to "pseudo-Joscelin."

[31] MS Paris, Bibliothèque Nationale lat. 13368 ff. 168ra1–179va21. MS Orléans, Bibliothèque Municipale lat. 266 (222), ff. 153a1–166a29.

[32] L. Minio-Paluello, *Twelfth Century Logic, Texts and Studies II: Abaelardiana Inedita* (Rome: Edizione di Storia e Letteratura, 1958), xli–xlvi, and esp. xliii.

is identified as the treatise *De generibus et speciebus*.[33] Most of the literature on these texts follows Cousin and King in assuming that they can be taken as a unit.[34] Yet I recommend that we adopt Minio-Paluello's more conservative attitude and that we treat these texts as discrete excerpts, unified only by theme, not by author or even school—unless, that is, we find some reason to treat them as a tighter unit. In fact, as I hope to show in what follows, we have good reasons *not* to unite sections 1–20 to sections 21–31.[35] In keeping with this conservative approach, I will identify the first twenty sections of King's edition as the Anonymous Fragment and sections 21 to 31 as *On the Destruction of Socrates*. I will reserve the title "*De generibus et speciebus*" for the third, larger fragment from Orléans 266.

Admittedly, "Anonymous Fragment" is far from an exciting title, but I would prefer not to prejudice future research by attributing this text to a particular author or school. In particular, I will insist that we do not identify sections 1–20 or 21–31 with Joscelin of Soissons or one of his students. In section 14, the text mentions the solution of a "Master G." Much has been made of this abbreviated reference to a twelfth-century master. Cousin prints "magistrum Willelmum," indicating that he thinks that Master G is some William, perhaps even Abelard's old teacher William of Champeaux. King thinks that "Master G" is a reference to a Master Goscelinus, or Joscelin. We know from John of Salisbury that one Joscelin of Soissons defended the theory that a universal is a collection of particulars. *On Genera* defends a sophisticated version of the theory that a universal is a collection of particulars.[36] Hence, according to this line of

33 We could have a fourth fragment, an excerpt on substantial *differentiae*, but Minio-Paluello elects to include this section of the Orleans manuscript (as well as the Paris manuscript) with *De generibus et speciebus* (*Twelfth Century Logic*, xliii, note 30).

34 King, *Peter Abailard and the Problem of Universals*, King, "Damaged Goods: Human Nature and Original Sin," *Faith and Philosophy* 24 (2007), 247–67, and Arlig, *A Study in Early Medieval Mereology*. Henry quotes three passages from the *Fragmentum Sangermanense*, two from *On the Destruction of Socrates* and one from *De generibus* (*Medieval Mereology*, pp. 109, 114, and 150–1), but because he uses them merely as foils for critiquing Abelard, his remarks should not be taken to constitute a study of these texts. The only study of these texts that does not assume that they form a unit is Andrew Arlig, "Early Medieval Solutions to Some Mereological Puzzles: the Content and Unity of the *De generibus et speciebus*," in Irène Rosier-Catach (ed.), *Arts du langage et théologie aux confins des XIe–XIIe siècles: textes, maîtres, débats* (Turnhout: Brepols, 2011, 485–508) (completed in 2008), but this study gets many important things wrong and it should be used with great caution.

35 There is some evidence that supports an ideological link between the *On the Destruction of Socrates* and *De generibus et speciebus* (see Arlig, "Early Medieval Solutions," esp. 506–7). But it is not certain that *On the Destruction of Socrates* and *De generibus* are parts of the same *treatise*.

36 See King, *Peter Abailard and the Problem of Universals*, part 2, chap. 8; and Arlig, *A Study in Early Medieval Mereology*, chap. 5.

argument, the Anonymous Fragment is from the school of Joscelin of Soissons. But I think we should not be so hasty. While I think that there are reasons to think that Master "G" is not William of Champeaux,[37] these reasons are not decisive. We know that William of Champeaux changed his views about universals over the course of his career. It is not inconceivable that here is another case where Abelard's old teacher changed his mind, perhaps again in the face of challenges from Abelard himself. Even if Master G is not William of Champeaux, it does not follow that he must be a Joscelin, let alone *the* Joscelin of Soissons. Currently, we do not have any evidence independent of these texts for what Joscelin of Soissons's views about part–whole dependence might have been. But even if "M. G." does refer to Joscelin of Soissons, as I will demonstrate below, I think there is reason to believe that most of section 1–20 is not by a student of Master Joscelin.

With these preliminaries in place, let us now turn to the Anonymous Fragment. The Fragment begins without any prefatory remarks. Instead, the first sentence explains that some integral wholes are continuous and some are discrete. The author then immediately announces that if we assume that a house is a continuous whole, then we can run the following argument:

If *house* is, *wall* is. And if *wall* is, half of *wall* is. And if half of *wall* is, half of half of *wall* is, and so on down to this *stone*. For these reasons, if this *house* is, *last stone* is. Therefore, if no *stone* is, then no *house* is.[38]

Later, the author presents a similar argument, which is based on the assumption that a house is discrete.[39]

My translation attempts to mimic the ambiguity of the argument as it appears in the original Latin. And as it happens the author of the Fragment notes one way in which the premises in the argument are ambiguous:

If this [argument] is taken as is, it is not disagreeable. But suppose the argument pertained to a determinate house, like so: If this house is, this wall is. And if this wall is, this half wall is. And so on to this little stone. And afterward suppose we drew the conclusion destructively that if this little stone is not, this house is not. Then we would fashion a disagreeable conclusion.[40]

[37] For the evidence see Arlig, "Early Medieval Solutions," 489–93 and 496.

[38] Anonymous Fragment § 3 (ed. Cousin, 507): *Si domus est, paries est; et si paries est, dimidius paries est; et si dimidius paries est, et dimidium dimidii est; et ita usque ad hunc lapillum. Quare si haec domus est, et ultimus lapillus est. Si ergo nullus lapillus est, etiam nulla domus est.*

[39] Fragment § 17 (ed. Cousin, 509–10).

[40] Fragment § 4 (ed. Cousin, 507).

What the author seems to mean by the argument taken "as is" is this: If a house is, it is a whole. In particular, the existence of a house entails the existence of some parts (walls, a floor, a roof, and so forth). Each of these parts is also complex, and so each part's existence will imply the existence of more parts: if a house is, some stones are. It would also be true that if there were no stones at all, then there would be no house. In other words, the agreeable version of the argument amounts to an acceptance of Priority Thesis 2A.

What our author rejects is the claim that the existence of *this* particular house implies the existence of *this* specific collection of parts. And given that this definite collection of parts need not exist if this house exists, it will not be the case that this house ceases to exist if one of these parts were to cease to be. The author then summarizes several strategies for resisting the conclusion about this particular house. We will only examine the interesting ones.[41]

The author of the Fragment reports that one way to try to resolve the puzzle is to employ the destructivist account of principal parts mentioned earlier.

> And again it should be set down that for continuous wholes one kind of part is principal, and another is secondary; and one kind of principal [part] is one that is principal in *essentia*, another principal in quantity, and another is [principal] in both ways. A part principal in *essentia* is one which when destroyed destroys its whole, as the heart or brain of Socrates, when destroyed, destroys Socrates.[42]

The interesting feature of this text is that the author distinguishes between parts principal in *essentia* and parts principal in quantity. Parts principal in quantity are merely large parts of a thing that has a size; so, for example, Socrates's upper half and his lower half are parts principal in quantity. Only parts principal in *essentia* entail the destruction of their whole, if they themselves are destroyed. Parts principal in quantity will only destroy their whole if they contain a part principal in *essentia*, since Socrates could lose a great portion of his lower half and yet survive the amputation.[43]

Armed with these distinctions, the destructivist proposes that the only things that follows from the existence of a whole are its parts principal in *essentia* and any essential principal parts of one of its essential principal parts.

[41] For a survey of all of the strategies, including the ones that in my judgment are far from promising, one may consult Arlig, "Early Medieval Solutions," but again with caution.

[42] Fragment §§ 6–7 (ed. Cousin, 507–8).

[43] Fragment §§ 8–9 (ed. Cousin, 508).

But [a part] principal either in *essentia* alone or in both [*essentia* and quantity] follows once a whole is posited. For if Socrates is, then his heart is and [his] brain is and the upper half, in which the heart and brain are contained, is. Likewise, any part principal in *essentia* of an [essential principal] part is posited once [the principal part] is posited, and if it is destroyed that [principal part] is destroyed.[44]

And hence, a whole exists only if its parts that are principal in *essentia* exist.

Therefore, we concede a consequence of this sort: if this house is, then this wall is, given that this wall is a part principal in *essentia*. But we do not accept this one: if this wall is, this half wall is. For we do not know whether this half wall is an essential part for this house.[45] For example, we see that often when doors or windows or entrances are made, more than half of the parts are subtracted, but nevertheless the same wall, which was there before, [still] exists—I do not mean "the same" in shape (*forma*) but the same in *essentia*.[46]

The idea is that if a particular house exists, then there is some particular thing that is its wall. But some halves of this particular wall could be removed without undermining the load bearing function of the wall, as one often does when one cuts out parts of the wall to make windows or entrances. Indeed, as the author of the Fragment observes, one might even remove more than half of the wall's parts and yet retain the wall, provided that one only removes half of its quantitative parts, not any of its essential parts. The same idea is more or less at work in section 16.

For let us posit that a wall is composed out of four stones, and thus each half wall will consist of two. Thus, one could destroy one of the two halves by removing one stone from [one of] the two [halves] while a wall nevertheless continues to exist in the three stones. But we concede in this kind of subtraction of a half wall that a wall would not be destroyed, only that a subtraction has occurred with the result that what remains suffices as an *essentia* of a wall. For a wall cannot remain the same only if a subtraction occurs with the result that what has been left cannot make a wall, whether something is added or not.[47]

In the imaged scenario the half wall that is destroyed has not been utterly destroyed, since one of the parts remains. Moreover, the part that remains allows the remaining three stones to carry on and continue to be a wall.

[44] Fragment §§ 9–10 (ed. Cousin, 508).

[45] It might at first seem striking that the author says that we do not know whether the half is essential to the house (*ad hanc domum*), since the previous quote talked about essential parts of essential *parts*. But clearly the author is merely cutting out a fairly obvious step: if P is an essential part of Q and Q is an essential part of R, then P is an essential part of R.

[46] Fragment § 12 (ed. Cousin, 508).

[47] Fragment § 16 (ed. Cousin, 509).

Thus, it appears again that the half wall has only been destroyed in its shape, or *forma*, not in its *essentia*.

The basic thought expressed in section 12, and reiterated in section 16, seems promising enough. But note that as the author of the Fragment presents things, the destructivist has no quarrel with the proposition that if this house exists, then this wall exists. His quarrel is with the proposition that if this wall exists, then this half wall exists. This does not seem to be an inadvertent slip, since the author reiterates the point in section 15.

> Thus, let us return to this [argument] and proceed as follows: "If this house is, this wall is." That is accepted. But this is rejected: "If this wall is, this half wall is." But suppose someone aimed to prove [the latter] by means of the destruction of the consequent as follows: "Clearly, if this wall is, also this half wall is, since if this half wall is not, this wall is not." But this does not follow. This half wall could be "destroyed" in the way that was just described. I do not mean that it is destroyed utterly—because then [the destruction of this wall] would follow—but that this half wall can be, I say, "destroyed" in form, but nevertheless this wall can remain in *essentia*.[48]

The claim that the utter destruction of the half wall entails the destruction of the wall is also not a slip.

> This half wall can be destroyed in two ways: With respect to one way, it is annihilated in such a manner that nothing of it remains, and in this way, when it is destroyed it can destroy its whole. But it can be destroyed in another way, so that the whole of its mass is not altogether taken away, but only its shape (*forma*) is altered because some of its parts remain—as when some timbers and stones are removed and doors or windows are made. When destroyed in this way, this half wall does not destroy this wall.[49]

It is puzzling that the destructivist appears to concede Priority Thesis 2B, if not something stronger.[50] As we observed earlier, it seems quite reasonable and indeed innocuous to assert that *some* essential principal parts, parts of the sort needed for there to be a house, are guaranteed to exist if a particular house exists. But the author concedes that "this wall" exists, not merely a wall of the right kind, if this house exists.

I do not know why the author seems to concede this much. Perhaps the thought might have been motivated like so: If Socrates exists, then we know not only that a heart exists, we know that *his* heart exists. Likewise, if this house exists, we know that *its* wall exists. "Which one is its wall?", a student

[48] Fragment § 15 (ed. Cousin, 509).

[49] Fragment § 13 (ed. Cousin, 508–9).

[50] I must thank the anonymous referee for helping me to appreciate how remarkable this concession is.

might have asked. The master turns and points to a house: "This one." Yet, even this line of thought does not explain why the Fragment's destructivist concedes that if this half of the wall were utterly destroyed, then "its whole" would also be destroyed. Why, in particular, does the destructivist not entertain the following thought? It seems that one could say that if this house exists, then some particular wall must exist. This particular wall, if a part of this house, is this house's wall. But it need not follow that this specific particular wall must exist if this house exists, so long as being this house's wall is merely a matter of being a part of this house. In other words, if parts are individuated by their wholes, then the destructivist can resist Abelard. But the destructivist in the Fragment seems to believe that the parts are at least on the same ontological par as the whole, if not the apparently fatal belief that wholes are individuated by and dependent upon their principal parts.

Once the destructivist concedes this much, it is hard to see how he can resist Abelard's conclusion about destructivism. If I concede that this particular (that is, the wall just pointed out) exists if this house exists, haven't I just conceded that this house depends upon a specific particular? But what makes this wall this particular wall other than a specific set of bricks or timbers? So, if we grant that this particular wall exists, it seems we must concede that this timber exists. As we have seen, Abelard grants that *a* wall could still persist if we perform the renovations alluded to above. But *this* wall is not *that* wall. And hence, Abelard would claim, if this timber is not, this wall is not, and if this wall is not, this house is not.

Again, if the house were a discrete whole, it appears that the author of the Fragment would accept a good portion of what our imagined Abelardian has just said.

Just as it is true that if one of these [e.g. the sheep] do not exist, this whole flock does not remain, so too if this house is taken to be a discrete whole consisting of a specific number of stones or posts, then every one of these discrete little parts should be posited upon positing the [house], and the destruction [of one of these] destroys the [house].[51]

Discrete wholes such as piles and flocks are identical to their parts, and hence, the existence of the whole entails the existence of each of the parts. If a house were a discrete whole, then it would seem to have some of the same persistence conditions of a pile of stones or a flock of sheep.

Yet, while the author of the Fragment concedes that a discrete whole entails the existence of every thing that is part of the discrete collection, the author makes much of the comparison of a house to a flock. A flock is

[51] Fragment § 17 (ed. Cousin, 510).

a discrete whole consisting of continuous wholes (individual sheep), and sheep have both essential and inessential parts.

It should be understood that just as every discrete part follows upon its whole, so too every essential part of every discrete part follows upon the same. For supposing it is true that if this flock is, this sheep is, it will also be true that if this flock is, the heart of this sheep is. Therefore, if the heart of this sheep does not exist, then this flock does not exist.[52]

Every discrete part of a discrete whole and every essential part of every discrete part of a whole is entailed by the existence of the whole. Thus, if a sheep is killed, the flock is destroyed; if the heart of one of the sheep in the flock is destroyed, this flock will be destroyed. However, our author denies that the collection of all the essential parts of the whole (whether they are essential parts of the whole or essential parts of parts of the whole) is identical to the collection of all the parts of the whole. So, for example, it will not follow that if this flock exists, that a specific hair of one of the sheep exists; nor will the flock perish if a hair is lost.

Similarly, our author insists, the existence of the house entails every essential part of the house. But even if we identify the house with a specific collection of stones or posts, it does not follow that every destruction of every half of a part belonging to the house will entail the destruction of the house. We could remove many of the non-principal parts of, for example, this post—namely, those that will not prevent it from bearing its share of the house's weight. Indeed, the post can lose a great deal of its quantity and yet persist, provided that the whole's *essentia* is not destroyed:

But let us return to the abovementioned. This does not follow: If this post is, the middle of this post is. For the middle can be destroyed—in the manner just now described, that is, not so much in relation to its whole mass but with respect to form—and nevertheless so long as some particles remain, this post will not be destroyed, since the whole matter of its middle does not perish even though the form perishes. Indeed, not even if a great amount were born off by the wind from one part, would the whole remaining part of the post follow once this post is posited. For according to the same reason, even this large part can be destroyed in form provided that it is not so much that the whole of its *essentia* is destroyed.[53]

Again, note that the author of the Fragment is committed to the claim that if any single post *as a whole* is removed, the house is destroyed. And, hence, while the author of the Fragment does not go as far as Abelard, the author concedes quite a bit to him. It also is at odds with a fairly common view

[52] Fragment § 18 (ed. Cousin, 510).
[53] Fragment § 20 (ed. Cousin, 510).

about houses, namely, that a house can persist even if a whole post is removed. Indeed, commonsense seems to tell us that a whole roof may be replaced, and yet the house that remains is still my house.

In short, the destructivist appears to be trapped by his commitment to a bottom-up analysis of things like houses. The being of this house comes from its essential principal parts. The being of these principal parts in turn comes from their essential principal parts. While the sum of all the principal parts and the principal parts of the house may not coincide with the house, it appears that the house is a lot less mereologically fluid than our ordinary conception of such things accepts.

One way to secure more flexible persistence conditions for houses and animals would be to give forms more of a role as the metaphysical glue of things. After all, in later medieval periods, it was a fairly common thought that substantial forms can imbue changing masses of matter and hence that particular substances can tolerate a great amount of mereological change.[54] Interestingly enough, there is some evidence that suggests some of Abelard's contemporaries did have something like this notion in mind.

A careful reader will have observed that I made no mention of what King's text presents as section 14 of the Fragment. Here it is:

> Or alternatively, according to Master G, first one ought to see what the words "if wall is, also this half wall" say. But it is not a composite of two or four stones and a form that is said to be "this wall", but rather a body imbued with the sort of property that makes [it] a wall. Therefore, whenever one finds this sort of form in some subject,[55] whether or not the quantity is augmented or diminished, the form [sic] that was before remains.[56] For example, if one head is amputated from a snake possessing two heads, the snake that was before will remain.[57]

[54] See Robert Pasnau, *Metaphysical Themes 1274–1671* (Oxford: Clarendon Press, 2011), 689–92.

[55] Master G does not specify that "this sort of form" (*talem formam*) is a substantial form. But then how could he? If a house is a continuous whole, then it is not true that all continuous wholes are substances, and hence, the forms that tolerate mereological fluctuations are not all substantial forms. Perhaps what this shows us is that the house being a continuous whole is merely a hypothetical exercise. The house is merely a placeholder for a continuous whole, even though houses are not themselves continuous. A precedent for this would be Aristotle, who famously uses artifacts as stand-ins for substances. But I am not so sure that there was a twelfth-century consensus on the status of artifacts like houses. The claim at the beginning of Fragment § 2 (ed. Cousin, 507) that "we could say a house is a discrete whole or a continuous one" could be read as an acknowledgment that there was disagreement among the schools on this point.

[56] The manuscripts read *forma quae prius fuerat remanet.* I would have preferred that it read that the subject (or perhaps substance) is what remains.

[57] Fragment § 14 (ed. Cousin, 509). The example of the two-headed snake is very odd. I have nothing helpful to say about why Master G might have given this particular example.

To my knowledge, no commentator on the Fragment has noticed how awkwardly this section fits into its surroundings.[58] In sections 11–13 and 15–16, the weaker kind of destruction—that is, the way of destroying the half wall that does not destroy the wall—is identified as destruction "in *forma*." Here in section 14, however, the form is the sign, if not the guarantor, that the whole has survived a mereological change. The discussion in sections 15 and 16 falls back on the distinction between being destroyed in form and being destroyed in *essentia* and, as I have just shown in my presentation of the Fragment, sections 6 to 13 plus sections 15 and 16 present one coherent line of thought once one omits 14. It should be remembered as well that when the discussion turns to the possibility that the house is a discrete whole, the preferred solution is the destructivist's. When all these facts are considered together, it is clear that section 14 is a non sequitur. The best hypothesis that I can offer for why section 14 appears in our manuscripts is that it was originally a marginal annotation which at some point found its way into the text. If this is so, then the attribution of the Fragment to a "pseudo-Joscelin" is on even shakier footing.

But the significance of this section goes beyond mere matters of attribution. The thesis hinted at in this fragment within a fragment is a marked step in the direction that one hoped that the destructivist would take. The house's wall does not depend upon this set of stones or that set; it depends upon there being some stones that retain the sort of form that imbues some things and makes them this wall.

It is odd, however, that Master G says that it is the *wall* that has a form. The example of the snake does not appear to illustrate a case of a part persisting because it retains its form (viz. the form of a head), but rather a case of an animal persisting because it retains the form of the whole animal. Master G might have an easier path ahead of him if he were to assert that only whole things have forms and that parts do not have their own forms. This would be the more natural way to describe what has happened to the snake. The amputated head is destroyed (or, in the terms of the rest of the Fragment, destroyed in *essentia*) since it no longer is attached to the snake. But the snake is not destroyed (in *essentia*), since the remaining body and head retain the property that allows it to be a snake. This could be what Master G actually meant to say in the case of the house. Unfortunately, we cannot know for certain, since section 14 is the only information that we have on the solution of Master G.

[58] Even I failed to appreciate the full import of this discrepancy. In my "Early Medieval Solutions," I treated sections 14–16 as if all three sections were presenting Master G's view (496–7).

4. A TOP-DOWN REJOINDER TO MEREOLOGICAL ESSENTIALISM

The notion that forms could be sufficient principles of persistence is a promising thought, but we only get a hint of it in the Fragment. In *On the Destruction of Socrates*, however, we find a sophisticated challenge to Mereological Essentialism that utilizes the thought that I suggested at the end of the last section.

As was mentioned above, the modern editors of this text have treated it as a part of a work also containing the Fragment. But it is far from clear that *On the Destruction* is a part of the same treatise as the Fragment. First, there is no transition between the two treatments of mereological issues. And whereas that fact might be explained away by hypothesizing that we have two excerpts from the same larger treatise, a second salient fact is harder to dismiss, for as I will show, the technical apparatus and indeed some basic metaphysical starting points in *On the Destruction* are noticeably different and arguably much more sophisticated than the apparatus employed by the destructivists. Therefore, I will treat *On the Destruction* independently from the Fragment. The question whether *On the Destruction* preserves a text from Joscelin's school is much more vexing. In keeping with my expressed conservatism about such matters, I prefer to remain agnostic.

Here is what is certain. *On the Destruction* is a short excerpt, both beginning and ending abruptly. In this excerpt we are invited to consider the body of Socrates at some time t_1. This body is composed out of a determinate number of "indivisible particles" that together are the "foundation" (i.e. the subject) of Socrates's whole quantity.[59] Every subset of Socrates's particles also forms some foundation for a specific quantity that is a portion of Socrates's whole quantity.

> Thus by adding [atoms] in this way and progressively creating new creations (*creaturas*), at some point one will arrive at some small bit (*particulam*) of Socrates, and at some point after that at a fingernail. And you will have one great nature, which is a part of Socrates but not Socrates, because the fingernail is not in the constitution of [this great nature], but this fingernail is a part of Socrates in addition to the great part.[60]

The fingernail is not Socrates, and the great nature is not Socrates. This Socrates-less-the-fingernail, which our anonymous author calls the "great

[59] *On the Destruction of Socrates* §§ 21–22 (ed. Cousin, 511).
[60] *On the Destruction of Socrates* § 22 (ed. Cousin, 511).

nature" or the "great part," collected together with the fingernail is Socrates at t_1.

The author of *On the Destruction* then asks us to consider what will happen if we sever Socrates's fingernail from the rest of him.

However if this fingernail is destroyed, the part is destroyed, the one belonging to a nature, of which the fingernail is a part—the nature which is Socrates—and thus Socrates is destroyed. But the great nature, which at first was a part of Socrates and not Socrates, remains Socrates, even though the fingernail is destroyed.[61]

The author's presentation of the puzzle is terse, but it appears that what we have is a dilemma. Socrates is a nature, specifically, the nature that is the composite of the fingernail and the great nature. If the fingernail is destroyed, the nature composed of the fingernail's nature and the great nature is destroyed. Therefore, Socrates is destroyed. But Socrates seems to persist. There he is, smiling and talking as he clips his fingernails. So, it seems that Socrates can be another nature. The obvious candidate is the great nature. So the great nature is Socrates. But we already assumed that the great nature is not Socrates, but only a part of Socrates. Thus, the great nature both is and is not Socrates. In sum, either (1) Socrates is not the great nature, and hence he is destroyed when the fingernail is destroyed, or (2) Socrates is not destroyed, but at the cost of asserting that something both is X and is not X.[62]

One obvious response to this dilemma is to note that the second horn has ignored the fact that there is a temporal dimension to this imagined scenario. The great nature is not Socrates at t_1. Whereas if Socrates persists at t_2, this must be because Socrates is the great nature at t_2. The proposition that the great nature is not Socrates at t_1 and is Socrates at t_2, is not an instance of the absurd claim that something both is X and is not X.

Interestingly, the author of *On the Destruction* indicates that this rejoinder would not suffice; for note how he solves the puzzle.

When one part of Socrates is destroyed, the ones that remain do not come to be Socrates, rather Socrates comes to be out of them. And, thus, on account of this we are neither forced to say that Socrates perishes, nor that a non-Socrates becomes

[61] *On the Destruction of Socrates* § 22 (ed. Cousin, 511).

[62] Why not allow that the great nature is a human (or even a Socrates) at t_1? The author does not say, but we can guess the answer. If we were to concede this, then we would have too many humans (or, worse, Socrates*es*) at t_1. In discussions like the one that we have preserved in *On the Destruction*, we should take care to distinguish a question of synchronic identity (e.g. How many humans or Socrates*es* are there at t_n?) from a question about diachronic identity (Can what is not this man at t_1 become this man at t_2?). The author of *On the Destruction* tacitly assumes an answer to the synchronic question. The issue on the table is the diachronic question.

Socrates, but only this: so long as the being (*essentia*) of Socrates is preserved, we agree that from these [sc. the loss of the part and the preservation of the *essentia*] the result is that Socrates is composed out of fewer [particles].[63]

Merely articulating the temporal dimension of the scenario will not suffice, since it still leaves us with the notion that a nature that is not-X has become a nature that is X. To see why this will not do for our author, it is crucial to appreciate that the whole treatment of mereological change in *On the Destruction* is framed in terms of natures, and not (as in the Fragment) particular things. Clearly, these natures are not abstract objects and they are not forms; they are concrete beings.[64] Nevertheless, they are stable concrete beings that belong to a particular natural class, or kind. Thus, the author is initially puzzled because to say that a nature that is not Socrates becomes Socrates seems to be a case of a nature changing its membership from one natural class to another. If we say that Socrates persists, it appears that we must assert that a nature that was not a member of the kind *human* (but only a member of a kind of human part), has become a member of the kind *human*. The solution that the author prefers allows him to avoid saying that a nature can cease to belong to one natural kind and to begin to belong to another. In a case where a man loses a fingernail no nature that was not human has become human; no nature has gone from belonging to one natural kind to belonging to another. Rather, a nature that belongs to the natural kind *human* is now composed out of fewer parts.

Yet there still seems to be a violation of the principle that no nature can change kind-membership. Now, at t_2, Socrates entirely coincides with the great nature, and hence, the great nature is no longer a part of Socrates.[65] Has the great nature lost its nature when it ceased to be a *part* of Socrates? The author of *On the Destruction* thinks this is an ill-formed question, because he rejects one of the key assumptions of the dilemma, namely, that every composite is a nature. First, he considers the finger.

In Socrates's finger, which is one of his members, a hundred indivisible particles are united, and out of these [particles] the finger is integrally composed. No nature below the finger is composed out of any one [or any collection of some] of these

63 *On the Destruction of Socrates* § 26 (ed. Cousin, 512). D. P. Henry reads this as the assertion that "Socrates" is "the proper name of the complete collection of the Socratic spatio-temporal parts" (*Medieval Mereology*, 114). I think that employing the modern notion of a spatio-temporal part in order to elucidate this medieval view is unwarranted.

64 This understanding of natures as *concreta* would not be unprecedented for readers of Boethius (see his *Contra Eutychen et Nestorium* 1).

65 This argument leans on the tacit, but quite common medieval assumption that no single part can be the whole. If Socrates is composed out of the composite that is the great nature and nothing more, then the great nature cannot be a part of Socrates.

hundred indivisible particles; rather all one hundred indivisible particles are bound up in the finger by means of the overlying form (*per supervenientum formam*).[66]

Even if the finger were a nature, it would not be composed out of smaller natures. A nature only exists if some particles are collected together and made one by a form. The same is true of larger composites of Socrates's body.

What was said about the finger can also be said about the palm and the remaining members. But it should be noted as well that one nature is not composed out of a finger and a palm, nor should a hand be thought to be one nature, and it should not be said that anything composed out of a palm and a forearm results in there being one nature. And the same holds for the other [parts of Socrates].[67]

The claim here seems to be quite general, and hence the point also applies to the part that is Socrates-less-the-fingernail-at-t_1. The "great nature," in other words, is not a nature after all, it is only a collection of things that can compose, either in whole or in part, Socrates. What determines the persistence of a nature is the form associated with that nature, and hence, what determines whether Socrates persists is whether his form persists and still manages to hold together some significant number of particles.

Seen in this light, the author of *On the Destruction of Socrates* is worried about something deeper than the relation of a thing to its parts. He is worried about the problem of change: if *X* is not *Y*, how can *X become Y*? Our author's answer is that if *X* and *Y* are natures, then indeed if *X* is at some time not of the same nature as *Y*, *X* can never become *Y*. However, it does not follow that *X* cannot change its accidents, including the accident of having these or those things as parts.

I will not pursue whether our author's answer to the problem of change is adequate. What is clear is that while the author's main target is change, of which mereological change is one kind, what the author of *On the Destruction* says about this issue has applications for the debate over Mereological Essentialism. Abelard's version of Mereological Essentialism—and perhaps all versions of the thesis—assume that the parts of *X* are intimately tied to, if not constitutive of, *X*'s nature. For example, Abelard concedes that forms are important for sustaining a succession of objects of a certain type across time, but he still insists that in order to track a particular object's trajectory through time one must trace the trajectory of its parts. The author of *On the Destruction* insists that this is the wrong way to look at things. Whether things are *parts* of some *X* is itself determined by *X*'s form and nature.

66 *On the Destruction of Socrates* § 23 (ed. Cousin, 511–12).
67 *On the Destruction of Socrates* § 25 (ed. Cousin, 512).

Notice as well that *On the Destruction* breaks from the approach of most of the anti-Essentialist theories preserved in the Fragment, and not just in how the puzzle is posed or with respect to the specific terminology that is employed (although this is not insignificant). With the possible exception of the mysterious Master G (who is mentioned *only* in section 14), the masters in the Fragment struggle to meet Abelard's challenge because they accept his way of framing the problem. Like Abelard, they start by thinking about the parts and then they look for something else—a glue we might say—that will hold enough of the parts together and arrange them in the right way to guarantee persistence. These thinkers never escape from the idea that what it is to be this individual is at least partially determined by the individual's actual constituents. The author of *On the Destruction* is much more definitive in his rejection of this approach. In the latter author's view, the emphasis should be placed on those wholes that are natures, and individuation should be determined by these natures and their forms, not by the parts of these natures. The parts of the natures cannot determine individuation because they are only what they are in virtue of being a part of a nature.[68] The promise of forms, which was only hinted at in the Fragment, has now been paid in full.[69]

Brooklyn College, The City University of New York

BIBLIOGRAPHY

Albert the Great. *Commentarii in librum Boethii De divisione: Editio princeps*, ed. P. M. von Loë (Bonn: P. Hanstein, 1913).

Arlig, Andrew. *A Study in Early Medieval Mereology: Boethius, Abelard, and Pseudo-Joscelin* (Ph.D. dissertation, The Ohio State University, Columbus, OH, 2005).

[68] The author of *On the Destruction* announces that when the finger is amputated, "new accidents are created and a new whole as made" (§ 25, ed. Cousin, 512). The added remark "just as it should be understood in the case of a corpse" makes it pretty clear that that which was the finger is the new whole. This suggests that the something is a finger only if it is a part of a nature and possesses the right sort of accidents.

[69] This paper is the result of many trials and much error. Earlier presentations of this material were given at the Eastern Regional Conference of the Society of Christian Philosophers (New York, NY, March 2011) and the eighty-sixth annual meeting of The American Philosophical Association, Pacific Division (Seattle, WA, April 2012). I wish to thank the individuals present (too many to name here) for their comments and questions. At the latter meeting I had the great fortune to have Calvin Normore as my commentator. His remarks and advice have been tremendously helpful. I also must thank the anonymous referee of *Oxford Studies*, whose probing questions and criticisms have been invaluable. Finally, I must thank Peter King, who introduced me to both Abelard and the *Fragmentum Sangermanense* so many years ago. Despite having such enviable mentors and critics, many errors and obscurities surely remain. All of these are mine alone.

—— "Abelard's Assault on Everyday Objects," *American Catholic Philosophical Quarterly* 81 (2007), 209–27.

—— "Early Medieval Solutions to some Mereological Puzzles: the Content and Unity of the *De generibus et speciebus*," in I. Rosier-Catach (ed.), *Arts du langage et théologie aux confins des XIe–XIIe siècles: textes, maîtres, débats* (Turnhout: Brepols, 2011), 485–508.

—— "Parts, Wholes and Identity," in J. Marenbon (ed.), *The Oxford Handbook of Medieval Philosophy* (Oxford: Oxford University Press, 2012), 445–67.

Boethius. *In Topica Ciceronis Commentaria*, in J. C. Orelli (ed.), Cicero, *Opera Omnia* 5.1 (Turin: Orelli, Fuesslini & Co, 1833).

—— *De divisione liber*, critical edition, translation, prolegomena, and commentary by John Magee (Leiden: Brill, 1998).

—— *Contra Eutychen et Nestorium*, in C. Moreschini (ed.), *De consolatione philosophiae. Opuscula theologica* (Munich: Saur, 2000).

Chisholm, Roderick M. *Person and Object: A Metaphysical Study* (LaSalle, IL: Open Court, 1976).

Cousin, M. Victor (ed.). *Ouvrages inédits d'Abélard* (Paris: Imprimerie Royale, 1836).

De Rijk, L. M. *Logica Modernorum: A Contribution to the History of Early Terminist Logic*, vol. II, part 2 (Assen: Van Gorcum, 1967).

Henry, D. P. *Medieval Logic and Metaphysics: A Modern Introduction* (London: Hutchinson, 1972).

—— *Medieval Mereology*, Bochumer Studien zur Philosophie vol. 16 (Amsterdam: B. R. Grüner, 1991).

Iwakuma, Yukio and Sten Ebbesen. "Logico-Theological Schools from the Second Half of the 12th Century: A List of Sources," *Vivarium* 30 (1992), 173–210.

King, Peter. *Peter Abailard and the Problem of Universals*, 2 vols. (Ph.D. dissertation, Princeton University, 1982).

—— "Damaged Goods: Human Nature and Original Sin," *Faith and Philosophy* 24 (2007), 247–67.

Marenbon, John. *The Philosophy of Peter Abelard* (Cambridge: Cambridge University Press, 1997).

Martin, Christopher J. "The Logic of Growth: Twelfth-Century Nominalists and the Development of Theories of the Incarnation," *Medieval Philosophy and Theology* 7 (1998), 1–15.

Mews, Constant. "On Dating the Works of Peter Abelard," *Archives d'histoire doctrinale et littéraire du Moyen Age* 52 (1985), 73–134.

Minio-Paluello, L. *Twelfth Century Logic, Texts and Studies II: Abaelardiana Inedita* (Rome: Edizione di Storia e Letteratura, 1958).

Pasnau, Robert. *Metaphysical Themes 1274–1671* (Oxford: Clarendon Press, 2011).

Peter Abelard. *Logica 'ingredientibus', pt. 1: Glossae super Porphyrium*, in B. Geyer (ed.), *Peter Abaelards Philosophische Schriften, Beiträge zur Geschichte der Philosophie des Mittelalters* (1919), no. 21, pt. 1 (Münster: Aschendorffshen Buchhandlung).

—— *Logica 'ingredientibus', pt. 2: Glossae super Praedicamenta Aristotelis,* in B. Geyer (ed.), *Peter Abaelards Philosophische Schriften, Beiträge zur Geschichte der Philosophie des Mittelalters* (1921), no. 21, pt. 2 (Münster: Aschendorffshen Buchhandlung).

—— *Logica nostrorum petitioni sociorum,* in B. Geyer (ed.), *Peter Abaelards Philosophische Schriften, Beiträge zur Geschichte der Philosophie des Mittelalters* (1933), no. 21, pt. 4 (Münster: Aschendorffshen Buchhandlung).

—— *Dialectica,* ed. L. M. de Rijk, 2nd edn. (Assen: Van Gorcum, 1970).

Why Are the Habits Necessary? An Inquiry into Aquinas's Moral Psychology

Jean Porter

According to Aquinas, virtues and vices are *habitus*, habits, that is to say, stable dispositions towards characteristic kinds of actions.[1] This claim is central to his overall moral theory, so much so that he devotes six questions of the *Summa theologiae* to habits generally considered, before turning to an extended consideration of the virtues and related concepts (*ST* I–II 49–54). Over the course of that analysis, he claims that habits are necessary to the rational creature, a claim that he explicitly applies to the will, as well as the intellectual faculties and the passions (*ST* I–II 49.4, 50.5). Almost from the beginning, Aquinas's commentators have questioned whether virtues, and by implication habits, are really necessary to the will. According to Aquinas, the will is a rational appetite, which depends on the intellect for its object, namely, the good as apprehended by reason (*ST* I–II 8.1, 9.1). Given this, why should the will need virtuous habits, or any habits at all, in order to act in the appropriate ways? It would seem that the intellect supplies all that the will needs in order to operate.

These and related questions originally motivated this paper, and Aquinas's analysis of the habits of the will does raise distinctive issues. But there is a more fundamental problem here. That is, it is not initially clear why Aquinas says that habits are necessary at all. It seems plausible to say that men and women can act more easily, with greater consistency and less struggle, once they develop settled dispositions of some kind. But Aquinas

[1] The term *habitus* is notoriously difficult to translate. 'Habit' carries the misleading suggestion that the *habitus* are more or less thoughtless dispositions towards stereotypical behaviors. 'Stable dispositions' is a better translation, but this too can be misleading, since as Aquinas notes, *habitus* are dispositions understood in one sense but not another (*ST* I–II 49.2 ad 3). In view of these difficulties, I have chosen to leave the term untranslated.

apparently believes that without habits, a rational creature cannot act at all, except perhaps in limited or rudimentary ways. This is a remarkably strong claim, and it raises a question that has not received the attention that it deserves.[2] Why does Aquinas believe that habits are necessary for the rational creature? In this paper, I will try to address this question, focusing especially on the habits of the appetites, that is to say, the passions and the will, which comprise the moral and theological virtues and their corresponding vices.

In the first section of this paper, I will examine Aquinas's analysis of the habits of the sensual appetites, that is to say, the passions. I will argue that for Aquinas, the passions need habits because the operations of the passions, which consist in their inclinations to particular goods, are intentional, that is to say, they are directed to objects mediated through sensory perceptions and imagination. Yet human desires and aversions are not spontaneously tied to specific objects, in the way that the passions of non-human animals apparently are. They need to be shaped through processes of formation, in such a way that they are directed towards certain kinds of imagined objects and not others.

The will is the characteristically human, rational appetite, and as such, it is importantly different from the passions. Nonetheless, like the passions, it is an appetite, which can only operate through inclinations towards some appropriate object. This suggests that habits are necessary to the will for the same basic reason that they are necessary for the passions. That is to say, the will operates through intentional inclinations, which can only take shape through processes of formation, through which the inchoate inclinations of the will are oriented towards determinate kinds of objects. More specifically, the formation of the habits of the will takes place through ongoing processes of choice, reflection, and further choice, which engage the will at every stage—thus, the will cannot acquire habits passively, through simple acquiescence in the good as presented by the intellect. These, at any rate, are the central claims to be developed in the second and third sections of this paper.

Finally, in the last section I will turn specifically to the virtues, seen as well-ordered habits of the passions and the will. Aquinas claims that virtues

[2] For example, in her extended treatment of the virtue of justice as Aquinas presents it, Eleonore Stump does not refer at all to Aquinas's claim that justice is a *habitus* of the will; see Stump, *Aquinas* (New York: Routledge, 2003), 309–38. Robert Pasnau comes closer to acknowledging the significance of *habitus* of the will in his analysis of human freedom, which he ties to the capacity of the will to subject immediate desires to our second-order desires (*Thomas Aquinas on Human Nature* (Cambridge: Cambridge University Press, 2002), 224–33). However, he does not explicitly link these to Aquinas's analysis of *habitus*, nor does he raise the question of whether these second-order desires themselves result from the activities of the will.

are necessary in order for the appetites to operate appropriately and well. This clearly means that the virtues are necessary in order for the appetites to operate in accordance with moral standards, since men and women can and do act effectively out of vicious habits. At the same time, Aquinas interprets the moral ideals of the virtues in such a way as to draw out the integral connections between these standards, and the exigencies of human activity more generally understood. His account of the virtues and vices can only be understood in terms of his overall moral psychology, as he himself indicates (I–II 6 introduction).

1. WHY ARE THE HABITS NECESSARY AT ALL? THE CASE OF THE PASSIONS

Aquinas identifies habits as one of two kinds of internal principles of human acts, the other being the capacities (*potentiae*) of the soul, including the powers of sensory and intellectual perception and the appetites (*ST* I–II 49 introduction).[3] These principles are not unrelated, of course, since Aquinas goes on to analyze habits as stable dispositions of the capacities of the rational creature, particularly those which are immediately oriented towards action (*ST* I–II 49). The idea of habits is complex in itself and comes to Aquinas with a long history of discussion, and I will not attempt to sort through all the details of his exposition. The most immediately relevant point is that for him, a habit properly so-called reflects a kind of development or formation, through which the powers of the intellect and the appetites are oriented towards certain characteristic kinds of activities (*ST* I–II 49.3). As such, habits presuppose capacities of some kind which are innately underdeveloped, together with some standard by reference to which they can be well formed, or else malformed (*ST* I–II 49.4). Aquinas goes on to say that habits are necessary to the rational creature, and not simply desirable enhancements, because the intellect and the appetites are not sufficiently well formed to generate the actions which are essential to the creature's ongoing operations (I–II 49.4). The relative indeterminacy of the intellect and the appetites reflects the fact that each is in some way

[3] For a good overview of the main lines of the debates over the relation between will and intellect, see Bonnie Kent, *Virtues of the Will: The Transformation of Ethics in the Late Thirteenth Century* (Washington, DC: Catholic University of America Press, 1993), 199–245; for an extended analysis of the development of Aquinas's own position, seen within its immediate context, see Odon Lottin, "Les fondements de la liberté humaine," 225–389 in *Psychologie et morale aux XII et XIII siècles*, Tome I (Louvain: Abbaye du Mont César, 1942), 255–62.

responsive to, or dependent on reason, rather than being fixed by its nature on some one specific object of apprehension or activity. This indeterminacy is thus by no means a defect, but it does leave a gap between the natural orientation of the intellectual power or appetite of the rational creature, and its actual use. Habits serve to fill that gap by orienting the capacities of the creature towards some kinds of operations, rather than others.

It is easiest to see what Aquinas means with respect to the intellectual capacities. To take one of his own examples, a normal human infant has the capacity to communicate linguistically, in the sense of having the capacity to learn a language. But until this capacity is developed in some specific way—until the child actually learns a language—he has no actual ability to communicate (*ST* I–II 56.3). In this kind of case, the habit in question, the stable disposition to grasp and use a language, represents a development of inchoate principles through training. Thus, the habits of the intellect represent a kind of development of innate natural principles, in such a way as to enable the agent to make use of his intellectual powers through skilled performances, intellectual perception and inquiry, and the like.

The habits of the appetites, likewise, represent developments of natural capacities, in such a way as to enable the agent to make actual use of these capacities. But we should be careful not to press the comparison too far, because as Aquinas goes on to say, the habits of the appetites are different from those of the intellect in one key respect (*ST* I–II 51.1). The habits of the intellect work by activating what would otherwise be inchoate principles of operation. The appetites, in contrast, are naturally oriented towards generic kinds of goods, and there is no need to activate this natural orientation through the formation of habits. However, the natural inclinations of the appetites cannot operate until these generic goods are specified, in such a way as to correlate the inclinations of the appetites with determinate objects. As Aquinas elsewhere explains,

> just as there is in the intellect some species which is the similitude of an object, so it is necessary that there should be something in the will, and in every appetitive power, through which it is inclined to its object, because the act of an appetitive power is nothing other than a certain inclination... Because it is necessary to the end of human life that an appetitive power should be inclined towards something determinate, to which it is not inclined from the nature of the power, which can orient itself towards many and diverse ends, therefore, it is necessary that there should be certain inclining qualities, which are called habits, in the will and the other appetitive powers. (I–II 50.5 ad 1)

We will return in the next section to Aquinas's remarks on the will. At this point, we need to consider the more basic issue raised here—that is, why does Aquinas say that every appetite needs habits in order to operate through inclinations towards specific objects? He acknowledges that the appetites are innately oriented towards generic kinds of goods, prior to any processes of formation. Why is this not sufficient to sustain the appropriate operations of the appetites? We can most readily see why Aquinas makes this claim by focusing initially on the passions, since these, unlike the will, can be found in both rational and non-rational creatures.

Aquinas refers to the passions as sensitive appetites, or the appetites of the sensitive part of the soul, in contrast to the will, which is a rational appetite, and as such, the appetitive power of the intellect (*ST* I 80.2, 81.1, 82.5; I–II 8.1). As such, the passions are capacities of desire and aversion arising out of images conveyed through the senses, directly or by way of memory and imagination. Aquinas's analysis of these passions follows a standard scholastic template, dividing the passions into two capacities for simple desire and aversion, on the one hand, and a kind of confrontational engagement with obstacles and threats of all kinds, on the other—that is to say, the passions of concupiscence and the passions of the irascible part of the soul, respectively (*ST* I 81.2). Because these inclinations stem from sense perceptions, they presuppose bodily change of some kind, if only through the functioning of the sense organs, and they are naturally targeted towards particular objects of desire and aversion (*ST* I–II 22.1, 3). In both respects, human passions are essentially similar to their counterparts in non-rational animals. Nonetheless, there is one crucial difference—that is, the passions of the rational creature are, so to say, responsive to reason, even though they also retain some independence from reasoned judgments and the commands of the will (*ST* I 81.3, I–II 56.4).

As we would by now expect, Aquinas wants to say that because human passions are responsive to reason, they both require habits disposing them to determinate objects, and are capable of being disposed in this way. But it is not immediately clear why this should be the case. On his account, the appetites, both sensual and rational, are dependent on perceptions of attractive or suitable goods, and operate through spontaneous inclinations towards naturally desirable activities and enjoyments. It would appear that these natural principles would be sufficient to generate action. We are drawn by objects and activities which we perceive or judge to be desirable, and we act accordingly—what more need be said?

Leaving aside the distinctively rational inclinations of the will, this way of analyzing activity would apply fairly well to the higher animals. Aquinas, following Aristotle, holds that animals interact with their environment on the basis of a sensate image, *phantasia*, to which they respond with spontaneous desire, aversion, or fear, leading to activities of pursuit or avoidance (*In de anima* III.6, paras. 655–70). Because the higher animals, unlike other kinds of non-rational creatures, move themselves to act on the basis of internal perceptions, they can be said to act on the basis of *arbitrium*, judgment. But unlike rational animals, they do not act in accordance with *liberum arbitrium*, free judgment, because they do not exercise deliberation and choice (*ST* I 83.1; I–II 6.2, 13.6). They do not need to do so; they perceive their world in terms set by their own natural needs and vulnerabilities, and these perceptions generate more or less fixed desires, aversions, and activities, coordinated by a kind of estimative sense (*ST* I 81.3). The key point here is that the passions of non-rational animals are capacities for intentional acts, that is to say, inclinations towards specific objects of desire, aversion, or alarm. As we have just seen, this kind of inclination is itself the proper act of an appetite—that is why Aquinas identifies the passions as the principles of those kinds of actions which the rational agent shares with non-rational creatures (*ST* I–II 6 introduction; cf. I–II 50.5 ad 1). At the same time, the appetites play a central role in the overall operations of a living creature, because they prompt the creature itself to action. Once elicited, an inclination initiates some kind of self-motion within the creature, through which it pursues, avoids, or resists some perceived desirable, noxious, or threatening object. Thus, animals are capable of moving themselves to activities, even though they are not fully masters of themselves in the same way as a rational creature is (*ST* I 80.1, 83.1).

Thus, the passions of non-rational animals are essentially capacities for intentional inclinations of a specific kind. It would seem that Aquinas would say the same about human passions. He certainly analyzes the passions in intentional terms, correlating each with its proper object (see *ST* I–II 26 for an overview), implying that passions are not simply inchoate feelings, but inclinations directed towards (or away from) appropriate objects. If this line of analysis is on target, then we can readily see why habits of the passions are necessary for creatures of our kind. Rational creatures, like non-rational animals, are tethered to their environment through spontaneous sensual perceptions, desires, and aversions. But these perceptions and feelings are not innately tied to particular objects, in the way that the passions of non-rational animals are. This indeterminacy is by no means a defect in itself—rather, it gives our perceptions and feelings a kind of plasticity, which enables them to be shaped by rational formation and reflection (*ST* I 81.3). At the same time, these unfocused desires and aversions cannot, in themselves, move the rational creature to act, precisely because they lack a determinate object, towards which (or away from which) the individual might direct her operations. These feelings are, at most, the incipient starting points for the passions. These capacities for responsive feeling need to be formed through ongoing processes of training and education, so that they will be elicited and expressed in appropriate ways, in accordance with perceived and imagined desirable and noxious objects. The child does not spontaneously perceive the world in terms of her needs and vulnerabilities, as a puppy would do. She must be taught how to feel, by being directed towards the appropriate objects of her desires and aversions, and trained in such a way as to associate, for example, hunger with nice tasty objects of consumption.

Habits are thus necessary to the passions, in order for them to take shape and to function properly as appetites, through inclinations towards or away from some perceived object. In the next section, I will argue that Aquinas applies essentially the same line of analysis to the will.

2. WHY ARE HABITS NECESSARY TO THE WILL?

We have already seen that Aquinas explicitly says that the will, like every other appetite, needs habits in order to direct itself towards some object in an appropriate way. By implication, the will, like the passions, is intentional in structure, insofar as its proper act consists in an inclination towards some determinate object. Yet—again, like the passions—the will cannot orient itself towards a determinate object unless it is disposed through habits to do so.

This, at any rate, is what Aquinas says at *ST* I–II 59.5 ad 1, and I will ultimately defend and expand on these claims. Nonetheless, it is not initially obvious that we should give so much weight to the similarities between the will and the passions. These are both kinds of appetites, but there are important differences between them. Most fundamentally, the will is a rational appetite, while the passions are sensual appetites. Thus, the passions are elicited by sensory images, which are shaped by rational judgments but remain irreducibly particular. The will, in contrast, responds to the good as presented to it by the intellect—that is to say, to something understood to be good in accordance with abstract, general criteria (*ST* I 80.2, I–II 9.1). We might say that whereas the passions are reason-responsive, the will is reason-dependent, at least in its positive exercise. Correlatively, the will is innately oriented towards the good as such, generally and abstractly considered, in contrast to the passions, which operate through inclinations towards particular objects. The will does extend to particulars, of course, through the exercise of *liberum arbitrium*, free judgment, which is the faculty of choice, directed to particular acts. Nonetheless, free judgment is a component of the will, although rationally distinct from it, and unlike the passions, it inclines towards particular objects and acts insofar as they represent means to, or instantiations of the good as such, understood in accordance with some rational idea of goodness (*ST* I 83.4).

Why are these distinctions relevant to a consideration of habits of the will? Taken in one way, they might imply that the will has no need of habits to function, since prior to the formation of any dispositions of the will, it is innately directed to a sufficient object, namely, the good as such. The exercise of the will in particular choices does presuppose inclinations towards more determinate objects, but these are chosen precisely as means to, or instantiations or components of a general conception of the good. Alternatively, we might acknowledge that the will's orientation towards the good stands in need of some further, substantive development, in order to incline towards a determinate object. But this does not require the formation of habits, except in a rudimentary sense, because the determinate good which is the object of the will is adequately specified by the intellect. These, at any rate, are the arguments that we will consider in this section.

Let us consider the first alternative. We might say that the will as such does not need to be perfected through habits, because it is innately oriented towards its object, namely, the comprehensive good as disclosed by reason. It is true that the will moves itself to act in and through the exercise of its capacities for free judgment, through which the agent chooses to pursue a particular object, regarded as a means to, or an instantiation of the good abstractly considered (*ST* I 83.4, I–II 9.3). Choice presupposes an extended process of discernment, in which practical reason and free judgment work in tandem, with the passions (perhaps) adding impetus to, or distracting from one's overall commitment to the rational good. These processes can break down in more than one way, through a deficiency in practical reason, or through distortions of judgment under the influence of contrary passions, leading to what Aquinas calls *incontinentia* or inconsistency (*ST* I–II 9.2, 77.1, II–II 156.1). But these kinds of failures cannot be attributed to the will properly so-called, that is to say, considered as a rational appetite directed towards the overall good. By implication, it would seem that the operations and choices of the rational creature can be adequately explained in terms of the habits of the passions, taken together with the intellect insofar as it contributes to human action through the habitual knowledge of first principles and through the operations of practical reason (I–II 58.4). We might think of these as providing the infrastructure, as it were, through which the innate orientation of the will towards goodness can be expressed in action.

Yet as we noted in the last section, Aquinas claims that the will, like other appetites, needs habits in order to operate through inclinations towards determinate objects. This claim implies that the innate orientation of the will towards a comprehensive good cannot, by itself, generate intentional inclinations. We might think that the deliberative processes of free judgment would be sufficient to do so, assuming that these are not hindered by disordered passions or other impediments external to the will itself. But this line of analysis presupposes that an abstract concept of the good would be sufficient, in itself, to provide a starting point for the processes of practical reasoning. This is by no means obvious. Practical reason always implies some kind of intelligible relation between general goals, ideals, or norms on the one hand, and the particular objects or actions which promote or instantiate them, on the other. Thus, it requires a conception sufficiently determinate to serve as the end in an ends–means relationship, or a general ideal in relation to a particular instantiation, or something of the sort.

In order to move forward at this point, we need to look more closely at the way in which Aquinas himself understands the general good, towards which the will is innately oriented. While he does hold that the will is oriented towards the good generally or abstractly considered, that does not mean that abstract goodness is itself the natural object of the will. Rather, Aquinas holds that the will is innately oriented towards the agent's own good, its perfection in accordance with the ideals of existence proper to it as a natural creature of a certain kind (*ST* I–II 7, 8; cf. I 5.1). In one sense, this innate orientation of the will towards the agent's perfection reflects a general metaphysical principle for Aquinas, since on his view every creature necessarily seeks its perfection in accordance with its natural form (I 5.1).[4] However, precisely because reasoned self-direction is natural to the human agent, she will necessarily pursue her final end through deliberative choices, formulated in the light of some conception of what it means for her to attain perfection, in accordance with some general idea of the kind of creature that she is (I–II 1.8, 91.2). What is more, since Aquinas identifies happiness with the perfection of a rational or intellectual creature, this is tantamount so saying that the will is innately oriented towards the agent's happiness—and indeed, Aquinas claims that every rational agent necessarily desires and seeks her own happiness (*ST* I 62.1, I–II 5.8).[5]

This is significant, because while "goodness as perfection, in accordance with a given kind of existence" is an abstract, comprehensive conception, it is not purely formal. Of course, most of us do not think in these metaphysical terms, but we are spontaneously drawn to satisfactions and activities

[4] As Robert Pasnau says, "One might suppose that this ascription of appetite to all of nature is some kind of crude anthropomorphism. . . . In fact, Aquinas' project is precisely the opposite. He is not trying to bring psychology to bear on the rest of nature, but rather to use his general theory of the natural order to understand human beings" (Pasnau, *Thomas Aquinas on Human Nature*, 201).

[5] Aquinas therefore holds that the desire for happiness, understood as the perfection of the rational or intellectual creature, is a metaphysical necessity, not simply an empirical fact as Pasnau claims (*Thomas Aquinas on Human Nature*, 219).

which sustain and express our existence as existing, living, and rational creatures (*ST* I–II 10.1, 94.2). These tendencies themselves constitute a kind of subjective orientation towards the perfection of the creature in accordance with its natural form of life, whether they are regarded in that light by the agent, or not. They inform the infant's earliest interactions with those around it, and they provide the raw materials for the processes of training and reflective appropriation which bring the adult to mature autonomy. They continue in some form even for those who are no longer, or perhaps were never able to engage in reasoned reflection and voluntary choice, until the death of the organism puts an end to any kind of natural striving for the good.

At the same time, the pre-rational operations and activities of the human agent are not, in themselves, sufficient to sustain rational action, grounded in some self-reflective sense of what one is doing, and why. These kinds of operations are targeted on particular objects, and if they are to be integrated into the inclinations of the rational appetite, the will, they need to be placed in relation to one another, through some general conception of what it means to live a good life, within which these diverse satisfactions have an appropriate place (*In de anima* III 16, paras. 840–2). Otherwise, the agent would have no basis for choice among disparate goods, and no way to deal with conflicts among incommensurable aims in an intelligent, consistent way. The innate orientation of the will provides starting points for developing a conception of the good, but they must be integrated in some way if the agent is to be capable of rational, fully voluntary action.

We can now see more clearly why Aquinas claims that the will needs habits in order to be rightly disposed towards its object. The will is innately oriented towards the agent's perfection or happiness, but in order for this innate orientation to sustain action, it must be specified through some determinate conception of perfection or happiness—not necessarily couched in those terms, but framed in terms general enough to be comprehensive, yet specific enough to provide a basis for effective practical reason (*ST* I–II 1.7, 8, 62.4). The agent's perfection or happiness, thus understood, constitutes the determinate object of the will. Clearly, the will is not innately oriented towards a determinate object of this kind—it needs to be directed in some way towards some plausible ideal of human existence, if it is to generate determinate inclinations which in turn move the agent to action.

This brings us to the second alternative suggested above. That is, let's grant that the will needs habits in order to specify its object, namely, the perfection of the agent, comprehensively considered. We might still conclude that these habits of the will play only a secondary and derivative role in shaping the operations of the will. As we have already observed, the will is dependent on the intellect for some conception of the agent's comprehensive good. Aquinas himself was aware that the will might therefore seem to be passive before the intellect, and in his mature thought he distinguished between the specification of the object of the will, which depends on the intellect, and the will's exercise of its act, which does not (*ST* I–II 10.2). On this view, someone who has an adequate grasp of the comprehensive good may fail to desire and pursue it, if she simply does not think of it. But given that someone has an adequate conception of what it means for her to attain her overall perfection, and is attentive to that conception, it would seem that this in itself should be enough to elicit the inclination of the will towards its proper end. The resultant dispositions of justice, hope, and charity might still count technically as habits, but they would not stem from the activities of the will itself, except in a very limited way.

Yet Aquinas apparently does not believe that even a sound grasp of the comprehensive good necessarily compels the will. This comes out most clearly in his analysis of the sin of settled malice (*certa malitia*), which as he explains is associated with (although not limited to) bad actions stemming from a vicious disposition towards one's overall good (*ST* I–II 78.2, 3). Sins of settled malice are thus contrasted with sins of inconsistent choice, mentioned above, which stem from a misjudgment of a particular seeming good under the influence of a badly integrated passion. In contrast, someone who sins out of a vicious habit does have a corrupt or disordered conception of his final good (*ST* II–II 156.3). It is all too possible to be sincerely committed to a sound ideal of self-restraint with respect to eating, while at the same time failing in a particular instance to apply that ideal in an effective way under the influence of passion, which focuses the mind on the immediately desirable aspects of this chocolate cream pie or that double cheese-burger. The inconsistent individual knows better, as we say, and soon comes to regret the inconsistent choice.

In contrast, someone whose desire for food has been perverted through gluttony has no commitment to live a life of self-restraint at all—rather, he consciously sets out to gratify his desires for certain kinds of flavors, or sensations of fullness, or the like, even when these cannot be pursued without cost to his overall well-being, comprehensively considered. Thus, the true glutton is not inconsistent or weak, inclined to over-indulge under the influence of a bad sweet tooth—rather, he is committed to a way of life which includes the pursuit of the pleasures of the table, even at the cost of sacrificing what he himself knows to be more exigent or important goods. Given what we have just said, we would expect Aquinas to say that settled malice, together with the vicious disposition with which it is correlated, is grounded in a simple mistake. The glutton simply does not know that there are more important things in life than fine dining or the satisfactions of being full, and if she could be reasoned out of her false beliefs, her dispositions and behavior would change accordingly. But Aquinas says nothing of the sort. According to him, the sin of settled malice presupposes that someone knows that he is acting contrary to the demands of reason and divine law, to the detriment of his overall perfection and ultimate salvation (*ST* I–II 78.1, II–II 156.3). Thus, someone who sins from settled malice is not simply inconsistent, nor is she just mistaken about the real character of her comprehensive good—on the contrary, it is entirely possible for someone to have a correct theoretical understanding of one's final end, and yet to incline towards a distorted or incomplete version of human perfection as one's own end (as Aquinas elsewhere says; *ST* I–II 72.5).

In one sense, a sin of settled malice does presuppose ignorance of the true good, since the agent believes that her sinful choice is more satisfying, or better suited to her, or in some other respect preferable to a choice consistent with the unqualified good—but this kind of ignorance would appear to follow from the disorder of the will, rather than causing it, and at any rate it does not obviate the agent's theoretical grasp of what the comprehensive good is (*ST* I–II 78.1 ad 1; cf. II–II 156.3 ad 1). In such a case, the distorted disposition of the will presupposes some kind of intellectual conception of the good, along the lines that this is the way of life that suits me, or the way of life that I really admire, or that I find rewarding here or now (*ST* I–II 78.3). But someone can hold this kind of belief, while also grasping that one's true end, comprehensively considered, is inconsistent with the final end that the will actually has. Intellectual judgments alone do not compel the will, even in its positive engagement.

Once again, it is helpful to compare the will with the passions. The passions, as appetites of the sensual part of the soul, emerge in response to images of desirable or noxious objects, as conveyed through sense perception, memory, and imagination. In the rational creature, these images do not emerge spontaneously—rather, they take shape through ongoing processes of experience and reflection. Even so, these reflective processes, through which we learn to perceive, are not in themselves sufficient to form the passions in the needed ways. We also need to learn to feel—that is, our innate tendencies towards desire and spirited engagement need to be shaped and directed towards appropriate images, and directed away from others. The passions are capacities for feeling in certain ways, in response to appropriate objects, and therefore they can only be developed through a kind of sentimental education, through which someone's feelings are elicited and encouraged in some circumstances, discouraged in others, and continually interpreted for the agent, in such a way that she comes to appreciate the significance of what she is feeling, and to direct her own feelings in a self-reflective way.

Similarly, the will, as the appetite of the intellectual part of the soul, emerges in response to some reasoned judgment regarding its proper object. But right judgments are not enough to shape the will in the needed ways—rather, the will, as an appetite, needs to be oriented towards the good disclosed by reason through processes of inclination towards that good. It can only develop stable dispositions towards the good presented to it by the intellect, in and through processes of inclining towards that good, in such a way that it eventually forms stable inclinations towards its comprehensive good, understood in this way, rather than that. Once we take account of this point, we can more easily see how someone could develop settled dispositions towards vice, even though she also has an adequate conception of what her comprehensive good, rightly considered, would look like. There is a difference between knowing abstractly that this or that way of life would be appropriate and salutary for me as a human being, and inclining towards that way of life as my final end. It may be that my will is actually drawn by some other alternative that my intellect presents, in such a way that I come to desire and pursue this as my end—*my own* ultimate end, in contrast to the abstract good for someone like me.

The difficulty at this point is that it is hard to say what these processes of formation, through which the will forms dispositions towards some determinate conception of happiness, would entail. We can see readily enough how the passions, which take shape through inclinations towards particular goods, could be exercised and shaped in the needed ways. But initially, it is hard to see how habits of the will could develop through any comparable process. We tend to assume that the will inclines towards its object, or it does not, and that does not leave a lot of scope for a developmental process. We turn to this issue in the next section.

3. VOLITION, CHOICE, AND THE DEVELOPMENT OF HABITS OF THE WILL

Aquinas does not offer an account of the processes of development that might lead to dispositions of the will. Yet he does offer the starting points for such an account, and these, taken together with contemporary work on practical reason, point the way towards a cogent analysis of the way in which habits of the will take shape, in such a way as to dispose the will towards one particular construal of the agent's comprehensive good. In order to develop this account, we will need to re-examine Aquinas's remarks about the relationship between the will's volition of the final end, and the choice of a particular good through free judgment. We will see that Aquinas's analysis of volition and choice implies a more intimate and reciprocal relation between the two than we might expect. Dispositions of the will do not just precede choice—they emerge and take shape in and through processes of choice, as the maturing agent develops her capacities for fully voluntary action. This, at any rate, will be the argument of this section.

In order to move forward at this point, we need to take a step back, in order to look more closely at Aquinas's conception of the good as happiness. Recall that Aquinas defines happiness as perfection, that is to say the appropriate and full development of the natural capacities of the rational or intellectual creature (*ST* I 62.1; cf. I–II 1.5). Thus understood, every rational or intellectual creature necessarily desires its own happiness, although not necessarily understood in those terms, and directs all its activities towards that end in some way or other (*ST* I–II 1.6,7; cf. I–II 5.8). Given the mode of activity proper to the rational creature, happiness can only be willed and pursued under some description or other, which need not be couched in metaphysical terms, but which will capture some idea of what it would mean to attain an ideal, proper to the kind of thing I take myself to be (*ST* I–II 1.7). The complexity of human existence guarantees that there will be more than one possible way of formulating one's ideal of a happy, or an admirable or desirable or praiseworthy life. At the same time, Aquinas clearly believes that this indeterminacy is not unbounded—we can formulate wrong conceptions of happiness, and literally drive ourselves to perdition in trying to pursue them.

Further on, Aquinas distinguishes between the attainment of happiness, and the object attained in a truly happy life. The latter consists in whatever objects or states or patterns of activity are appropriately fulfilling for the kind of creature that we are—whatever it is, in other words, that will draw out and sustain the full and integral development of our natural potentialities (*ST* I–II 3.1). Considered in terms of the creature's attainment, happiness is identified with sustained activities which express and sustain the creature's natural capacities in the fullest possible way—its perfection, in other words (*ST* I–II 3.2). The language of perfection can be misleading in this context, and so it is worth underscoring that for Aquinas, perfection is always linked to activity in accordance with some normative ideal—paradigmatically, the ideal proper to a specific kind of existence. Thus, Aquinas claims that seen from this standpoint, all human persons seek the same end, that is to say, perfection as agents of a specific kind. What is more, we share the same end, formally considered, with every other creature, since everything naturally desires its continued existence and full development as a creature of a certain kind—keeping in mind that "desire" does not necessarily presuppose sentience (*ST* I–II 1.7, 8). In this way,

Aquinas places the rational appetite of the will, and the comprehensive good towards which it is ordered, within the wider context of desire, activity, and fulfillment which for him comprise the necessary structures of created existence at every level.

In the last section, we noted that the human agent is naturally drawn to the particular goods and satisfactions which are necessary to the organic life and well-being of the human creature. These are necessary to any kind of comprehensive perfection, and they represent perfections of a kind in themselves, in the sense that they foster and support the actualization of human capacities and powers. Similarly, human activities of any kind can be said to perfect the agent in some respect, insofar as they represent the actualization of human capacities for action. What is more, the indefinite variety of human ideals, possibilities, and experiences offer many ways of construing one's overall perfection, or happiness—many different ways to envision a life that is fulfilling, or praiseworthy, or admirable, or suitable, or whatever terms one uses to describe the kind of life one seeks.

The point I want to make here is that both the agent's comprehensive good and the concrete possibilities for pursuing that good here and now can be understood in multiple ways by the same person at any given point in her life. What is more, the agent's overall perfection can credibly be understood in more than one way, involving distinct and even incompatible ways of realizing the open-ended possibilities of human nature. Whenever it is engaged in some act of volition or choice, the will necessarily presupposes some rational conception of the good, but it will normally have more than one such conception available to it, and more than one level on which to focus its attention (*ST* I–II 13.6). At the same time, formally considered, the comprehensive good towards which the will is necessarily inclined is the agent's own perfection, in accordance with the ideal of existence proper to the kind of creature that he or she is. Whatever else it means, this perfection implies activity, through which the agent's potentialities are developed and expressed in appropriate ways. Seen from this standpoint, any activity on the part of the human creature can be construed in some way as a means to, or an exemplification of one's final end, since any human action represents a limited yet real perfection of natural capacities.

Once we appreciate this point, we can more easily make sense of what seem at first to be inconsistent claims regarding the agent's orientation towards the final end. Aquinas claims that each person necessarily desires happiness, understood as his own perfection, and directs every action towards attaining that final end (*ST* I–II 5.8). What is more, he claims that the rational agent necessarily pursues his final end under some description or other, in accordance with a reasoned conception of the good (*ST* I–II

1.6, 7, 10.2). Yet he also explicitly says that there are some kinds of voluntary, rational acts that are inconsistent with the agent's overall conception of the good—actions of inconsistent choice, and also venial sins (*ST* I–II 72.5). We can reconcile this seeming inconsistency, however, in terms of a distinction between the pursuit of some object as the pursuit of one's final end, and the activities which are in some way constitutive of the agent's final end. The key point is that any act can be considered from some perspective as promoting or exemplifying the agent's happiness, understood in terms of perfection, equated with activity. Any action perfects the agent in some way or other, and can therefore be construed and willed—in however distorted a fashion—as a moment of happiness.

For Aquinas, the ideal of rationality is set by a mature, self-reflective agent who has a well-developed and sound conception of her final end, and who governs her deliberations and choices by reference to this end. This is pretty clearly an ideal, and yet it is not so far outside the bounds of possibility as to be unrealistic or unpersuasive. We know what it would mean to live a life of integrity, consistency, and conscious purpose, and without trying to argue the point, I would suggest that even at the subjective level, this is the most satisfying way that a person can live. Most of us are not going to live up to this ideal, but we can approximate it, sufficiently to develop a taste for this kind of autonomy and self-command. In contrast, we have the ideal, if that is the word, of the inconsistent person, whose general idea of the good is sound, but who fails to follow through on his best insights. The point is that even someone who chooses inconsistently can be said to pursue his final end of perfection in a qualified sense—the problem is, he does so in terms of whatever strikes him as fulfilling here and now, under a rational description which is tweaked to reflect his immediate desires. At the same time, however, someone who chooses badly in this way, under a distorted conception of the good, is not wholly mistaken or irrational. In one sense, at least, the activity that he chooses is indeed a component of his overall subjective happiness, understood as the realization of his capacities as a given kind of creature.

This brings us to a critical point. Someone who chooses inconsistently does so because her overall conception of the ideal life, which she normally finds attractive and compelling, does not in this instance attract her (*ST* II–II 156.1, 2; cf. I–II 10.3). As Aquinas suggests, her will is not exercised in the right way, at the critical moment, because for whatever reason, it is engaged by some alternative possibility for satisfying activity (*ST* I–II 78.3). In itself, this failure need not reflect a vicious disposition. Nonetheless, this kind of inconsistency is only possible because the attractive alternative does offer a kind of happiness, in the qualified sense of an activity which fulfills some human potentiality. As such, it implies an alternative to the agent's own (by hypothesis, sound) ideal of life, an alternative that would allow for the pursuit of many more such satisfactions. Admittedly, most of us would not seriously consider a way of life centered around the unrestrained pursuit of candy. Nonetheless, it is easy to imagine other, more serious and alluring temptations that might draw someone away from a sound comprehensive ideal to pursue a life of pleasures, excitement, or power.

At any rate, the case of inconsistent choice is relevant here, because it prompts us to look more closely at the relation between the volition of the will towards a final end, and the exercise of free judgment, through which this volition is pursued and realized. We tend to assume the unqualified priority of the volition of the will over the exercise of free judgment, the latter being in every way dependent on the former. Thus, when Aquinas says that the will moves itself to act through choice, he does not seem to leave any space for the kind of self-reflective processes of formation that we would associate with habits. It would appear that the processes of practical reason presuppose that the will already is disposed, well or badly, towards its object, the final end as understood intellectually. This line of analysis, in turn, suggests that at this ultimate level, and seen in relation to its active exercise, the will is passive with respect to the intellect. This interpretation suggests that the will inclines towards the intelligible good through a kind of transcendental meta-choice, which it then expresses in time through the processes of actual choice. But Aquinas does not say anything of the sort. On the contrary, he observes that just as the intellect can only grasp general concepts as these are mediated through particulars, so the will can only be moved through the mediation of particulars (*ST* I 80.2 ad 3). He does not explain how this process might work, but his analysis of the relation between will and choice points the way towards a fuller account of the processes through which the will arrives at the volition of the final end through the mediation of choice.

On Aquinas's view, rational action presupposes that the agent's act can be justified in relational terms—one chooses this determinate act for the sake of that wider aim, in terms of which the particular choice is rationally justified. But this structure need not imply that the wider aim is clearly formulated in advance. On the contrary, we can, and we often do, discover what we really care about, respect, or love in and through processes of choice. Once again, we need to bear in mind that every choice involves an inclination towards activity, which is in some way perfecting. That is why it draws the will, and by the same token, that is why it can be regarded intellectually as a means to, or a component of, a wider ideal of life. At the same time, most of our choices are framed by natural and social contexts, in such a way as to open up further possibilities for fulfilling activity, together with unexpected deprivations and sacrifices. These, too, are experienced by the will as in some way fulfilling, or not, and these inclinations prompt further reflection on the kind of life that they imply. My point is that through this process, the inclinations of the will begin to take on a patterned shape, characterized by the tendency of the will to engage itself with respect to these kinds of activities, to turn actively from other, inconsistent or damaging activities, and not to engage others. The will thus disposes itself to its act in and through processes of inclining towards certain kinds of subjective perfections and rejecting, or simply failing to advert to, others.

Until recently, the claim that we might arrive at some sense of our own desires, aims, and commitments in and through the processes of choice would have seemed very odd to most of our contemporaries. Recently, the philosopher Elijah Millgram has offered a persuasive way of thinking about these processes, in terms of what he describes as practical induction.[6] Millgram's theory is meant to challenge the widespread assumption that practical reason in itself is always limited to means–end reasoning, which takes its starting points from predetermined ends. On the contrary, he argues, our choices themselves provide the starting points for genuine reasoning about the aims for which we act. Through experience and reflection, we build up an extensive sense of the kinds of activities which we find rewarding, and we also get a sense of which out of a range of incommensurable values are most important to us. This extended practical sense provides the basis for practical induction, through which we form conclusions about the overall ends which have prompted our choices, and in terms of which they can be rationally justified.

Aquinas would have no difficulty with this way of construing practical reason. It fits well with his overall account of the way in which the intellect moves from apprehension of particulars to a grasp of specific forms, seen as exemplified in these specific ways, an account which he explicitly extends to practical reasoning (*in de anima* III.16, para. 842). He would add that the processes that Millgram describes also involve the operations of free choice and will, operating in tandem with practical and speculative reasoning (*ST* I–II 13.1). Millgram emphasizes that the agent learns what she really wants, in and through induction from her specific choices. Aquinas would add that this only works, because the agent really wants something—that is to say, her free choice and will are engaged through her inclinations towards some kinds of choices and her aversion or distress at others, inclinations which themselves provide the starting points for the processes of practical

[6] In particular, see Elijah Millgram, *Practical Induction* (Cambridge, MA: Harvard University Press, 1997), 43–66 for an analysis and defense of the idea of practical induction.

induction that Millgram describes. The agent's natural desire for happiness sets the processes of activity in motion, and informs her activities and reflections at every point. We act, most fundamentally, because we naturally desire life and effective operation in accordance with the structuring principles of our existence. Through our experiences of our actions, we come to regard certain kinds of activities as appropriately fulfilling, and others as not worth our pursuit, or even downright noxious.

At the same time, practical induction cannot be limited to the level of reflection on diverse courses of action, considered seriatim.[7] Every human life offers a range of alternative choices, incommensurable and at least potentially incompatible. If we are to sustain a course of activity over time, with any degree of reasoned self-determination and consistency, we need to be able to arrive at some comparative judgments regarding priorities—which courses of activity should be privileged, which are to be rejected, and how do we deal with the indeterminate middle range of options? Aquinas offers both a way of thinking about this problem, and an indication of how it is that we address it. On this view, what we are thinking about, as we reflect on options and priorities, is nothing other than the true meaning of happiness, given what we understand ourselves to be, and how we reflectively experience ourselves in our active engagement with the world. This line of reflection will necessarily move in the direction of comprehensive integration, because only in this way can we arrive at the needed sense of the overall meaning and purpose of our lives—needed, if we are to take possession of ourselves, determining the course of our lives autonomously, through the exercise of reasoned judgments. By the same token, this orientation towards happiness sets general parameters for the kinds of reflections that Millgram envisions. As we reflect on which activities are satisfying or not, we also place these experiences in wider contexts, testing our options for consistency and placing them in a wider framework of meaning and purpose.

[7] Throughout his analysis of practical induction, Millgram argues cogently that unity of agency presupposes ongoing processes of deliberation, through which one's choices and desires are related coherently to one's past dispositions and associated, in some suitable way, with a future trajectory: "Unity of the self in the practical domain will in like manner be exhibited in one's ability to—and in the likelihood that one actually *will*—bring to bear, in the course of practical deliberation, one's practical judgments... as they become relevant to the question one is considering" (*Practical Induction*, 53). Although I cannot defend the point here, I would add that Aquinas's theory of the metaphysical unity of the self, expressed through natural inclinations towards one's final end of perfection, provides the formal structure of desire and deliberation needed to account for the possibility and rationality of Millgram's practical induction.

At this point, the will begins to form stable dispositions, that is to say, habits, through processes of ongoing interaction between the intellect and the inclinations of the will itself. Prompted by a judgment that this or that desideratum is in some way good, the will determines itself towards a particular way of realizing its capabilities through a given choice, and then experience subsequently either confirms or calls into question the soundness of the initial judgment. The agent's experiences thus inform his sense of what the true good is, while his ongoing inclinations towards the good, thus understood, dispose him towards activities which promote that overall good or at least do not undermine it. Once again, it is worth emphasizing that at every point in this process, the operations of the will are to some extent independent of the intellect, and play an independent role in shaping the agent's conception of, and his active desire for his final end. It is true that the will cannot positively incline towards anything, unless the intellect presents it as being in some way good. Yet as we have already noted, nothing that the intellect can offer by way of an image of the good can compel the exercise of the will. Even though the agent grasps that one alternative is rationally more compelling or more fulfilling than other possibilities, he may not desire that alternative, because he prefers an alternative option which he also grasps to be good in some way. These volitions, and the choices they inform, will in turn shape the agent's further reflections, in such a way as to incline him progressively to construe his life and his choices in terms of what he actually loves, in contrast to other, perhaps objectively better objects of love.

The will naturally and necessarily inclines towards happiness, that is to say, the agent's perfection, which can be attained in more than one way. It moves itself to act through processes of choosing specific acts, each of which is in itself an actualization, a perfection of the agent's active powers, and each of which is regarded in some more specific way as a means to, or an element of the agent's overall happiness as she understands it. Seen from this perspective, the dispositions of the will, its virtuous or vicious habits, can be understood as dispositions to pursue one's objective final end in characteristic ways, implying the pursuit of some kinds of activities rather than others. The habits of the will dispose it to choose well or badly, in accordance with the agent's best judgments about who and what she is, which courses of action will best promote her overall happiness, and what boundaries are placed on her choices. The virtues of the will dispose her to choose well; vices of the will dispose her to choose badly.

This brings us to one further issue. Aquinas claims that habits are necessary to the rational creature. This is not tantamount to saying that good habits, virtues, are necessary, and indeed, it seems that they are not. Aquinas does however say that the virtues are necessary in order to enable the appetites to function well, to incline to their object in appropriate ways (*ST* I–II 56.4, 6). In the next section, we turn to a (necessarily brief) consideration of what he means by this claim

4. THE CONDITIONAL NECESSITY OF THE VIRTUES

Aquinas apparently believes that the habits of the appetites are always either virtues or vices—that is to say, there are no morally neutral habits of the appetites (*ST* I–II 54.3; cf. I–II 18.9). Why should this be the case? Most fundamentally, because we are most characteristically moral and spiritual beings, whose overall perfection depends critically on our own, self-reflective desire for and pursuit of appropriate ends (*ST* I–II 90.2). Aquinas does not say that the only thing of value is a good will, but he does clearly say that the overall perfection of the human agent depends on right desires, and not on right knowledge except insofar as right desire presupposes some knowledge of one's true end (*ST* I–II 56.3). The habits of the passions and will are always either virtuous or vicious, because they always operate in such a way as to either support the agent's overall desire for, and pursuit of her comprehensive good, or to undermine it in some way.

The virtues are necessary in order for the appetites to function appropriately and well, and yet apparently they are not necessary for basic functioning, since we can and do act out of vicious habits. The key idea here is that a habit develops some faculty in such a way as to bring order and direction to its operations, focusing them in such a way as to direct them to act. A well-formed, salutary habit—that is to say, a virtue—will perfect its subject faculty in a full, unqualified sense. It will dispose the faculty to function in accordance with its own innate natural tendencies, and to do so in such a way as to promote the overall development, integration, and expression of the natural tendencies of the agent, taken as a whole (*ST* I–II 49.3, 55.1, 3). In the words of the scholastic formula, the virtue renders both the agent's actions, and the agent herself, good without qualification (*ST* I–II 56.3). Vicious habits similarly bring order and direction to the agent's appetites, sufficient to direct them to act in characteristic ways. Thus, they also represent a kind of development and completion of innate capacities, and in that sense they are also perfections of the faculty. However, by hypothesis, vicious habits orient the appetites towards actions which are in some way at odds with the agent's overall integrated functioning (*ST* I–II 55.3 ad 2). Seen from the limited perspective of the faculty they inform, the vices are perfections, but from the perspective of the agent's overall perfection, they are distortions, which undercut the agent's overall perfection.

Once again, Aquinas's analysis of inconsistent choice helps us to see what motivates this line of analysis. The inconsistent person, we recall, has a good overall grasp of his comprehensive good, and is sincerely committed to pursuing it. However, for whatever reason, his passions have been formed in such a way that he finds it difficult to maintain his commitments in certain situations. For example, a long history of bad eating has oriented his appetite for food in such a way that he keeps choosing fish and chips, even though he really should not. This deficiency is not the same thing as gluttony, which implies a settled commitment at odds with one's overall good, but it does reflect some kind of malformation of the passions. This malformation, in turn, skews the agent's judgments in particular situations, in such a way that he chooses a course of action contrary to his true good, without realizing it at the time. This kind of malformation of the passions is all too possible, because in themselves the passions are oriented towards particular objects disclosed through sense perception. Therefore, they need to be formed through the acquisition of habits, in order to incline to objects which are genuinely in accordance with the individual's overall good.

The will is innately oriented towards the individual's comprehensive good, and it does not need habits to direct its inclinations accordingly (*ST* I–II 56.6). However, the will is also the faculty for actions *ad extra*, which bring the individual into relation with other people, community and commonwealth, and ultimately God. It is not innately oriented towards right relations in all these contexts, and that is why it too needs virtues in order to act appropriately and well. The virtues of the will, including the cardinal virtue of justice and the theological virtues of hope and charity, all dispose the agent, in diverse ways, to choose in accordance with a right understanding of his place in the community and the cosmos, and his proper relations to others. Aquinas believes that in each case, the intellect provides the necessary starting points for determining what this means. He regards the first principles of justice, comprising fundamental norms of non-maleficence and obligation, as *per se nota* specifications of the principles of practical reason as applied to interpersonal relationships (*ST* I–II 100.3 ad 1, 100.5 ad 4; II–II 79.1). The starting points for determining our right relation to God, and to ourselves and others seen in reference to God, are provided by the theological virtue of faith, which is necessary for both hope and charity (*ST* I–II 65.5; II–II 3.3, 17.7). At every point, the agent's choices are formed by reference to some conceptions of what she owes to other people, and perhaps also by reference to the basic truths of faith. Yet these are not compelling—she may choose to act in ways that are unjust or unloving, because she inclines to some activity which she cannot pursue within the bounds of justice or charity. One such action does not a vicious disposition make, but the agent who consistently prefers activities contrary to justice or charity will dispose herself, over time, to act in ways that are unjust or unloving—not necessarily out of bad motives, but simply because she prefers a way of life that cannot be realized in a just and loving way.

Aquinas associates this kind of disposition with the traditional category of settled malice, as we have seen. We are not compelled to choose the highest good, or even to choose an adequate or compelling good—we can freely dispose ourselves, knowingly, towards ways of realizing our human potential which are in some way perverse, even self-destructive over the long term. By the same token, however, through our free choices to act in accordance with justice and charity, we can freely dispose ourselves over time to incline towards upright and loving activities, and to find our greatest satisfactions in a life lived in right relation to God and others. In this case, too, the dispositions of the will are genuinely habits of the will, presupposing the judgments of the intellect but also dependent on an irreducible exercise of volition, through which the will is disposed towards its object in a particular way. Right knowledge about the human good, even a correct grasp of one's own true and comprehensive good, does not in itself make anyone a good person—we must freely love and pursue the comprehensive good that we see, through a way of life in which we attain our own objective fulfillment while maintaining right relations with others (*ST* I–II 56.3).

University of Notre Dame

BIBLIOGRAPHY

Kent, Bonnie. *Virtues of the Will: The Transformation of Ethics in the Late Thirteenth Century* (Washington, DC: Catholic University of America Press, 1993).

Lottin, Odon. *Psychologie et morale aux XII et XIII siècles* (Louvain: Abbaye du Mont César, 1942).

Millgram, Elijah. *Practical Induction* (Cambridge, MA: Harvard University Press, 1997).

Pasnau, Robert. *Thomas Aquinas on Human Nature: A Philosophical Study of* Summa theologiae *1a 75–89* (Cambridge: Cambridge University Press, 2002).

Stump, Eleonore. *Aquinas* (The Arguments of the Philosophers) (New York: Routledge, 2003).

Thomas Aquinas. *Opera omnia* (Rome: Commissio Leonina, 1882–).

Olivi on Consciousness and Self-Knowledge: The Phenomenology, Metaphysics, and Epistemology of Mind's Reflexivity

Susan Brower-Toland

The theory of mind that medieval philosophers inherit from Augustine is predicated on the thesis that the human mind, in its nature and in its functioning, bears the image of the divine trinity. This thesis, which Augustine develops at length in the latter books of his *De Trinitate*, has at its core a picture of human intellect and human thought as essentially self-reflexive. Indeed, on the Augustinian picture, this self-reflexivity is the very locus of mind's trinitarian structure. And this is because, on Augustine's view, the human mind (*mens*) is such that it bears a thee-fold relation to itself: "it always remembers itself, always understands itself, and always loves itself."[1] Among Augustine's medieval successors (as among current commentators) there is no consensus regarding either the proper interpretation of this thesis, or even the details of the cognitive theory attendant on (or required for) it. Even so, medieval philosophers accept the

[1] See, e.g., *De Trinitate* 14.9. This thesis is the conclusion at which Augustine arrives at end of Book 10 of *De Trinitate* (see 10.18). However, he returns to it and further expounds it in Book 14. English citations of *De Trinitate* are from Augustine, *The Trinity*, ed. J. E. Rotelle, tr. E. Hill (Hyde Park, NY: New City Press, 1991). For further discussion of this thesis see Charles Brittain, "Intellectual Self-Knowledge," in E. Bermon and G. O'Daly (eds.), *Le De Trinitate de saint Augustin exégèse, logique et noétique* (Paris: Vrin, 2012), 322–39; Gerard O' Daly, Augustine's Philosophy of Mind (Berkley: University of California Press, 1987), 209–11. A brief précis of the whole of *De Trinitate* can be found in Mary Clark, "De Trinitate," in E. Stump and N. Kretzmann (eds.), *The Cambridge Companion to Augustine* (Cambridge: Cambridge University Press, 2001), 91–102.

basic Augustinian thesis about the reflexivity of the mind and, likewise, generally agree that—whatever else it involves—such reflexivity entails that the mind (or intellect, or rational soul)[2] is such that it is aware of itself and (at least some of) its occurrent states. Indeed, because self-knowledge of this sort comes to be taken as essential to a proper account of the mind as the *imago Dei*, such knowledge comes to figure among the basic *explananda* in later medieval cognitive theory.[3]

For the same reason, questions concerning the precise nature and scope of the mind's access to itself are widely discussed throughout the later medieval period. How does the mind reflexively cognize itself? Does such self-cognition depend on representational or inferential processes? Is awareness of one's states to be explained by the introduction of numerically distinct, higher-order acts of inner-awareness? Does reflexive awareness extend to all one's subjective states—both dispositional and occurrent, sensory and intellective?[4] Medieval discussions of these (and related) questions serve as one of the primary contexts for medieval theorizing about the nature of consciousness. Admittedly, to characterize medieval interest in mind's reflexivity in this way is to frame it in a terminology

[2] Although, strictly speaking, these terms are not equivalent, the differences in their meanings are not salient here. In fact, Olivi himself often uses them interchangeably (see, for example, passage A below). In what follows, therefore, I shall move freely between them (and related adjectives).

[3] To be sure, Augustine's *De Trinitate* is not the only source of influence on medieval discussions of self-knowledge. Other influential treatments include Aristotle's discussion of intellectual self-knowledge in *De Anima* (III.2 and 4), relevant portions of the *Liber de causis*, as well as Avicenna's treatment of self-awareness in his *Liber de anima*. It is fair to say, however, that Augustine's *De Trinitate* is particularly authoritative—a fact which owes, no doubt, to the theological significance of his thesis about mind's reflexivity. For further discussion of the influence of Augustine's *De Trinitate* on later medieval philosophical psychology see Pekka Kärkkäinen, "Interpretations of the Psychological Analogy from Aquinas to Biel," in P. Kärkkäinen (ed.), *Trinitarian Theology in the Medieval West* (Helsinki: Luther-Agricola-Society, 2007), 256–79; John O'Callaghan, "Imago Dei: A Test Case for St. Thomas's Augustinianism," in M. Dauphinais, B. David, and M. Levering (eds.), *Aquinas the Augustinian* (Washington, DC: Catholic University of America Press, 2007), 100–44; Edward Booth, "Saint Thomas Aquinas's Critique of Saint Augustine's Conceptions of the Image of God in the Human Soul," in J. Brachtendorf (ed.), *Gott und sein Bild: Augustins De Trinitate im Spiegel gegenwärtiger Forschung* (Paderborn: Ferdinand Schöningh, 2000), 219–40; and Burkhard Mojsisch, "Dietrich von Freiberg: ein origninelle Reezipient der *Mens-* und *Cogitatio-*Theorie Augustinus," in J. Brachtendorf (ed.), *Gott und sein Bild: Augustins De Trinitate im Spiegel gegenwärtiger Forschung* (Paderborn: Ferdinand Schöningh, 2000), 241–8.

[4] For an overview of medieval discussions of these issues see my "Self-Knowledge, Self-Consciousness, and Reflexivity," in R. Friedmann and M. Pickavé (eds.), *Companion to Cognitive Theory in the Later Middle Ages* (Leuven: Leuven University Press, forthcoming).

that, while familiar to us, is foreign to their own discussions.[5] Still, the phenomena targeted in medieval treatments of mental reflexivity share a great deal in common with what, in contemporary philosophy, goes under the heading of "phenomenal consciousness". What is more, the analyses medieval philosophers develop to account for mental reflexivity often bear a striking resemblance to those found in contemporary discussions of phenomenal consciousness. Or so it seems to me.

I cannot, in the space of a single paper, undertake to fully substantiate these broad remarks about the connections between medieval accounts of mind's reflexivity and contemporary discussions of consciousness. Nonetheless, I propose to make *some* progress on that project by taking a closer look at the treatment these issues receive in the work of one particularly influential late-medieval philosopher, Peter John Olivi (1248–98).[6] In what follows, therefore, I trace the details of Olivi's account of the nature of reflexive awareness.[7] I begin by identifying the various phenomena Olivi associates with mind's self-reflexivity (Section 1). Here I argue that there are

[5] Indeed, to my knowledge, medieval philosophers have no single Latin expression corresponding to our own term "consciousness". I do, however, think their usage of the term "*experior*" often expresses a kind of awareness that contemporary philosophers would associate with phenomenal consciousness. For a discussion of the history and etymology of the contemporary notion of "consciousness" see the introductory essay in S. Heinämaa, V. Lähteenmäki, and P. Remeseds (eds.), *Consciousness: From Perception to Reflection in the History of Philosophy* (Dordrecht: Springer, 2007).

[6] For details about Olivi's biography and historical context see David Burr, "The Persecution of Peter Olivi," *Transactions of the American Philosophical Society* 66 (1976), 3–98 and David Burr, *Olivi and Franciscan Poverty: The Origins of the Usus Pauper Controversy* (Philadelphia: University of Pennsylvania Press, 1989). For an overview of Olivi's philosophical writings and distinctive positions see François-Xavier Putallaz, "Peter Olivi," in J. Garcia and T. Noone (eds.), *A Companion to Philosophy in the Middle Ages* (Oxford: Blackwell, 2007), 516–23 and Robert Pasnau, "Peter John Olivi," in E. N. Zalta (ed.), *The Stanford Encyclopedia of Philosophy* (Fall 2008 Edition) <http://plato.stanford.edu/archives/fall2008/entries/olivi/>. Finally, for a survey of Augustine's influence on Olivi see Juhana Toivanen, "Peter John Olivi," in W. Otten (ed.), *The Oxford Guide to the Historical Reception of Augustine* (Oxford: Oxford University Press, 2013).

[7] It is widely acknowledged that self-reflexivity is a prominent theme in Olivi's philosophy of mind; it runs through his treatment of the senses, the intellect, and even—indeed, especially—his theory of the will. For Olivi's account of reflexivity in the faculty of will see Mikko Yrjönsuuri, "Free Will and Self-Control in Peter Olivi," in H. Lagerlund and M. Yrjönsuuri (eds.), *Emotions and Choice from Boethius to Descartes* (Dordrecht: Kluwer, 2002), 99–128. For reflexivity at the level of sense cognition see Juhana Toivanen, *Animal Consciousness: Peter Olivi on Cognitive Functions of the Sensitive Soul* (Ph.D. dissertation, University of Jyväskylä, 2009) and Juhana Toivanen, "Perceptual Self-Awareness in Seneca, Augustine, and Olivi," *Journal of the History of Philosophy*, forthcoming. Because of the emphasis Olivi places on reflexivity in his philosophical psychology he's more explicit than most regarding how he understands its central features—most notably its phenomenology. For the same reason, his account of

clear connections between his understanding of the phenomenological character of reflexive awareness and that associated our own notion of "phenomenal consciousness". With these connections in mind, I then turn, in the remainder of the paper, to his analysis of the metaphysical structure (Section 2) and the epistemological status (Section 3) of phenomenally conscious states.

1. OLIVI ON THE PHENOMENA OF REFLEXIVITY: CONSCIOUSNESS AND SUBJECTIVITY

In contemporary discussions, theories of "consciousness" often address very different sorts of mental phenomena. Much the same is true of medieval discussions of mind's reflexivity. Thus, despite widespread medieval acceptance of the thesis that mind or rational soul is self-reflexive, there is little or no consensus about the nature or proper characterization of the phenomena entailed by such reflexivity. For the same reason, any comparison between medieval discussions of reflexivity and contemporary discussions of consciousness requires clarity about the mental phenomena under consideration in both contexts. I want to begin, therefore, by getting clearer about the various types of psychological phenomena Olivi associates with the self-reflexivity of the rational soul.[8]

Olivi, like most of his contemporaries, takes for granted that the reflexivity that characterizes the mind entails self-knowledge of two kinds, namely, (1) knowledge of itself and (2) knowledge of its own occurrent acts.[9] Whereas self-knowledge of the first sort involves reflexive awareness

reflexivity is particularly useful as a point of comparison to contemporary discussions of phenomenal consciousness.

[8] Olivi does not suppose that reflexive awareness is unique to intellective faculties. Indeed, he's quite explicit that even in the case of non-human animals there is a minimal (*semiplene*) form of self-reflexive awareness associated with sensory cognition. In the case of humans, however, he holds reflexive awareness (even of sensory states) owes ultimately to the intellect. See below, nn. 12 and 23.

[9] In calling the intellect's knowledge of itself "self-knowledge," I do not mean to commit myself to the view that Olivi identifies the human person (i.e. that to which the first-person pronoun refers) exclusively with the rational soul. Indeed, I suspect this is not the case. However, because Olivi's account of the metaphysics of human beings—and, in particular, his account of the soul, its parts, and their various relations to the body—is extremely complicated, and because nothing in my discussion requires taking a stand on these matters, I set them to one side. Detailed treatment of Olivi's account of the soul and its relation to the body can be found in Robert Pasnau, "Olivi on the Metaphysics of the Soul," *Medieval Philosophy and Theology* 6 (1997), 109–32. For discussion of Olivi's notion of self and self-hood, see Mikko Yrjönsuuri, "Locating the Self Within the Soul:

of oneself (or of one's own mind), knowledge of the second sort is reflexive awareness of a particular event or state that occurs within oneself. Although Olivi takes there to be a close connection between these two kinds of self-knowledge, it will be important to mark the difference between them. In what follows, therefore, I speak of the former as "*subject*-reflexive" since it involves knowledge or awareness of oneself as the subject of thought; I speak of the latter as "*state*-reflexive" since it is knowledge or awareness of a given state occurring within oneself.

a. Subject-reflexive self-knowledge: nature and types

Olivi identifies a variety of different types of reflexive awareness associated with each of these two broad categories of self-knowledge. In connection with subject-reflexive knowledge, for example, he distinguishes between (1a) a *quasi*-perceptual or experiential mode of knowing one's own mind or soul, and (1b) a conceptual or *quiddative* knowledge regarding the nature of a mind or rational soul in general.[10] The following passage, which contains Olivi's most explicit and most detailed characterization of each of these two modes of subject-reflexive knowledge, is worth quoting at length:

Thirteenth-Century Discussions," in P. Remes and J. Sihvola (eds.), *Ancient Philosophy of the Self* (Dordrecht: Springer, 2008), 225–41 and Mikko Yrjönsuuri, "Types of Self-Awareness in Medieval Thought," in V. Hirvonen, T. J. Holopainen, and M. Tuominen (eds.), *Mind and Modality: Studies in the History of Philosophy in Honor of Simo Knuuttila* (Leiden: Brill, 2006),153–69; Sylvain Piron, "L'expérience subjective selon Pierre de Jean Olivi," in O. Boulnois (ed.), *Généalogies du sujet: de saint Anselme à Malebranche* (Paris: Vrin, 2007), 43–54.

[10] This distinction is not unique to Olivi. Aquinas, to take just one example, draws a similar distinction in his treatment of self-knowledge at *De veritate* 10.8c and *Summa theologiae* I.87.1c. (Interestingly, despite the fact that Olivi is clearly aware (and critical) of Aquinas's discussion, he fails to note that Aquinas marks the very same sort of distinction—a failure which vitiates much of his critique of Aquinas's views.) Very likely, the distinction has its source in *De Trinitate* 10, where Augustine—as part of a solution to a paradox of self-inquiry—distinguishes between two kinds of self-knowledge: (i) mind's subjective awareness of its own existence and occurrent activities and (ii) its knowledge of the nature of minds in general. For further discussion of the relationship between Olivi and Aquinas's views on mind's knowledge of itself see François-Xavier Putallaz, *La connaissance de soi au XIIIe siècle: de Matthieu d'Aquasparta à Thierry de Freiberg* (Vrin: Paris, 1991), chap. 2, and Christian Rode, "Der Begriff der inneren Erfahrung bei Petrus Johannis Olivi," *Bochumer Philosophisches Jahrbuch für Antike und Mittelalter* 13 (2008), 123–41. For an illuminating discussion of Augustine's account of the mind's search for itself in *De Trinitate*, see Gareth Matthews, "Augustine on Mind's Search for Itself," *Faith and Philosophy* 20 (2003), 415–29.

[A] It should be recognized that the soul (*anima*) knows (or can know) itself in two ways. The first (1a) is in the manner of an experiential perception—similar, in a way, to touch (*per modum sensus experimentalis et quasi tactualis*). In this way, the soul senses with complete certainty that it exists, lives, thinks, wills, sees, hears, and moves the body and likewise concerning other acts of which it knows and senses itself to be the principle and subject. And this is so inasmuch as there is no object and no act that it can occurrently know or consider without it always thereupon knowing and sensing itself to be the subject of the very act by which it knows and considers that thing. Accordingly, in its act of thinking, it always shapes the force of this proposition: "I know this" or "I opine this" or "I have a doubt about this". And the soul has this knowledge of itself through the immediate inward turn of its intellective gaze (*per immediatam conversionem sui intellectualis aspectus*) upon itself and upon its acts. Indeed, so long as one is vigilant in use of free choice of the will, it remains always and continually turned inward upon the soul. Nevertheless, because the essential characteristics and properties of the soul are not sufficiently clear to everyone, they must be distinguished and studied. Thus, although the mind (*mens*) senses and feels itself immediately through itself, it does not, nevertheless, know its nature by *genera* and *differentia* so as to distinguish it from all other things by the *genera* and *differentia* of those other things.... The second way (1b) of knowing itself is via discursive reasoning. Through this reasoning it investigates the *genus* and *differentia*, which it does not know by means of the first way of knowing itself.... [In this reasoning process] it begins first from those things that it grasps about itself through the first way of knowing and holds these as primary, infallible, and indubitable principles—for example, that it is a living thing, and that it is the principle and subject of all the aforementioned acts.[11]

As this passage makes clear, on Olivi's view, these two modes of subject-reflexive awareness differ both in their content and in the means by which they come to be possessed. Thus, in the first case, (1a), the mind's awareness of itself is both *de se* (that is, *essentially* and *exclusively* self-directed) and utterly immediate. As Olivi explains, one is directly acquainted with oneself as the "principle and subject" of one's various mental states (e.g. thinking and willing) and bodily activities (e.g. seeing and hearing).[12] Although this

11 *Summa* II, q. 76 (III, 146–7). The critical edition of Olivi's question-commentary on the *Sentences* of Peter Lombard is published in several volumes. My discussion draws from several questions from book two of this work, which is published in *Quaestiones in secumdum librum Sententiarum* [= *Summa* II], ed. B. Jansen (Florence: Collegium S. Bonaventurae, 1922–6).

12 That subject-reflexive awareness includes awareness of oneself as the subject of both sensory as well as intellective states is something to which Olivi calls attention in a number of other contexts as well. In all such contexts Olivi explains the existence and unitary nature of the soul's subject-reflexive awareness as a function of its intellective power. Cf. *Summa* II, q. 51 (II, 122): "We sense within ourselves, through intimate and perfectly certain experience, that the sensory part is restrained, ruled, and directed by the superior [intellective] part as something intimately implanted in its nature. Its being

sort of subject-reflexive knowledge is characteristic of the mind or rational soul, Olivi relies on metaphors involving sensory modes of awareness to illuminate its nature. Such metaphors are, I take it, intended to illustrate both the immediacy as well as the non-conceptual, non-propositional nature of such knowledge.[13] Indeed, as his remarks in text A make clear, this sort of experiential subject-reflexive knowledge lacks any sort of conceptual or cognitive structure: "the mind *senses* and *feels* itself immediately through itself." The mind is, in other words, aware of *itself* via direct experience of its occurrent thoughts and activities. For clarity, in what follows, I refer to this first type of awareness as 'experiential' subject-reflexive awareness.

By contrast with this immediate and *experiential* awareness of one's self or mind, subject-reflexive knowledge of the second type, (1b), is distinctly conceptual or thought-like in nature. It is, as Olivi characterizes it, intellectual knowledge of the very nature of the mind itself—its "essential character and properties" (or *genus* and *differentia*). Acquiring such knowledge requires both "discursive reasoning" and "investigation." One begins, Olivi claims, from experiential awareness of one's own mind and, *via* rational investigation, eventually arrives at knowledge of the *quiddity* or

implanted at the root of our superior part (because that is the root of our subsisting part) is sensed to such an extent that the superior part itself intimately senses and declares that the acts of the sensory part are its own. Thus it says, 'it is I who understands, sees, and eats'." In general, Olivi seems to appeal to the highest power in the soul (e.g. the common sense in non-rational animals, the intellect in humans) as the source of the unity of its subject-reflexive awareness. For further discussion of this point see Juhana Toivanen, "Peter Olivi on Internal Senses," *British Journal for the History of Philosophy* 15 (2007), 427–54. See also passage D and n. 23 below.

[13] Olivi's use of sensory metaphors in passage A to characterize intellect's self-reflexive awareness is typical. See, for example, the passage cited from q. 51 in n. 12 just above as well as the text cited in passage B below. Similar language can be found in his discussion at *Summa* II, q. 74 (III, 126): "cum quis sentit se scire et videre et amare, ipse sentit tunc identitatem et, ut sic loquar, suitatem sui ipsius, in quantum cognitum et in quantum suppositum activum, ad se ipsum hoc advertentem et sentientem." Likewise, the comparison to a tactual modality of awareness is repeated elsewhere. Olivi's inclination to compare the intellect's reflexive awareness to the sense modality of touch is not surprising since, on his view, the sense of touch is itself a self-reflexive mode of awareness. See Mikko Yrjönsuuri, "Perceiving One's Own Body," in S. Knuuttila and P. Kärkkäinen (eds.), *Theories of Perception in Medieval and Early Modern Philosophy* (Dordrecht: Springer, 2008), 101–16 and Toivanen, *Animal Consciousness*, 299–308. In a passage from Olivi's *Impugnatio quorundam articulorum Arnalidi Galliardi* [= *Impugnatio*], he characterizes the intellect's experiential subject-reflexive awareness not only in terms of a "tactual mode" of awareness, but also as a kind of "very bleary-eyed, obscure" sort of vision. (*Noster enim apprehendit se et substantiam mentis nostre quasi per modum tactus, aut quasi per modum visus valde lippiet caliginosi....*) See *Impugnatio* 19.16.

the very definition of mind.[14] Unlike the first sort of subject-reflexive self-knowledge, this quiddative self-knowledge is neither direct (since it is mediated by conceptual and inferential processes) nor exclusively self-directed. Its content applies to minds in general—not just one's own. In this sense, quiddative self-knowledge is a type of access one has to one's mind *via* a description or definition of minds in general. Although not distinctively first-personal in nature, Olivi, nevertheless, counts this as a type of subject-reflexive self-knowledge since to know the essence or quiddity of mind in general is to know the very nature of *one's own* mind.

b. State-reflexive self-knowledge: nature and types

When it comes to *state*-reflexive self-knowledge, it is more difficult to find a single passage in which Olivi explicitly considers the character and types of knowledge mind has of its own states. We may begin, however, by considering what passage A above already suggests about Olivi's views on the nature of state-reflexive knowledge.

For starters, it is clear that Olivi takes for granted not only that we possess knowledge or awareness of a wide range of our occurrent states, but also that such *state*-reflexive awareness is always accompanied by experiential *subject*-reflexive awareness. As we have already noted, he holds that it is precisely in virtue of being aware of one's occurrent mental states that one is immediately, subjectively aware of one's own mind. Thus, in passage A, he insists "there is no object and no act that it can occurrently know or consider without it always thereupon knowing and sensing itself to be the subject of the very act by which it knows and considers that thing." On his view, then, state-reflexive self-knowledge—*whatever* form it takes—is such that it always includes, constitutively as we'll see, subject-reflexive awareness of this sort. This is something Olivi emphasizes in a variety of contexts, but his remarks in the following passage are representative in this regard:

[B] I never apprehend my acts (for example, acts of seeing, speaking, and so on) except by apprehending myself seeing, hearing, thinking, and so on. And, it would seem that, in the natural order, an apprehension of the subject itself is prior to this apprehension. And for this reason when we want to convey these states to others, we do so in a way that presupposes a subject by saying "I think this" or "I see this" (and so on with other cases).... For we apprehend our acts only as being predicated or

[14] Following Augustine, Olivi holds the mind's search for *quiddative* self-knowledge (i.e. knowledge of the nature of one's mind) presupposes that it already knows itself in some way. Thus, for example, in *De Trinitate* 10.6, Augustine argues that: "Since the mind, in seeking what mind is, knows that it is seeking itself, it follows that it knows that it is itself a mind."

attributed to us. Indeed, when we apprehend our acts by a certain inner and quasi-experiential awareness, we distinguish between the acts themselves and the substance on which they depend and in which they exist. Thus, we are perceptibly aware that these acts are derived from and dependent on a substance and not the other way around, [for we perceive] that the substance is fixed and permanent in itself, whereas the acts are continuously in the making.[15]

Here, Olivi begins by arguing for the connection between state- and subject-reflexive awareness by appealing to the phenomenology of his own experience: "I never apprehend my acts (for example, acts of seeing, speaking, and so on) except by apprehending *myself* seeing, hearing, cognizing, and so on." As further evidence for the subject-reflexive character of state-reflexive awareness, Olivi points to the fact that we can and do report the occurrence of our mental states using first-person attributions: "*I* think this," "*I* see that." And, while Olivi thinks that our subjective experience of our states is such that we can distinguish phenomenologically between the mental act and our soul as its subject, nevertheless, awareness of the former never occurs without some implicit awareness of the latter. Indeed, the subject-reflexive, or first-personal character of state-reflexive awareness is a feature that characterizes even our experience of sensory activities and states. And this is because, as he explains, "the superior part itself intimately senses and declares that the acts of the [lower] sensory part are its own. Thus it says, 'it is I who understands, sees, and eats'."[16]

Olivi's insistence on the connection between state-reflexive and subjective subject-reflexive awareness owes, ultimately, to his views about the nature of the mind itself. Olivi holds, as a metaphysical thesis, that the mind is a power whose very nature is characterized by a kind of permanent self-orientation or self-directedness. Thus, in a number of places, Olivi describes the mind as "always and continually turned inward" and, hence, as the ever-present object of its own "reflexive" or "inwardly turned" regard. This innate metaphysical or structural self-reflexivity is, on Olivi's view, both distinct from and prior to episodic acts of subject- and state-reflexive awareness. That it is distinct is evident not only from his emphasis on its being a fixed, or permanent feature of the mind as such, but also from the fact that, unlike subject- and state-reflexive awareness, such

[15] *Impugnatio* 19.11. See also Olivi, *Summa* II, q. 59 (II, 540): "It is a natural apprehension by which, through reason, I apprehend myself seeing and sensing just as, through reason, I apprehend myself understanding and willing, and do so in such a way that through reason I apprehend and sense that it is the same one who sees and understands, namely, me. This sense would be false, unless these actions were truly from the same subject which is called 'I'."

[16] *Summa* II, q. 51 (II, 122).

structural reflexivity does not, by itself, constitute any kind of experienced, or *phenomenal*, self-awareness.[17] Rather, it is a non-cognitive feature of the mind that grounds or explains its capacity for occurrent acts of phenomenal self-awareness. Thus, Olivi claims in passage A above, for example, that the soul's experiential subject-reflexive awareness arises "through the immediate inward turn of its intellective gaze on itself."[18] Elsewhere, he claims that acts of state- and subject-reflexive awareness in general are "*caused* by the ever-recurrent actuality of the intellect's [orientation] toward itself and its knowing."[19]

[17] If structural reflexivity amounted to phenomenally or consciously experienced self-awareness, each person would at all times be directly aware of her own soul. But I can find no evidence that Olivi thinks this is the case. What is more, his account of the two types of subject-reflexive awareness in passage A seems to rule it out. After all, in that passage, Olivi allows for only two types of subject-reflexive awareness, experiential and quiddative. But neither of these two modes of subject-reflexive awareness constitutes an innate, permanent, phenomenally conscious grasp of one's self or soul.

[18] Olivi habitually characterizes the mind's innate self-reflexivity as a function of the self-directedness of its "gaze" or "regard" (*aspectus*). This way of speaking might seem to vitiate my contention that the mind's permanent or structural self-directedness is not a type of *awareness*. It is important to keep in mind, however, what Olivi refers to as "*aspectus*" of a cognitive power is distinct from the *act* of such a power. Hence, the mere self-directedness of the soul's *gaze* does not by itself entail the existence of an *act* of self-cognition. (Interestingly, there are even contexts in which Olivi characterizes the directedness of the *aspectus* as "hidden" or unconscious. For example, in the course of discussing angelic communication, he speaks at one point of a cognitive power's possessing an "unnoticed directedness" (*occulta conversia*). See his *Quaestio de locutionibus angelorum*, ed. S. Piron, *Oliviana* 1 (2003), § 32, <http://oliviana.reues.org/document18.html>.) Indeed, in general Olivi thinks that directing of the focus (or the attention) of a given cognitive power is a necessary condition for the production of its act. For discussion of the role of attention in Olivi's account of intentionality in general see Dominik Perler, *Théories de l'intentionnalité au moyen âge* (Paris: Vrin, 2003), 44–75; and José Filipe Silva and Juhana Toivanen, "The Active Nature of the Soul in Sense Perception: Robert Kilwardby and Peter Olivi," *Vivarium* 48 (2010), 245–78.

[19] *Summa* II, q. 76 (III, 149). More precisely, what Olivi claims in the passage from which this line is taken is that *both* the soul's habitual self-knowledge *as well as* its occurrent acts of self-knowledge arise through the essence of the mind as a self-reflexive power. Olivi is particularly concerned to establish that mind's capacity self-reflexive awareness is not to be identified as a mere disposition for (or a habitual form of) self-knowledge. Rather, he argues this capacity is part of very nature or essence of the mind itself: "Licet autem habitualis notia sui sit eius accidens inseparabilie... non tamen aestimo quod sit necessaria ad producendum actum sciendi se, sed potius habitus praedictus causetur ex redundanti actualitate intellectus ad se et sua sciendum." His insistence on this point is significant in light of the broader issues he is addressing in the context of q. 76. This question is addressed to a broader debate over whether the soul knows itself through species or through its own essence. The claim that intellect's innate, essential reflexivity is the causal source of its occurrent and habitual self-knowledge is central to his defense of the latter of these two positions. For a survey of this debate over the nature and source of the soul's knowledge of itself see Putallaz, *La Connaissance*; Cyrille Michon, "Ego Intelligo (lapidem). Deux conceptions de la réflexion au Moyen

There are two respects in which mind's permanent, structural reflexivity grounds or explains its episodic acts of phenomenal reflexivity. First, Olivi holds that it entails the mind's state-reflexive awareness. In fact, on his view, the mind's innate self-directedness guarantees the ubiquity of state-reflexive awareness. Thus, according to Olivi, if I think about (desire, or perceive) something, my thought (desire, or perception) will register in phenomenal awareness. And this is because, as Olivi sees it, if the mind is essentially reflexively directed toward *itself,* it must be reflexively directed upon anything that occurs in itself. Consider his remarks in the following passage (which is embedded in a larger context to which we will have occasion to return later—see passage J below):

> [C] A power that is reflexively directed on itself can see everything that presently arises and exists in itself at the moment [it arises and exists]. Both from itself, and given the very fact that it is turned toward itself, this power is turned toward all those things that exist or arise in it.[20]

According to Olivi, for a cognitive power to be essentially self-reflexive is for it to be structured in such a way that it falls within the scope its own potential *field of view* (what Olivi refers to as its *aspectus*). Such self-directedness entails that when the cognitive power is actualized in cognition—that is, in actually cognizing a given object—its act of cognizing will yield awareness not only of the *object* thus cognized, but also of the act of cognizing it.

In addition to explaining the existence and ubiquity of state-reflexive awareness, the mind's structural reflexivity also explains why reflexive awareness of one's states always involves awareness of oneself as its subject. Olivi seem to think that, because state-reflexive awareness arises out of the soul's structural self-directedness, awareness of its states must also include their self-attribution. Thus, to be aware of a given state is to be aware of it *as one's own*—as a state *of oneself.* For this reason, Olivi insists (in passage B) that "we apprehend our acts only as being predicated or attributed *to us*" and, likewise, (in passage A) that the soul "in its act of thinking, always shapes something with the force of this proposition: 'I know this' or 'I think this'." On his view, the reflexive structure of the mind accounts for the first-person or subject-reflexive phenomenal structure of its state-reflexive awareness.

Age," in O. Boulnois (ed.), *Généalogies du sujet: de saint Anselme à Malebranche* (Paris: Vrin, 2007), 114–47; and Therese S. Cory, *Aquinas on Human Self-Knowledge* (Cambridge: Cambridge University Press, forthcoming), chap. 1.

[20] *Summa* II, q. 79 (III, 159–60).

What the foregoing shows, then, is that, for Olivi, experiential subject-reflexive awareness is a constitutive feature of *any* kind of *state*-reflexive awareness. The two simply cannot be separated. Awareness of one's occurrent states of thinking, or desiring, or perceiving something *just is* a kind of awareness of *oneself*—namely, as thinking about, desiring, or perceiving that thing. Or, to put it otherwise, it is awareness of these states as states *of* oneself.

That said, it must be emphasized that Olivi does recognize different types or levels of state-reflexive awareness. As I noted earlier, there is no single passage in which Olivi expressly or systematically distinguishes among the different ways in which mind knows its own states. Nevertheless, he does implicitly presuppose and rely on such distinctions in a variety of contexts. As a case in point, consider the following passage:

> [D] All (or, many) of the [soul's] powers are very frequently (indeed, almost always) engaged in their acts. Thus, often when I see, I simultaneously hear, smell, touch, and taste. At the same time, alongside each of these [acts], there is also the common sense running about discerning among these various faculties and among their objects. Thus, at that very same moment, I am aware, through the intellect, of all of these acts and their objects. Likewise, at that same time, I am also aware (or I can be aware) that I am intellectively aware of them [. . .] And, with respect to all of these acts, I am always aware of these acts as mine. As a result, I always apprehend myself as the subject of these acts. Therefore, the intellect apprehends, simultaneously, a whole plurality of acts as well as their objects.[21]

In the broader context from which this passage is taken, Olivi is attempting to establish the possibility of the simultaneous occurrence of a plurality of acts in a single power (a view that was hotly debated in his day).[22] In the passage itself, Olivi identifies various sorts of psychological acts or states that he thinks can occur at the same time. Interestingly, on his list of simultaneously occurring acts are *two* distinct kinds of (intellective) state-reflexive awareness; one of which he thinks accompanies any occurrent state (including sensory states), whereas the other only sometimes does. Here, again, is the relevant distinction:

> I am [2a] aware, through the intellect, of all of these acts [viz., seeing, hearing, smelling, etc.] and their objects. Likewise, at that same time, I am [2b] also aware (or I can be aware) that I am intellectively aware of them.

21 *Summa* II, q. 37 (I, 659).

22 For discussion of this debate among later medieval thinkers, see Russell Friedman, "On the Trail of a Philosophical Debate: Durandus of St.-Pourçain vs. Thomas Wylton on Simultaneous Acts in the Intellect," in S. Brown, T. Dewender, and T. Kobusch (eds.), *Philosophical Debates at Paris in the Early Fourteenth Century* (Leiden: Brill, 2009), 433–61.

It should be clear that the first of these two kinds of state-reflexive awareness, (2a), is just the ubiquitous first-person state-reflexive awareness that Olivi thinks is entailed by mind's structural reflexivity. Thus, what he has in mind by it is roughly this: for any occurrent states–e.g. my simultaneously seeing and touching some object, the pen in my hand, say—I will be aware not only of the *object* of such states (namely, the pen) but also, at some level, of *my seeing and touching* it. Thus, even when attention is explicitly directed outward at some external object, as it is when I am seeing and touching the pen, I am nonetheless at some level aware of my seeing and feeling it.[23]

Olivi then goes on to call attention to the fact that, *in addition* to this, I can also become focally aware of my inner acts or states so as to make them explicit objects of cognition. In order to contrast this second sort of state-reflexive awareness (namely, 2b) with the first sort (namely, 2a) let us refer to the former as "pre-reflective" awareness and to the latter as "reflective" or "introspective" awareness. One of the differences between the two is that whereas the first sort is ubiquitous, the second is not. On the contrary, Olivi thinks that introspective awareness is a type of state-reflexive awareness of which we are capable, but not necessarily always exercising. Interestingly, however, as passage D makes clear, he does think that both sorts of state-reflexive awareness can occur simultaneously. That is, Olivi seems to think that I can, for example, experience seeing and feeling the pen and at the same time (introspectively) attend to my experience of seeing and feeling it.[24]

Similarly, I think it is this same basic distinction—that is, between pre-reflective versus introspective type of state-reflexive awareness—that Olivi

[23] Although Olivi insists (in passage D and elsewhere) that (i) we are conscious of sensory states and (ii) that our consciousness of them owes to the intellective faculty, it is nevertheless not altogether clear precisely *how* he understands the role of intellect in rendering such states conscious. He claims, for example, that "it is by one power that we say inside ourselves, 'the same I who understands, also wills and sees', namely, the intellective power. By apprehending its own subject and its own acts, as well as the acts of other powers, it is able to say this. But it is able to bring this about even though it is not the case that it is the whole subject and even though it is not the case that it elicits the acts of the other powers" (*Summa* II, q. 54 (II, 241)). Thus, even if acts of sensory perception belong to different faculties or powers than acts of thinking and willing, the rational soul's reflexive awareness of all of these acts (and of itself as their subject) is explained by the reflexivity of the intellective power. His point, I take it, is that the reflexive capacity of the whole derives from the reflexive capacity of its chief (or highest) part. Thus, the rational soul (or perhaps even the soul/body composite—whatever is the referent of the first-person pronoun 'I') is capable of self-reflexive awareness (of itself and of its states) in virtue of its possession of a self-reflexive power (namely, the intellect).

[24] But he clearly does not presuppose that the co-occurrence of these two types of awareness is ubiquitous. Or, in any case, Olivi seems willing to recognize the possibility that one is not always introspectively aware of one's inner states.

has in mind when he distinguishes between the following two sorts of state-reflexive knowledge:

[E] . . . just as my knowing that the sun exists is one act of knowing, and my knowing myself to know this is another, so also it is one act to assert "the sun exists", and another to assert "I know that the sun exists". The first [act of assertion] is based on the first act of knowing, the second based on the second along with the first. But the second act of knowing (which is closely related to the mode set out in a preceding question) includes in itself a plurality of acts of knowing: (i) the act by which I know myself, (ii) the act by which I know the knowing of the sun, and (iii) the act by which I know myself to be the subject of that act. Although perhaps in this case the third is not really distinct from the second.[25]

Here, Olivi marks the distinction between the two types of state-reflexive awareness—namely, pre-reflective vs. reflective—by calling attention to a difference in their object.[26] In the case of the first type, the object of awareness is something external to the knower—in Olivi's example, the sun (or the sun's existence or presence); in the second case, the object of awareness is a state of the knower herself—namely, her knowledge or awareness of the sun. Although, in the former case, the act of knowledge is directed at something external (viz., the sun), the subject is, nevertheless, pre-reflectively aware of her knowledge since she is able to express it when she asserts: "the sun exists."[27] By contrast, in the latter case, the subject is introspectively aware of her *knowing* the sun's existence. Hence her assertion of this fact: "I know the sun exists." In both cases, moreover, it is clear that state-reflexive knowledge includes subject-reflexivity as well. In the pre-reflective case, the subject experiences herself as knowing the sun; in the introspective case, she experiences herself as knowing her knowledge of the sun. The inseparability of these two types of knowledge is no surprise, of course, since as we have already noted state-reflexive awareness is always given as a first-personal or subject-reflexive experience.

c. State-reflexivity as self- or subjective consciousness

As the foregoing makes clear, Olivi recognizes various types of both subject-reflexive and state-reflexive self-knowledge. They are not, however, all equally fundamental. Experiential subject-reflexive awareness is, for

25 *Summa* II, q. 79 (III, 165).

26 This distinction, between pre-reflective and reflective or introspective awareness of what one knows, is evident throughout Olivi's discussion in q. 79. I will return to Olivi's discussion in q. 79 presently.

27 Elsewhere in the same discussion, Olivi claims that asserting "the sun exists" is equivalent to "I know the sun exists". See *Summa* II, q. 79 (III, 167).

example, more fundamental than quiddative; pre-reflective state-reflexive awareness is more fundamental than introspective. Indeed, in both cases, the latter form of self-knowledge depends on (or derives from) the former. On Olivi's view, moreover, the most fundamental types of subject- and state-reflexive awareness, while conceptually distinct, are mutually entailing. To be reflexively aware of a given state is to be aware of it *as one's own*—that is, as a state of oneself. Again, experiential subject-reflexive awareness is nothing other than acquaintance with oneself as "the principle and subject" of one's states. This is a point that we have seen Olivi emphasize repeatedly. As he says (in passage D): "I am aware . . . of all of [my] acts and their objects. . . . [and] I am always aware that these are my acts"; or again (in passage A) "there is no object and no act that [the soul] can occurrently know or consider without it always thereupon knowing and sensing itself to be the subject."

Thus, while Olivi allows (in text B above, for example) that one can, in some sense, distinguish between oneself (or one's mind) and states thereof, nevertheless, at the phenomenal level, state-reflexive and experiential subject-reflexive awareness are inseparable. They occur as two aspects of a single conscious experience. Indeed, there is, to my knowledge, no evidence that Olivi thinks awareness of oneself (or one's mind) ever occurs independently of awareness of some occurrent state. Like Hume, who famously argues "I never catch myself without a perception," Olivi appears to deny that one ever cognizes—or "catches"—one's self or soul independently of awareness of one's occurrent states.[28] It is not surprising, therefore, that the phenomenon Olivi identifies most centrally and fundamentally with the reflexivity of the human mind is one's subjective (or subject-reflexive), pre-reflective awareness of one's occurrent states.

If this is right, however, there is good reason for thinking that the phenomenon Olivi targets in connection with mind's self-reflexivity shares much in common with that targeted in contemporary discussions of consciousness. To be sure, contemporary philosophers recognize a wide range of so-called "conscious" phenomena, and there is a great deal of disagreement about which is most fundamental or most central. Even so, there is significant overlap between the kind of self- and state-reflexivity that Olivi fixes on and the mode of awareness nowadays associated with *phenomenally conscious states.*

[28] See David Hume, *Treatise of Human Nature* (I, IV, vi). Unlike Hume, however, Olivi does not infer from this that one does not, therefore, catch oneself *with* an occurrent state. In being aware of one's states, one is aware of oneself being in that state—and this, for Olivi, amounts to a kind of self-awareness.

Admittedly, current treatments of phenomenal consciousness are very often focused around qualia—that is, the purely qualitative features associated with phenomenally conscious states. And it is not obvious that anything in Olivi's discussion bears on current discussions of qualia. Typically, qualitative character is associated with the "what it's like" or the "feel" of our mental or intentional states. (To take a few standard examples: the *bluish character* of my visual experience of the sky, or the particular *sharpness* or *pulsing feel* of my headache.) So understood, it is fairly clear, I think, that Olivi's notion of reflexivity is *not* an approximation of the contemporary notion of qualitative character.[29]

But, it is also widely acknowledged that there may be more to phenomenal consciousness, more to our experience of our mental states, than qualitative character. Thus, philosophers from Franz Brentano to Colin McGinn have called attention to the self-conscious or subjective character of phenomenally conscious states. The core idea here is just that phenomenally conscious states are states one is aware of oneself as being in. Conscious experiences have, as Colin McGinn puts it, a kind of "Janus-faced" character. Not only do they direct their subject outward to the external world, but they also present a subjective face to their subject. On McGinn's view, therefore, phenomenally conscious states "involve presence to a subject, and hence a subjective point of view. Remove the inward looking face and you remove something integral—what the world *seems* like to the subject."[30]

Inasmuch as conscious experiences are *present* to a subject, we may say they are states of which a subject is *aware*. And inasmuch their presence is *to a subject* they possess a kind of "for-*me*-ness" where this entails implicit awareness of oneself as their subject. This for-me-ness quality features prominently (though not uncontroversially) among the phenomena

29 This is not to say that Olivi would reject the notion that our states have what we call 'qualitative character'. But he certainly does not single out this feature of conscious experience for explicit consideration. By contrast, his account of the phenomenal character of reflexive awareness focuses rather on its first-personal or subjective character. It is not clear to me, moreover, that among medieval philosophers in general we can find anything approximating our contemporary notion of qualia. A *possible* exception to this rule might be Peter Auriol who, in defending his (notorious and controversial) notion of "apparent being" (*esse apparens*), is quite expressly concerned with the need to explain *the way things appear* in cognition. And he seems to think that this feature of cognition cannot be explained merely by explaining the intentional or representational features of cognitive states. See Auriol's *Scriptum super primum Sententiarum*, dist. 35, a. 1.

30 Colin McGinn, "Consciousness and Content," in N. Block, O. Flanagan, and G. Güzeldere (eds.), *The Nature of Consciousness: Philosophical Debates* (Cambridge, MA: MIT Press, 1997), 300.

targeted in current discussions of phenomenal consciousness.[31] To take just a few examples from the recent literature:[32]

[G] Let's take my current visual experience as I gaze upon my red diskette case, lying by my side on the computer table. I'm having an experience with a complex qualitative character, one component of which is the color I perceive. Let's dub this the aspect of my experience its "reddish" character. There are two important dimensions to my having this reddish experience. First, as mentioned above, there is something it's like for me to have this experience. Not only is it a matter of some state (my experience) having some feature (being reddish) but, being an experience, its being reddish is "for me," a way it's like *for me* in a what that being red is like nothing for—in fact is not in any way "for"—my diskette case. Let's call this the *subjectivity* of conscious experience. Nagel (1974) himself emphasized this feature by noting that conscious experience involves our having a 'point of view'. The second important dimension of experiences that requires explanation is qualitative character itself. Subjectivity is the phenomenon of there being something it's like *for me* to see the red diskette case. Qualitative character concerns the "what" it's like for me: reddish or greenish, painful and pleasurable, and the like.[33]

[H] The other component of phenomenal consciousness [in addition to its qualitative character] is subjective character: the *for-me-ness* of conscious experiences. What

[31] To be sure, the thesis that phenomenal consciousness is or entails self-consciousness or subjectivity (or even that the latter pair of concepts are mutually entailing) is quite controversial. Even so, inasmuch as there are a number of contemporary proponents of such a view it is fair to say that Olivi's theory of mind's reflexive awareness counts as *a* theory of phenomenal consciousness. (Contemporary discussion and defense of this sort of view include: Uriah Kriegel, *Subjective Consciousness* (Oxford: Oxford University Press, 2009); Uriah Kriegel, "Consciousness and Self-Consciousness," The Monist 87 (2004), 185–209; Uriah Kriegel, "Consciousness as Intransitive Self-Consciousness: Two Views and an Argument," *Canadian Journal of Philosophy* 33 (2003), 103–32; Tim Bayne, "Self-Consciousness and the Unity of Consciousness," *The Monist* 87 (2004), 224–41; Dan Zahavi, "Self and Consciousness," in D. Zahavi (ed.), *Exploring the Self: Philosophical and Psychopathological Perspectives on Self-Experience* (Amsterdam: J. Benjamins, 2000), 55–74; Owen Flanagan, *Consciousness Reconsidered* (Cambridge, MA: MIT Press, 1992); Rocco Genarro, "Consciousness, Self-Consciousness, and Episodic Memory," *Philosophical Psychology* 5 (1992), 333–47.) Since there is no universally accepted characterization of the phenomenology associated with phenomenal consciousness there is, likewise, no single criterion for specifying what constitutes a theory of phenomenal consciousness (or when a theory has been given that captures all the relevant phenomena). For my purposes, then, it is sufficient to establish that the phenomena Olivi's theory targets overlap significantly with those targeted by theories prominent in contemporary discussions of phenomenal consciousness.

[32] This first-personal aspect of phenomenal consciousness gets particular emphasis from those within the phenomenological tradition. For an overview, see Shaun Gallagher and Dan Zahavi, "Phenomenological Approaches to Self-Consciousness," in E. N. Zalta (ed.), The Stanford Encyclopedia of Philosophy (Winter 2010 Edition) <http://plato.stanford.edu/archives/win2010/entries/self-consciousness-phenomenological/>.

[33] Joseph Levine, *Purple Haze: The Puzzle of Consciousness* (Oxford: Oxford University Press, 2001), 6–7.

is this *for-me-ness*? On the view I want to take it is a form of awareness. In virtue of being aware of my experience of the blue sky, there is something it is like for me to have that experience.[34]

> [I] However, there is more to experience than the fact that what it is like to perceive a black triangle is subjectively distinct from what it is like to perceive a red circle (cf. Nagel 1974). . . . all of these phenomenal experiences involve a reference to a subject of experience. In perceiving or imagining an object consciously one is aware of the object as appearing in a determinate manner to oneself. . . . One reason these experiences are said to be subjective is because they are characterized by a subjective mode of existence, in the sense that they necessarily feel like something *for somebody*. Our experiential life can consequently be said to entail a primitive form of self-referentiality or for-me-ness.[35]

As should be clear, the phenomenon targeted in these passages—namely, an awareness of one's occupying one's mental states—is precisely the sort of phenomenon that Olivi singles out in his characterization of reflexive awareness. Insofar as we find in Olivi a theory of *this* sort of phenomenon, we find what can fairly be characterized as a theory of ("subjective" or "self-") consciousness.

2. OLIVI ON THE METAPHYSICS OF REFLEXIVITY: A ONE-LEVEL THEORY OF CONSCIOUSNESS

To this point, I have been focusing on Olivi's understanding of the phenomenology of reflexive awareness. I have argued, moreover, that his notion of state-reflexive awareness is central in this understanding and corresponds directly to what we nowadays term "phenomenal consciousness". I now want to turn from questions about the phenomenology of state-reflexive awareness to questions about its proper analysis. Nowadays, those who think that phenomenal consciousness is or entails subjective-awareness can be roughly divided according to whether they accept a two-level or one-level theory. Thus, according to two-level—or "higher-order"—theories of consciousness, one's awareness of a given state owes to that state serving as the object for a distinct, higher-order state. By contrast, on one-level—or "same-order"—theories, awareness of a given states owes to some intrinsic feature of the state itself. In this section of the paper, I want to consider whether Olivi's analysis of state-reflexive awareness yields a one- or two-level theory of consciousness.

34 Kriegel, *Subjective Consciousness*, 47.

35 Shaun Gallagher and Dan Zahavi, *The Phenomenological Mind* (London: Routledge, 2008), 49–50.

To anticipate, I argue that Olivi is committed to a one-level analysis. It is worth saying, however, that while I think we can glean Olivi's views on this matter from what he does say in the texts, he rarely addresses the issue head-on. What is more, in one of the (perhaps the only?) contexts in which he does consider questions about the analysis of state-reflexive awareness, he does not make explicit *which type* of state-reflexive awareness is under consideration (i.e. pre-reflective or introspective).

The text I have in mind, and on which my discussion shall hereafter focus, is q. 79 of his commentary on Book II of Lombard's *Sentences*. As we'll see, Olivi's discussion in this question suggests, on the face of it, a commitment to a higher-order theory of consciousness. In fact, commentators have taken his remarks in this context as evidence for just such an interpretation.[36] But, as careful attention to the details of his argument in several key passages shows (see texts J and K below), Olivi is, in fact, committed to *rejecting* a higher-order account of consciousness. Establishing this claim will require clarity both about what sort of state-reflexive awareness is at issue in this context, and where exactly the key passages occur in the overall (and rather complicated) dialectical structure of the question as a whole. Before turning to details of the text, therefore, I begin with some general remarks about the topic and general structure of q. 79 itself.

In q. 79 Olivi considers whether a given (intellective) state can take itself as its object.[37] As the ensuing discussion makes clear, the issue at stake is that of explaining state-reflexive awareness.[38] Olivi takes as given that we do possess knowledge regarding our current mental states. The issue, then,

[36] See Christian Rode, "Peter of John Olivi on Representation and Self-Representation," *Quaestio: Yearbook of the History of Metaphysics* 10 (2010), 155–66. Christopher Martin, while not expressly interested in Olivi's theory of consciousness, nevertheless seems to presuppose that Olivi is committed to a higher-order analysis. See his "Self-Knowledge and Cognitive Ascent: Thomas Aquinas and Peter Olivi on the KK-Thesis," in H. Laugerland (ed.), *Forming the Mind: Essays on the Internal Senses and the Mind/Body Problem from Avicenna to the Medical Enlightenment* (Dordrecht: Springer, 2007), 93–108. On Martin's interpretation, Olivi's notion of (pre-reflective) state-reflexive awareness is a matter of the subject standing in the relation of knowing to her first-order (or world-directed) acts of cognitive awareness.

[37] Olivi's own, more elaborate, statement of the question runs as follows: "Can an act of knowledge or love have itself for its object? For example, when I know myself to know or to love, or when I will myself to love, is the act that is designated using the infinitive the same as that which is designated using the indicative?" *Summa* II, q. 79 (III, 158).

[38] Although Olivi uses the terms "knowledge" and "knowing" (*scientia/scire*) throughout his discussion, the context makes clear that he's using these terms generically to indicate *intellective* awareness in general. Their usage is not indicative of any attempt on his part to single out a type of intellective awareness with any special epistemic status (other than that associated with all forms of intellective cognition).

is to explain this. Does one's knowledge or awareness of a given state come by way of an act numerically distinct from, and directed upon it? Or can an act be directed upon, and thus include awareness of, itself? Olivi associates a negative answer to this latter question with Augustine. As he says, "the opinion of Augustine" is that "one and the same act of knowing *cannot* take itself as an object."[39] Olivi himself, however, is ambivalent about the correct answer and, so, after first advocating for the Augustinian line and carefully rebutting all arguments that suggest that an act *can* be directed upon itself, he reconsiders. In fact, he goes on to advance the opposite view, and endeavors to refute all the preliminary arguments in favor of the Augustinian line. At the end of the discussion, he confesses that "it is not easy to judge which of these opinions is more likely true"[40] and, so, ultimately sides with authority, that is, with Augustine.

That Olivi ultimately takes the Augustinian side—adopting the view that reflexive awareness of one's states comes by way of a numerically distinct, higher-order act of awareness—might, at least on the face of it, suggest that he adopts a higher-order theory of consciousness. It is clear, in any case, that he is adopting a higher-order analysis *of whatever type of state-reflexive awareness is at issue in this question.* It is less clear, however, that the type of state-reflexive awareness at issue is that associated with ordinary, pre-reflective consciousness. In fact, as I read it, the kind of state-reflexive knowledge under discussion in q. 79 is *not* phenomenal consciousness but introspection. Thus, while Olivi *is* claiming that introspective awareness of one's states comes by way of numerically distinct, higher-order acts of awareness, nothing follows from this about his analysis of ordinary phenomenal consciousness (i.e. pre-reflective, state-reflexive awareness). Indeed, to the extent that Olivi's discussion in q. 79 does bear on the nature of our non-introspective experience of our states, it suggests a one-level analysis.

The best evidence for this reading comes from a passage in which Olivi is defending the Augustinian view (i.e. the view that an act never takes itself as object) against what he clearly takes to be a particularly worrisome objection. The objection in question charges that the Augustinian view must be rejected on the grounds that it leads to an infinite regress in higher-order states. Although the statement of the objection is rather lengthy, it is worth quoting in its entirety.[41]

39 *Summa* II, q. 79 (III, 163).

40 *Summa* II, q. 79 (III, 169).

41 As I indicated earlier, this is part of a larger discussion within which passage C is imbedded.

[J] If [A_2] the act by which I know my knowing of the sun differs from [A_1] the act of knowing the sun itself, and likewise if [A_3] the act by which I know the act of knowing by which I know the act of knowing the sun differs from [A_2] the reflexive knowing of the knowing of the sun, and so on into infinity, then, it is impossible that a person actually knows, or could know, every act of knowing that he currently has—unless, of course, he has an infinity of acts. After all, the final act of knowing by which the mind gazes on the preceding act of knowing could not itself actually be known unless it were to know itself or unless, in addition to it, there were some further act of knowing—but then it would not be final. [...] Hence, either one must grant that there is no *final* act of knowing... or that, if there is a final act, then it cannot actually be known. [...] But it does not seem true that... there could exist some act of knowing in me that I could not know. For, a power reflexively directed on itself can see everything that presently arises and exists in itself at the moment [it arises and exists]. Both from itself, and from the very fact that it is turned toward itself, this power is turned toward all those things which exist or arise in it—much as the gaze of the eye, by the very fact that it is turned toward the wall and toward the surrounding air, is by that fact turned toward those things which arise visibly or pass through it. Moreover, if I do not know the final act, I cannot enumerate the number of my reflective acts. But that is contrary to experience, and contrary to Augustine...[42]

Although Olivi's statement of the argument is not particularly felicitous, nevertheless, its central line of reasoning is fairly straightforward.

The argument takes its start from the assumption that the mind's state-reflexive knowledge extends to *all* its occurrent acts or states. Since this assumption figures importantly in the discussion to come, let us refer to it as the 'ubiquity principle'.[43] Now, if a given mental act cannot take itself as object, as the Augustinian claims, knowledge of a given mental act, A_1, will require the introduction of a numerically distinct, higher-order act, A_2—one which takes A_1 as its object. Of course, if the mind knows *all* of its acts, as the ubiquity principle requires, it will know A_2. But, again, if a mental act cannot take itself as an object, then knowledge of A_2 will require the introduction of a further, higher-order state, A_3, and so on. Hence the regress. As the objector points out, the only recourse for the Augustinian is either to deny the ubiquity principle or to bite the bullet and allow an infinite series of higher-order mental states. Insofar as neither option looks very attractive, the opponent concludes that we should instead reject the

[42] *Summa* II, q. 79 (III, 159–60).

[43] Not surprisingly, the motivation for this assumption comes from the—now familiar—point from passage C above regarding the structural reflexivity of the mind: "A power reflexively directed on itself can see in everything that presently arises and exists in itself."

Augustinian line in favor of the view that a given mental act or state *can* take itself as object.

So much for the objection. Of more interest for present purposes is Olivi's response to it. In this connection, I want to advance two claims. First, that Olivi's response to the regress argument makes clear that the type of state-reflexive awareness at issue in q. 79 is introspective (rather than pre-reflective) in nature and, hence, when he defends the Augustinian view, he is defending a higher-order theory of introspective knowledge, not a higher-order theory of phenomenal consciousness.[44] The second claim is this: to the extent that Olivi's response to the regress argument does bear on his views about consciousness it suggests a one-level theory.

Here is what Olivi says by way of reply to the regress argument:

> [K] It should be said that the final act of knowing, which follows as many reflections as the intellect is capable of, cannot be known by a further [act of] reflection. But this does not occur because of a defect in its knowability, but rather because of a defect of the power for producing a final reflective act simultaneous with those preceding it. Nonetheless, concerning any act of knowing, a person can be said to be certain and can know that act with certainty. Not just because he has certain knowledge of it in habit, but also because certitude about the act is contained in some way in certitude about its object. For being certain of the one necessarily and infallibly implies the truth of the other.... Moreover, to the extent that an act of knowing proceeds from the intellect as something actually structured for knowing (*actualiter coordinato ad scire*) what proceeds from it, to that same extent it can be said that it knows that very act of knowing—namely, because the intellect generates and contains it [i.e., its act] in the manner of something both able to be known and productive of knowing. But what is further added is not true, namely, that a power reflexively directed on itself can see whatever arises in itself only if its reflection is such that it actually regards all such things as objects. For although the power is turned toward the act which it brings about (as cause to its effect), nevertheless, it does not follow from this that it is turned toward it as toward an object it is actually able to think of or does think of.[45]

As this passage makes clear, Olivi concedes that there can be only a finite number of simultaneously occurring mental acts and, hence, that "the final act" in any series of higher-order states, as such, "cannot be known." As he says: "the final act of knowing, which follows as many reflections as the intellect is capable of, cannot be known by a further [act of] reflection."

[44] There are, however, a plenty of medieval thinkers who do develop higher-order theories. William Ockham, for example, holds that consciousness is a matter of higher-order perception. For discussion of his views and their place within broader medieval debates about consciousness see my "Medieval Approaches to Consciousness: Ockham and Chatton," *Philosopher's Imprint* 12 (2012), 1–29.

[45] *Summa* II, q. 79 (III, 164).

Thus, Olivi's response to the regress argument essentially involves denying its starting assumption—namely, the ubiquity principle. But note: if the kind of state-reflexive knowledge or awareness at issue here were that associated with ordinary (pre-reflective) consciousness, this would be an *extraordinary* concession for Olivi to make. Indeed, it would contradict what he says elsewhere about state-reflexive awareness. While it may be commonplace among contemporary philosophers to allow that we are completely unconscious of some (indeed, perhaps a great many) of our occurrent states—this is not the view Olivi endorses. As I have argued, Olivi is committed to the view that consciousness of some sort is ubiquitous: insofar as mind is reflexively directed on itself, it is *always* (pre-reflectively) aware of its occurrent states. He does not, however, suppose that introspective awareness is likewise ubiquitous. In fact, as we have seen (e.g. passage D above), Olivi holds that while we may be able to introspect our states, we do not always do so. In light of this, it is natural to read his rejection of the ubiquity principle as rejection of the claim that we possess *introspective* knowledge regarding all our states—a reading which is consistent with what he says about both pre-reflective and introspective awareness elsewhere.[46] If this is the right reading of the passage, however, it should be clear that the kind of state-reflexive knowledge at issue in q. 79 is not consciousness, but introspection. Hence, to the extent that Olivi is defending a higher-order or two-level theory of state-reflexive awareness in this context, it is a higher-order theory of introspection that he defends, not a higher-order theory of consciousness as such.

This is not to say, however, that q. 79 reveals nothing about Olivi's analysis of consciousness itself. In fact, I think his remarks in this very passage (namely, passage K) demonstrate that, when it comes to pre-reflective state-reflexive awareness, Olivi is committed to a same-order or one-level theory. To see this, notice that when Olivi concedes to his opponent that some acts "cannot be known" by the mind, he immediately goes on to qualify this concession in a significant way. He insists that while not all of our acts are (or even can be) taken as objects for further higher-order states (on pain of regress), nevertheless, it does not follow that such acts are not known *in any way*. Consider, for example, what he says mid-way through text K:

Moreover, to the extent that an act of knowing proceeds from the intellect as something actually structured for knowing (*actualiter coordinato ad scire*) what proceeds from it, to that same extent it can be said that it knows that very act of

[46] See passage D above, for example.

knowing—namely, because the intellect generates and contains it [i.e., its act] in the manner of something both able to be known and productive of knowing.

Here, Olivi expresses his agreement with his opponent that the intellect, as a reflexive power, is oriented toward its own states in such a way that it is always aware of the acts that proceed from or arise within itself. But then (toward the end of the passage) he denies that this sort of reflexive knowledge or awareness entails any *higher-order* awareness of such acts. As he says in the last line, "although the power is turned toward the act which it brings about" it does not follow from this that the power is "turned toward it as toward an object that it actually can think of or does think of." Here again, it seems to me the best way to understand these remarks is to read them in light of our distinction between two kinds of state-reflexive awareness: pre-reflective consciousness vs. introspective awareness of one's states. Read this way, we can see that while Olivi does think that the latter, introspective variety of state-reflexive awareness requires the introduction of a numerically distinct higher-order state, he denies this is the case when it comes to pre-reflective awareness of one's states. Indeed, he insists to the contrary that we can know or be aware of a given state even in the absence of any further, higher-order state that relates to it as its object. And this just reinforces the conclusion that he rejects a higher-order theory of consciousness.

But, then, if consciousness of one's states is not to be explained by appeal to a relation such states bear to other, higher-order states, what does explain it? One obvious way to respond to this question—an approach frequently taken by contemporary advocates of one-level theories—is to argue that conscious states are conscious in virtue of some representational (or intentional) relation they bear to themselves.[47] This is just to say that states are

[47] On this view, conscious states are conscious in virtue of their possession of some kind of higher-order self-referential content. Historically, Brentano is the thinker most frequently associated with this sort of view. (See Amie Thomasson, "After Brentano: A One-Level Theory of Consciousness," *European Journal of Philosophy* 8 (2000), 190–209 and Dan Zahavi, "Back to Brentano?" *Journal of Consciousness Studies* 11 (2004), 66–87.) The view has, however, also been attributed to both Aristotle and even to Locke. (For its attribution to Aristotle see Victor Caston, "Aristotle on Consciousness," *Mind* 111 (2002), 751–815; it is attributed to Locke by Angela Coventry and Uriah Kriegel in "Locke on Consciousness," *History of Philosophy Quarterly* 25 (2008), 221–42.) Current proponents of a same-order approach to consciousness include Uriah Kriegel, Rocco Gennaro, and Robert Van Gulick. See, for example, Kriegel, *Subjective Consciousness*, and Uriah Kriegel and Kenneth Williford (eds.), *Self-Representational Approaches to Consciousness* (Cambridge, MA: MIT Press, 2006).

conscious in virtue of taking themselves as object.[48] Although Olivi's rejection of a higher-order analysis might seem to imply his acceptance of just such a view, I think it is clear that his discussion in q. 79 precludes it.[49] To be sure, Olivi does explicitly entertain the possibility that intellective states can take themselves as object, but he entertains this possibility as an analysis of *introspective* knowledge, not consciousness. What is more, when it comes to pre-reflective awareness of one's states, Olivi rejects not only the idea that such awareness owes to a state's serving as object for some higher-order state, but also and more generally that it owes to that state serving as an intentional *object* of any sort. This, I take it, is the point of his remark in passage K, when he says that it is "not true that a power reflexively directed on itself can see whatever arises in itself only if its reflection is such that it actually regards all such things as objects." Hence, even if our subjective states *can* (and, in cases of introspection, do) function as intentional objects of numerically distinct acts of awareness, nevertheless, our being conscious of them does not require this. Hence, consciousness is not, apparently, to be explained by appeal to any sort of *act–object* relation or structure—whether higher- or same-order.

But if consciousness is not to be explained on an act–object model of awareness, what remains? One further interpretive possibility is to read Olivi as defending something like an adverbial theory of consciousness. On this reading, consciousness would be an intrinsic, unstructured feature of intellective acts or states such that one's subjective experience of a given state is a matter of her having or occupying that state *in a certain way*.[50] For example, my conscious experience of seeing the pen owes to the fact that the act of seeing itself occurs in a *subjective*, or *conscious way*. Inasmuch as consciousness turns out, on the adverbialist view, to be a non-relational

[48] Thus, on such a view, conscious intentional states (say, my consciously seeing the pen in my hand) will often have two intentional objects: a primary, external object (namely, the pen) and a secondary, inner object (namely, itself).

[49] Putallaz seems attracted to some such a reading of Olivi. As he interprets Olivi, pre-reflective consciousness is an internal feature of conscious states (and so not a matter of higher-order awareness) and is such that it involves some kind of self-referring, intentional (indeed, universal, or conceptual) content. In fact, it is in this latter respect that Putallaz locates the principle difference between Aquinas and Olivi's conception of pre-reflective consciousness. See his discussion of the two-fold or "double aspect" of Olivi's notion pre-reflective awareness in *La Connaissance*, 96 ff.

[50] This sort of approach to consciousness is developed and defended by a number of thinkers in the phenomenological tradition. See David W. Smith, "The Structure of (Self-) Consciousness," *Topoi* 3 (1986), 73–85; Zahavi, "Back to Brentano?," 81–5. As Thomasson describes the view, consciousness of some act is "ontologically, something like a property of the first act—a way the first act is, rather than an independent act of its own" ("After Brentano," 203).

feature of conscious states, attributing such a view to Olivi would certainly explain his unwillingness to characterize (pre-reflective) state-reflexive awareness in terms of any sort of act–object relation.[51] Even so, I think we must resist this interpretation as well. While Olivi does reject the notion that consciousness is to be explained in terms of a state's holding the object-place in some intentional, or act–object relation, it does not follow from this that he rejects a relational analysis *tout court.* In fact, as I read Olivi, consciousness does turn out to be kind of relation: namely, one that holds between the mind or intellect, on the one hand, and its subjective states on the other. Consider, for example, his remarks in the following passage:

[L] Every act of knowing includes a relation on the part of the act to its subject—not merely [a relation] as to a subject but also as to something known, since no one knows anything unless he knows himself knowing it (and included in this is knowing himself existing and knowing himself existing as one knowing).[52]

The central claim of this passage is by now familiar: Olivi is once again calling attention to the fact that all acts of intellect (i.e. "acts of knowing") are both subject- and state-reflexive in character. What is particularly noteworthy in his remarks here, however, is that he analyzes such reflexive awareness as a type of relation—namely, one that holds between the subject and the act itself. The question, of course, is what exactly the nature of this relation is. Olivi tells us only that it is a relation "not merely as to a subject but as to something known."[53] Of course, such remarks do not, by themselves, go very far toward clarifying matters. Yet, taken in conjunction with what we have seen so far, and in particular both (i) Olivi's insistence that we experience our mental acts or states, and (ii) his steadfast refusal to construe such experience it in terms of any *act–object* model of awareness, it is natural, I think, to take his remarks here as a way of calling attention to a distinctive, sui generis mode of access the soul has to its own subjective states. Indeed, that Olivi takes the mode of awareness in question to be sui generis is suggested precisely by the fact that the

51 It is not clear to me, however, how this account is supposed to yield an analysis that explain or fits the target phenomena. How could an intrinsic, unstructured feature of some act explain *my* being *aware-of* that act?

52 *Summa* II, q. 103 (III, 236).

53 Insofar as occurrent acts or states are episodic, medieval philosophers typically identify them with accidental forms inhering in the soul as their subject (typically, forms in the Aristotelian category of quality). Thus, I take it, when Olivi characterizes the relation in terms of it being "as to a subject," he's referring to the fact that a given act relates to the soul as a subject of inherence. The relation it bears to the soul "as something known" is, by contrast, its presence to the soul as something subjectively experienced.

relation in question is, on his view, *categorically different* from the kind of access or awareness relation a subject bears to the objects of ordinary intentional or representational states.[54] On this way of reading him, then, consciousness turns out to be a primitively subjective mode of access or awareness—the kind he is at pains to characterize throughout his writings in terms of its distinctive first-personal, experiential quality.

If this is the right way to read Olivi, the theory of consciousness he holds clearly does qualify as a one-level theory. Consciousness of one's subjective states is not a function of those states serving as objects for any further, higher-order acts of awareness. Nor is it an unstructured monadic property or adverbial feature of them. Rather, consciousness is a special, sui generis relation that a subject (or rational soul) bears to its own states: a primitive kind of subjective access. In this regard, then, Olivi can be understood as drawing a distinction between two irreducibly distinct types of awareness: one the one hand, there's the sort of awareness one has of objects *via* her occurrent acts or states (e.g. my awareness of, say, *the pen*) and, on the other hand, the sort of awareness one has *of* her occurrent acts themselves (e.g. my awareness *of seeing* the pen). Each type of awareness, moreover, is a distinct type of relation: the former, an act–object relation; the latter, a subject–act relation. And, clearly, on Olivi's analysis, ordinary conscious experience includes both. Thus, my consciously seeing the pen in my hand involves (i) my having an act of visual awareness, one that takes the pen as its object, and (ii) my subjective experience of this visual awareness, one that takes my seeing the pen as its terminus or relatum.

3. OLIVI ON THE EPISTEMOLOGY OF REFLEXIVITY: CONSCIOUSNESS AND THE INFALLIBILITY OF SELF-KNOWLEDGE

Having explained what I take to be Olivi's account of both the phenomenology and proper analysis of reflexive awareness. I now want to show that Olivi's particular understanding of the phenomenal character and ontological structure of state-reflexive knowledge is motivated by his broader commitment to Augustinian views about the *epistemology* of self-knowledge.

[54] Perhaps there is here something akin to Husserl's distinction between perceiving and experiencing. See Zahavi, "Back to Brentano?," 82. See also Dan Zahavi, *Self-Awareness and Alterity: A Phenomenological Investigation* (Evanston, IL: Northwestern University Press, 1999).

Augustine's thesis about the mind's self-reflexivity is, at bottom, a theological thesis. It is a thesis about the essential and ultimately trinitarian structure of the human mind. As Augustine sees it, however, this thesis carries important epistemological implications. In particular, it entails that self-knowledge is epistemically distinctive in a number of ways—most notably in its being more secure or more certain than knowledge of anything else.[55] As Augustine famously remarks: "What is more present to thought than what is present to mind, and what is more present to the mind than the mind itself?"[56] Olivi clearly takes this part of the Augustinian legacy seriously. Thus, echoing Augustine, he claims "our mind... immediately sees itself as its inmost and most immediate object."[57] Accordingly, he holds that the nature of mind's access to itself is such that knowledge regarding not only itself but also its subjective states is utterly certain. Thus, for example, when it comes to knowledge of oneself, Olivi claims, "a person knows that he exists and lives so infallibly that he is unable to be in doubt about this."[58] Likewise, when it comes to the extent and nature of our knowledge of our mental states, Olivi is equally sanguine. On his view, "we possess superlative knowledge and experience of what it is to understand, what it is to will, and what it is to believe."[59] Not surprisingly, moreover, Olivi takes these two types of self-knowledge to be intimately connected. Indeed, it appears that certainty about the former—that is, about our own existence—is ultimately grounded or included in the security of our experience of the latter, namely, our subjective states. As he explains,

[M] no one is certain in knowledge of something unless he knows himself to know it—that is, unless he knows that he is the very one who knows it. But certitude

[55] Augustine holds that this is so both for subject-reflexive and state-reflexive self-knowledge of ourselves. Thus, he thinks that we know the proposition "I exist" with utter certainty, and he also maintains that knowledge of our own states is among the few examples of knowledge that proves immune to skeptical doubt. See Gareth Matthews, *Augustine* (Oxford: Blackwell, 2005), chaps. 2 and 5, and Gareth Matthews, *Thought's Ego in Augustine and Descartes* (Ithaca: Cornell University Press, 1992) for further discussion of these issues in Augustine.

[56] *De Trinitate* 10.10. See also 10.5 and 10.16. The certainty of self-knowledge is crucial to Augustine's overarching project in this work. As he makes clear in Book 8, the doctrine of the trinity is, of necessity, an article of faith, but in order to ensure that our "faith is not fabricated" such faith must be secured or anchored in something we know. On his view, our faith in the trinity is anchored in what we know and experience of our own minds, since it in the human mind that the image of the trinity is located.

[57] *Impugnatio* 19.5.

[58] *Impugnatio* 19.11. Cf. *Impugnatio*, 19.10: "We know most certainly and intimately that we exist."

[59] *Impugnatio*, 19.11.

concerning the subject [of one's states] runs universally through the apprehension of each one of our acts.[60]

When it comes to the epistemology of self-knowledge, therefore, state-reflexive awareness plays a foundational role. And this is because (i) subject-reflexive awareness is included constitutively in state-reflexive awareness and (ii) state-reflexive awareness itself is utterly secure, epistemically speaking. As he claims (in passage K above): "concerning any act of knowing, one can be said to be certain and can know it with certainty."

Here Olivi's commitment to a broadly Augustinian account of the epistemology of reflexive awareness drives much of Olivi's theory of consciousness and self-knowledge. This is clearest, I think, in the case of his account of the nature of introspective knowledge. To see this, let us return briefly to his account of introspective (state-reflexive) knowledge in q. 79. Recall that the question at issue in this context has to do with whether a given mental act or state can take itself as object. As we have now seen, a negative answer to this question amounts to two-level, or higher-order, account of introspective knowledge whereas an affirmative answer yields a same-order theory. It is perhaps to Olivi's credit that he ultimately comes down on the side of a negative answer, since a one-level theory of introspection looks rather implausible phenomenologically. After all, on such a view, mental states turn out to be such that they are not only always subjectively experienced by their subject, but they are also—at all times—introspectively known to her as well. And this is because on such a view both pre-reflective and introspective awareness are entailed by the occurrence of the state itself. In siding with the higher-order theory, however, Olivi explicitly allows that we lack introspective knowledge for at least some of our states.

And yet, as we have seen, Olivi does take the same-order theory seriously. In fact, he defends it at length and, were it not for the authority of Augustine, he might very well have come down in favor of it. This is somewhat surprising both because, as just noted, the view is implausible, *prima facie*, and also because this sort of view was widely rejected in Olivi's day. That said, we can, I think, begin to make sense of the appeal of such a view for Olivi if we consider it in the context of his commitments to an Augustinian account of the epistemology of self-knowledge.[61] After all, whatever else may be said for it, the one-level theory of introspection easily

[60] *Impugnatio*, 19.11. See also passages A and L above.

[61] This is not to say that epistemic considerations are the only features that render this sort of view attractive to Olivi. Indeed, it seems clear that his commitment to the reflexive character of acts of will is playing an important role here too. For more on Olivi's views about reflexivity in connection with acts of willing, see Yrjönsuuri, "Free Will and Self-Control," 100–3 and 118–23.

accommodates the pristine epistemic status accorded to self-knowledge on the Augustinian picture. That this is the case is clear, first, from the fact that on the one-level model of introspection mental states turn out to be self-intimating—that is to say, they are such that, necessarily, being in a given mental state entails knowing this very fact. Thus, on the one-level theory of introspection, whenever a subject is thinking of something, she thereby inevitably forms an introspective judgment to the effect that she has just such thought. What is more, such judgments are guaranteed to be both indubitable and infallible. After all, it is not possible for the subject to doubt the truth of her introspective judgment if that judgment coincides with conscious experience of the very state she attributes to herself. Likewise, it is not possible for her self-attributing judgment to be false if the judgment in question contains or includes the state she attributes to herself. It is, I think, the fact that the one-level analysis of introspective knowledge secures such a robust privilege for self-knowledge that explains Olivi's willingness to defend (even if not, ultimately, to endorse) such a view.[62]

While Olivi eventually rejects the one-level theory of introspection, it is worth noting that his account of phenomenal consciousness nevertheless preserves—albeit in slightly weakened form—much of the epistemic profile associated with it. His insistence on the ubiquity of (pre-reflective) consciousness, for example, entails that mental states are, in an important sense, still self-intimating. While it is not the case (as it is on the one-level theory of introspection) that merely being in a mental state suffices for one's forming a self-attributing judgment regarding that state, it does, nevertheless, suffice for *some form of awareness* of it—namely, the sort that constitutes one's conscious experience of it. And even if, on Olivi's final view, being in a mental state is not sufficient for the actual possession of infallible introspective knowledge of that state, nevertheless, it is sufficient for one's *being able* to have such knowledge. After all, on his analysis, consciousness is a very special type of access to one's states—access that not only grounds, but also guarantees our *ability* to attend to and to judge indubitably and infallibly about our subjective states. This is clear, for example, from the fact that even when Olivi is forced to admit—on threat of regress—that there are states which one cannot actually introspect (say, the final state in a higher-order series), he insists nonetheless that *with*

[62] The importance of such epistemic considerations in shaping Olivi's analysis of reflexive awareness is even more clear in his debate with those who hold that the soul's awareness of itself is in some way mediated by intelligible species or phantasms. Olivi insists that such a view fails precisely because it fails to preserve the certainty traditionally associated with self-knowledge. See *Impugnatio* 19 *passim.*

respect to any such state "one can be said to be certain and can know it with certainty." His insistence on this point owes, I believe, to the fact that he takes consciousness as a kind of privileged access. Thus, the "certainty" Olivi ascribes even to states that are not introspectively known owes to the fact that they occur consciously. Since consciousness serves as the grounds for introspective judgments, it follows that whether or not a subject actually introspects a given state, her access to that state is such that she "can know it with certainty." Whether or not a subject *actually* forms any introspective judgment is, therefore, (epistemically) irrelevant. Either way, the epistemic grounds for such a judgment remain the same. As Olivi himself puts it (in passage K), the mind's access to its states is such that its states are by nature "productive of [introspective] knowing":[63]

To the extent that an act of knowing proceeds from the intellect as something actually structured for knowing what proceeds from it, to that same extent it can be said that it knows that very act of knowing—namely, because the intellect generates and contains it [i.e. its act] in the manner of something both able to be known and productive of knowing (*scibilem et scivitum*).

It is no doubt for this same reason that Olivi claims (in the last lines of passage A) that consciousness—that is, one's experiential, subject-/state-reflexive awareness—yields "primary, infallible, and indubitable principles" for more introspective varieties of self-knowledge.

In the end, therefore, it is clear that Olivi's commitment to the privileged status of self-knowledge illuminates—and, indeed, partly motivates—his specific views about the nature and structure of state-reflexive awareness. Such a commitment not only explains his attraction to the controversial, one-level analysis of introspection but also, I believe, ultimately motivates his account of consciousness as a sui generis type of access to one's subjective states—one meditated neither by representation nor inferential processes. At the end of the day, it is this access that anchors the certainty associated with self-knowledge in general—both experiential and *quiddative* forms of subject-reflexive knowledge as well as introspective and non-introspective forms of state-reflexive awareness.

4. CONCLUSION

Although Olivi's treatment of these issues forms just one part of a much longer tradition of medieval reflection on the nature of mind's self-

[63] I am grateful to Scott MacDonald for calling my attention to the way in which Olivi's remarks here illuminate precisely this feature of his view.

reflexivity, his account serves to illustrate the way in which questions about mind's reflexivity provide an important context for theorizing about the nature of self-knowledge in general and consciousness in particular. What is more, attention to the details of Olivi's discussion helps to clarify some of the connections that can (and cannot) be drawn between medieval theories of self-reflexivity and contemporary theories of consciousness. As we have seen, the core phenomenon at stake in Olivi's theory of reflexivity—namely, the subjective or self-conscious character of experience—overlaps with that targeted in a number of current theories of phenomenal consciousness. Still, insofar as contemporary notions of *quale* or qualitative character have no obvious correlate in his account of reflexive awareness, we must resist any unqualified assimilation of his notion of reflexivity to the current notion of consciousness.

Again, we have also seen that because Olivi, like other medieval philosophers, admits various types of reflexive awareness, a proper understanding of his theory of consciousness and its relationship to contemporary theories requires that we pay attention to which among these various modes of awareness is at issue at any given point in his discussion. Thus, whereas higher-order and even same-order or self-representationalist analyses of consciousness are widely accepted among philosophers today, we can now see that Olivi rejects such analyses.[64] Although he does endorse a higher-order approach to *introspective* knowledge, and even entertains adopting a same-order account of introspection, nonetheless, phenomenal consciousness, for him, is distinct from (and presupposed by) such introspective awareness. Indeed, on his analysis, consciousness is distinct from all other forms of awareness. Hence, on his view, it cannot be explained or analyzed in terms of any other, more familiar, form of intentional or representational awareness—whether higher- or same-order in nature.

Finally, as the discussion of Olivi helps us to see, even if debates about self-reflexivity are a natural place to look for medieval treatments of consciousness, discussions of such reflexivity include much else besides. At bottom, the traditional thesis that the mind is self-reflexive in nature is a thesis about the essential character of the mind as such. It is in the course of exploring the broader implications of this thesis (metaphysical, theological, epistemological, and phenomenological) that questions relating to

[64] In this regard, however, he is not representative of medieval approaches generally. There are a number of medieval thinkers who quite explicitly develop and defend higher-order theories. See n. 44 above.

consciousness often come to the fore. Even so, self-consciousness is but one among many philosophical and theological themes associated with the traditional thesis about the reflexivity of mind.[65]

Saint Louis University

BIBLIOGRAPHY

Augustine. *De Trinitate libri quindecim*, ed. J. W. Mountain, CCSL 50-50A (Turnhout: Brepols, 1968).

—— *The Trinity*, ed. J. E. Rotelle, tr. E. Hill (Hyde Park, NY: New City Press, 1991).

Bayne, Tim. "Self-Consciousness and the Unity of Consciousness," *The Monist* 87 (2004), 224–41.

Booth, Edward. "Saint Thomas Aquinas's Critique of Saint Augustine's Conceptions of the Image of God in the Human Soul," in J. Brachtendorf (ed.), *Gott und sein Bild: Augustins De Trinitate im Spiegel gegenwärtiger Forschung* (Paderborn: Ferdinand Schöningh, 2000), 219–40.

Brittain, Charles. "Intellectual Self-Knowledge," in E. Bermon and G. O'Daly (eds.), *Le De Trinitate de saint Augustin exégèse, logique et noétique* (Paris: Vrin, 2012), 322–39.

Brower-Toland, Susan. "Medieval Approaches to Consciousness: Ockham and Chatton," *Philosopher's Imprint* 12 (2012), 1–29.

—— "Self-Knowledge, Self-Consciousness, and Reflexivity," in R. Friedmann and M. Pickavé (eds.), *Companion to Cognitive Theory in the Later Middle Ages* (Leuven: Leuven University Press, forthcoming).

Burr, David. "The Persecution of Peter Olivi," *Transactions of the American Philosophical Society* 66 (1976), 3–98.

—— *Olivi and Franciscan Poverty: The Origins of the Usus Pauper Controversy* (Philadelphia: University of Pennsylvania Press, 1989).

Caston, Victor. "Aristotle on Consciousness," *Mind* 111 (2002), 751–815.

Clark, Mary. "De Trinitate," in E. Stump and N. Kretzmann (eds.), *The Cambridge Companion to Augustine* (Cambridge: Cambridge University Press, 2001), 91–102.

Cory, Therese S. *Aquinas on Human Self-Knowledge* (Cambridge: Cambridge University Press, forthcoming).

Coventry, Angela and Uriah Kriegel. "Locke on Consciousness," *History of Philosophy Quarterly* 25 (2008), 221–42.

Flanagan, Owen. *Consciousness Reconsidered* (Cambridge, MA: MIT Press, 1992).

[65] I would like to thank Jeffrey Brower, Juhana Toivenen, and an anonymous referee for OSMP for very helpful comments on an earlier draft of this paper. I have also benefited from presenting parts of this paper at the 2012 Cornell Colloquium in Medieval Philosophy and at the third SSALT (Subjectivity and Selfhood in the Latin and Arabic Traditions) workshop. I am grateful to the audiences on both of these occasions for valuable discussion and feedback.

Friedman, Russell. "On the Trail of a Philosophical Debate: Durandus of St.-Pourçain vs. Thomas Wylton on Simultaneous Acts in the Intellect," in S. Brown, T. Dewender, and T. Kobusch (eds.), *Philosophical Debates at Paris in the Early Fourteenth Century* (Leiden: Brill, 2009), 433–61.

Gallagher, Shaun and Dan Zahavi. *The Phenomenological Mind* (London: Routledge, 2008).

—— "Phenomenological Approaches to Self-Consciousness," in E. N. Zalta (ed.), *The Stanford Encyclopedia of Philosophy* (Winter 2010 Edition) <http://plato.stanford.edu/archives/win2010/entries/self-consciousness-phenomenological/>.

Genarro, Rocco. "Consciousness, Self-Consciousness, and Episodic Memory," *Philosophical Psychology* 5 (1992), 333–47.

Heinämaa, Sara, Vili Lähteenmäki, and Pauliina Remes (eds.), *Consciousness: From Perception to Reflection in the History of Philosophy* (Dordrecht: Springer, 2007).

Hume, David. *A Treatise of Human Nature*, ed. P. H. Nidditch, 2nd edn. (Oxford: Clarendon Press, 1978).

Kärkkäinen, Pekka. "Interpretations of the Psychological Analogy from Aquinas to Biel," in P. Kärkkäinen (ed.), *Trinitarian Theology in the Medieval West* (Helsinki: Luther-Agricola-Society, 2007), 256–79.

Kriegel, Uriah."Consciousness as Intransitive Self-Consciousness: Two Views and an Argument," *Canadian Journal of Philosophy* 33 (2003), 103–32.

—— "Consciousness and Self-Consciousness," *The Monist* 87 (2004), 185–209.

—— *Subjective Consciousness* (Oxford: Oxford University Press, 2009).

Kriegel, Uriah and Kenneth W. Williford. *Self-Representational Approaches to Consciousness* (Cambridge, MA: MIT Press, 2006).

Levine, Joseph. *Purple Haze: The Puzzle of Consciousness* (Oxford: Oxford University Press, 2001).

McGinn, Colin. "Consciousness and Content," in N. Block, O. Flanagan, and G. Güzeldere (eds.), *The Nature of Consciousness: Philosophical Debates* (Cambridge, MA: MIT Press, 1997), 295–308 [reprint of "Consciousness and Content," *Proceedings of the British Academy* 76 (1988), 219–39].

Martin, Christopher. "Self-Knowledge and Cognitive Ascent: Thomas Aquinas and Peter Olivi on the KK-Thesis," in H. Laugerland (ed.), *Forming the Mind: Essays on the Internal Senses and the Mind/Body Problem from Avicenna to the Medical Enlightenment* (Dordrecht: Springer, 2007), 93–108.

Matthews, Gareth. *Thought's Ego in Augustine and Descartes* (Ithaca: Cornell University Press, 1992).

—— "Augustine on Mind's Search for Itself," *Faith and Philosophy* 20 (2003), 415–29.

—— *Augustine* (Oxford: Blackwell, 2005).

Michon, Cyrille. "Ego Intelligo (lapidem). Deux conceptions de la réflexion au Moyen Age," in O. Boulnois (ed.), *Généalogies du sujet: de saint Anselme à Malebranche* (Paris: Vrin, 2007), 114–47.

Mojsisch, Burkhard. "Dietrich von Freiberg: ein origninelle Reezipient der *Mens-* und *Cogitatio*-Theorie Augustinus," in J. Brachtendorf (ed.), *Gott und sein Bild:*

Augustins De Trinitate im Spiegel gegenwärtiger Forschung (Paderborn: Ferdinand Schöningh, 2000), 241–8.

O'Callaghan, John. "Imago Dei: A Test Case for St. Thomas's Augustinianism," in M. Dauphinais, B. David, and M. Levering (eds.), *Aquinas the Augustinian* (Washington, DC: Catholic University of America Press, 2007), 100–44.

O'Daly, Gerard. *Augustine's Philosophy of Mind* (Berkeley: University of California Press, 1987).

Pasnau, Robert. "Olivi on the Metaphysics of the Soul," *Medieval Philosophy and Theology* 6 (1997), 109–32.

—— "Peter John Olivi," in E. N. Zalta (ed.), *The Stanford Encyclopedia of Philosophy* (Fall 2008 Edition) <http://plato.stanford.edu/archives/fall2008/entries/olivi/>.

Perler, Dominik. *Théories de l'intentionnalité au moyen âge* (Paris: Vrin, 2003).

Petrus Ioannis Olivi. *Quaestiones in secundum librum Sententiarum*, vols. I–III, ed. B. Jansen, Bibliotheca Franciscana Scholastica Medii Aevi IV–VI (Florence: Collegium S. Bonaventurae, 1922–6).

—— *Quaestio de locutionibus angelorum*, ed. S. Piron, *Oliviana* 1 (2003) <http://oliviana.revues.org/document18.html>.

—— *Impugnatio quorundam articulorum Arnalidi Galliardi, articulus 19*, ed. S. Piron, *Oliviana* 2 (2006) <http://oliviana.revues.org/document56.html>.

Piron, Sylvain. "L'expérience subjective selon Pierre de Jean Olivi," in O. Boulnois (ed.), *Généalogies du sujet: de saint Anselme à Malebranche* (Paris: Vrin, 2007), 43–54.

Putallaz, François-Xavier. *La connaissance de soi au XIIIe siècle: de Matthieu d'Aquasparta à Thierry de Freiberg* (Vrin: Paris, 1991).

—— "Peter Olivi," in J. Garcia and T. Noone (eds.), *A Companion to Philosophy in the Middle Ages* (Oxford: Blackwell, 2007), 516–23.

Rode, Christian."Der Begriff der inneren Erfahrung bei Petrus Johannis Olivi," *Bochumer Philosophisches Jahrbuch für Antike und Mittelalter* 13 (2008), 123–41.

—— "Peter of John Olivi on Representation and Self-Representation," *Quaestio: Yearbook of the History of Metaphysics* 10 (2010), 155–66.

Silva, Filipe José and Juhana Toivanen. "The Active Nature of the Soul in Sense Perception: Robert Kilwardby and Peter Olivi," *Vivarium* 48 (2010), 245–78.

Smith, David W. "The Structure of (Self-) Consciousness," *Topoi* 3 (1986), 73–85.

Thomasson, Amie. "After Brentano: A One-Level Theory of Consciousness," *European Journal of Philosophy* 8 (2000), 190–209.

Toivanen, Juhana. "Peter Olivi on Internal Senses," *British Journal for the History of Philosophy* 15 (2007), 427–54.

—— *Animal Consciousness: Peter Olivi on Cognitive Functions of the Sensitive Soul* (Ph.D. dissertation, University of Jyväskylä, 2009).

—— "Peter John Olivi," in W. Otten (ed.), *The Oxford Guide to the Historical Reception of Augustine* (Oxford: Oxford University Press, 2013).

—— "Perceptual Self-Awareness in Seneca, Augustine, and Olivi," *Journal of the History of Philosophy* (forthcoming).

Yrjönsuuri, Mikko. "Free Will and Self-Control in Peter Olivi," in H. Lagerlund and M. Yrjönsuuri (eds.), *Emotions and Choice from Boethius to Descartes* (Dordrecht: Kluwer, 2002), 99–128.

—— "Types of Self-Awareness in Medieval Thought," in V. Hirvonen, T. J. Holopainen, and M. Tuominen (eds.), *Mind and Modality: Studies in the History of Philosophy in Honor of Simo Knuuttila* (Leiden: Brill, 2006), 153–69.

—— "Locating the Self Within the Soul: Thirteenth-Century Discussions," in P. Remes and J. Sihvola (eds.), *Ancient Philosophy of the Self* (Dordrecht: Springer, 2008), 225–41.

—— "Perceiving One's Own Body," in S. Knuuttila and P. Kärkkäinen (eds.), *Theories of Perception in Medieval and Early Modern Philosophy* (Dordrecht: Springer, 2008), 101–16.

Zahavi, Dan. *Self-Awareness and Alterity* (Evanston, IL: Northwestern University Press, 1999).

—— "Self and Consciousness," in D. Zahavi (ed.), *Exploring the Self: Philosophical and Psychopathological Perspectives on Self-Experience* (Amsterdam: J. Benjamins, 2000), 55–74.

—— "Back to Brentanno?" *Journal of Consciousness Studies* 11 (2004), 66–87.

Duns Scotus on Essence and Existence

Richard Cross

That there is some kind of distinction between essence and existence is a centerpiece of the metaphysics of many medieval philosophers. Duns Scotus has very little to say about it, and his position—and apparent lack of interest in the question—has puzzled commentators since his own time. For example, one of his most significant early followers, Francis of Meyronnes, attempts to make sense of Scotus's inchoate views by claiming that existence is an "intrinsic mode" of an essence. According to Meyronnes,

> an intrinsic mode is that which, coming to some form or quiddity, does not alter its formal notion,[1]

and he includes both existence (*exsistentia*) and haecceity (the explanation for individuation) in this category.[2] On this view, actual existence is a modalization of an essence; an existent individual is an essence with a certain mode.

This interpretation is found in a great deal of more recent reflection on Scotus's teaching too. For example, Etienne Gilson states,

> It appears that, according to Scotus, existence is but an intrinsic modality of essence or, as some of his disciples will be fond of saying, a "degree" (*gradus*) of essence. And it is truly so, if existence is but an essence in its ultimate degree of determination.[3]

[1] Francis of Meyronnes, *Tractatus formalitatum* (Venice, 1520), fo. 263vb.

[2] See *Tractatus formalitatum* (fo. 263vb); also Meyronnes, *In libros sententiarum* I, d. 8, q. 5 (Venice, 1520), fo. 49rb.

[3] Etienne Gilson, *Being and Some Philosophers*, 2nd edn. (Toronto: Pontifical Institute of Medieval Studies, 1952), 91. See too A. J. O'Brien, "Duns Scotus' Teaching on the Distinction Between Essence and Existence," *The New Scholasticism*, 38 (1964), 65–77; W. Hoeres, "Wesen und Dasein bei Heinrich von Gent und Duns Scotus," *Franziskanishe Studien* 47 (1965), 171–9; John F. Wippel, "Essence and Existence," in N. Kretzmann, A. Kenny, and J. Pinborg (eds.), *The Cambridge History of Later Medieval Philosophy* (Cambridge: Cambridge University Press, 1982), 406. The argument in each

An early addition, almost certainly not by Scotus, added in some manuscripts of Scotus's *Quodlibet*, puts the position nicely:

> It can be said that, in creatures, an essence and its existence are related as quiddity and mode, and for this reason are distinguished. In God, however, existence belongs to the concept of the essence.[4]

This passage is cited by Allan B. Wolter in his account of the issue, in defense of the modalization reading.[5]

As far as I know, there is no evidence that Scotus himself explicitly thought of the matter in this way. Scotus's discussion of intrinsic modes applies in cases where an essence is modified not by any added reality (as, e.g., in the case of a specific difference added to a genus) but in some other way,[6] and (as Gilson points out) paradigmatically by some kind of degree or amount of the essence (as, e.g., in the case of degrees of heat, or of intensity of color).[7] And it is not clear that something's existence could be some kind of intensification of the thing.

In what follows I will attempt to gather together all the things Scotus actually says, in order to come to some kind of conclusion as to what Scotus thinks about the whole issue. Basically, Scotus puts the apparatus of his so-called "formal" distinction to work, claiming that there is a formal distinction between essence and existence (and between the individual and its existence)—a distinction that is neither real nor merely rational, and that, by way of background to the main discussion, I introduce in Section 1, where I discuss too Scotus's views on individuation (since it is in the context of this that he discusses the essence/existence question most explicitly). In Section 2—the core of this essay—I outline Scotus's main treatment of the essence/existence distinction, found in his discussion of individuation. Scotus rejects any kind of real distinction between essence and existence, and in Section 3 I highlight a text in which Scotus talks about this. My fourth section considers what Scotus has to say about the question of essence and existence in God (not much, as it turns out, though what he does say is surprising). The remaining two substantive sections fill out

case is largely that Scotus's claims about formal and modal distinctions (on which, see below) require that he *ought* to have asserted a modal distinction between essence and existence. But here I focus on what he does in fact say, and in consequence I come to a different conclusion.

4 Scotus, *Quodlibet* [= *Quod.*] 1, n. 4 (Wadding XII, 5).

5 See Allan B. Wolter, "Is Existence for Scotus a Perfection, Predicate, or What?," in Wolter, *The Philosophical Theology of John Duns Scotus*, ed. M. M. Adams (Ithaca, NY: Cornell University Press, 1990), 281.

6 See Scotus, *Ordinatio* [= *Ord.*] I, d. 8, p. 1, q. 3, n. 136 (Vatican IV, 221).

7 See Scotus, *Ord.* I, d. 17, p. 1, q. 2, n. 28 (Vatican IV, 150).

ways in which the discussion relates to notions of potency and actuality (Section 5), and to the question of a thing's existence being caused (Section 6). A final section offers some brief concluding reflections.

1. THE BASIC METAPHYSICAL FRAMEWORK

In his rather involved discussion of the question of individuation, Scotus devotes some space to a consideration of the view that actual existence individuates, and this is the focus for his main discussion of the essence/existence question.[8] So to begin with, I describe briefly what Scotus has to say about individuation, so that we can understand what he does and does not reject in the view that existence individuates. The general idea is this. There are common natures, in some sense shared by different particulars. Since such natures are supposed to perform some kind of explanatory function—explain kind-membership—Scotus reasons that they must have some kind of *entity*: they must be real in some sense, and thus nominalism on the question of common natures be false:

In the thing [viz. in extramental reality] the nature according to [its primary] entity has true real being outside the soul. And according to that entity, it has a unity in proportion to it.[9]

Thus, a nature as such, the common nature, has some kind of reality prior (in some sense) to its instantiations. Scotus does not mean that the primary entity of the nature is something that it has *independently* of its instantiation. Existing as this or that particular is accidental to the nature in the sense that, although the nature cannot exist without being one or more particulars, there is or are no one or more particulars that it is necessary that the nature be. The entity that Scotus talks about is just *essence*: what it is to be such-and-such a kind of thing; the thing that is what is signified by a definition. Both of these points are made here:

Although [the nature] is never without [particularity, nevertheless . . .] it is not [particular] . . . but is naturally prior to [it]. . . . In accordance with this natural

[8] For a brief exposition of this text (which I discuss in detail below), see William O'Meara, "Actual Existence and the Individual according to Duns Scotus," *Monist* 49 (1965), 659–69.

[9] Scotus, *Ord.* II, d. 3, p. 1, q. 1, n. 34 (Vatican VII, 404–5; translation in Paul Vincent Spade, *Five Texts on the Mediaeval Problem of Universals: Porphyry, Boethius, Abelard, Duns Scotus, Ockham* (Indianapolis: Hackett, 1994), 64–5).

priority, the what-the-thing-is is the *per se* object of the intellect and is *per se*, as such, considered by the metaphysician and expressed by the definition.[10]

(For all practical purposes in this discussion, Scotus uses "essence" and "nature" interchangeably, and I follow his usage here.) Scotus appeals to a well-known *dictum* of Avicenna to illustrate what he means, using as an example what it is to be a horse:

"Equinity is just equinity. Of itself it is neither one nor several, neither universal nor particular."[11]

The claim about the unity of equinity ("neither one nor several") is a way of picking out, for Scotus, the unity that is a "proper passion" of the nature, a *proprium* or necessary feature that is explained by the nature itself; and this is the "unity" that is "in proportion to" the nature (as Scotus puts it in the first quotation in this section):

[Non-numerical] unity is a proper passion of the nature according to its primary entity. Consequently, the nature is intrinsically *this* neither from itself nor according to its proper unity, which is necessarily included in the nature according to its primary entity.[12]

The nature's primary entity and unity are in some sense distinct from the entity and unity of the individual itself: if they were identical to the entity and unity of the individual, then there could be only one instance of the nature:

Whatever from its own notion is in something *per se* is in it in every instance; therefore, if the nature of stone were of itself "this," then whatever the nature of stone were in, that nature would be this stone. The consequent is nonsense.[13]

Rather, Scotus proposes, the nature gets tied to particular individuals by means of an individuator; in virtue of its possession of such an individuator, a complete particular is of itself distinct from every other complete particular. And the nature gains its own particularity in virtue of its union with the individuator:

Whatever is in this stone is numerically one, either primarily or *per se* or denominatively. Primarily, say, as that through which such a unity belongs to this

[10] Scotus, *Ord.* II, d. 3, p. 1, q. 1, n. 32 (Vatican VII, 403; Spade 63, translation slightly altered).

[11] Scotus, *Ord.* II, d. 3, p. 1, q. 1, n. 31 (Vatican VII, 403; Spade 63), quoting Avicenna, *Metaphysica* V, c. 1 (ed. van Riet II, 228, ll. 32–6).

[12] Scotus, *Ord.* II, d. 3, p. 1, q. 1, n. 34 (Vatican VII, 404–5; Spade 64–5).

[13] Scotus, *Ord.* II, d. 3, p. 1, q. 1, n. 3 (Vatican VII, 392; Spade 58).

composite. *Per se*, the stone itself, of which what is primarily one with this unity is a *per se* part. Only denominatively, what is potential and is perfected by the actual and is so to speak denominatively related to its actuality.[14]

The item that is primarily numerically one is the individuator; the item that is *per se* numerically one is the complete, concrete, individual substance, including the essence and the individuator—e.g. this human being; and the item that is denominatively numerically one is the (individualized, abstract) essence: something—e.g. *this humanity*—that gains its individuation from an item extrinsic to it (namely, the individuator, intrinsic to the complete item but extrinsic to the nature-component of the complete item). As Scotus understands individuation, the individuator is a *haecceity* or thisness, a wholly non-qualitative property of the concrete entity whose individuation it is supposed to explain.

Clearly, this posits a cluster of entities in a whole substance that, while not separable from each other, are nevertheless not strictly speaking identical. Scotus develops a very complex theory, both metaphysical and semantic, that distinguishes different varieties of numerical sameness, and he uses this theory to explain something of what he means in the individuation case. In a central passage, Scotus gives an exhaustive list of the different kinds of numerical unity that he acknowledges:

Just as we can find many degrees of unity—

firstly, the minimal degree is unity of aggregation; in the second degree is unity of order; in the third is accidental unity, which adds to order the informing, albeit accidental, of one by the other of those things that are thus one; in the fourth is the *per se* unity of something composed of essential principles one of which is *per se* act and the other *per se* potency; in the fifth is the unity of simplicity which is truly sameness (*identitas*) (for whatever is there is really the same as each thing [there], and is not merely one with it by the unity of union, as in the other modes)

—so, further, not every sameness is formal. I call that sameness formal when, [in the sixth degree], that which is said to be thus the same includes, *per se* in the first mode, that with which it is the same in its formal quidditative notion.[15]

The idea is that the first four types of unity involve really distinct components united to each other by means of certain real relations. The criterion for real distinction is separability, construed in the following sense: two things are really distinct if (and only if) at least one of them can survive without the other,[16] and real relations are ties really distinct from the items

[14] Scotus, *Ord.* II, d. 3, p. 1, qq. 5–6, n. 175 (Vatican VII, 477–8; Spade 103).

[15] Scotus, *Ord.* I, d. 2, p. 2, qq. 1–4, n. 403 (Vatican II, 356–7).

[16] See e.g. Scotus, *Quod.* 3, n. 15 (Wadding XII, 81).

that they tie together.[17] The fifth type of unity is of things really the same (i.e. inseparable), and this is distinguished from the sixth and final case, that of definitional inclusion or complete definitional coincidence. (It might be thought that talk of "definitions" here means that Scotus sees the domain of formal sameness/difference as concepts. But this would be wrong: as we saw above, he believes that the subjects of definition are extramental—e.g. common natures.)

In order to understand what follows, we need to be clear about the fifth and sixth cases here, so I pause to consider them more closely. And the situation is made a little harder than it might otherwise be by Scotus's terminology. Basically, the unity of simplicity—that unity which is (according to Scotus) "truly sameness"—is a kind of sameness that falls short of identity (in our sense). Scotus usually labels it "real" or "unqualified" sameness, and it is, I think, his basic sense of sameness. Two things are really the same if they are naturally counted as one thing, or counted as one thing under standard natural-kind sortals, and a necessary condition for this is that the items are inseparable.[18] But Scotus does not believe that, for two items to be really the same, they need to be *identical*. And it is the sixth kind of unity—formal sameness—that encompasses identity in our sense. The domain of items that can exhibit this last kind of relation includes not merely complete things and their concrete constituents, but also abstract properties (individual natures, substantial or accidental). Roughly, two abstract particulars satisfy the sixth kind of unity if they have the same definition, just as concrete objects are identical if they have exactly the same properties.

But, sadly, the situation is yet more complex than this, because Scotus elsewhere, in a text rather later than most of those that I consider here, distinguishes two varieties of the sixth kind of sameness (only one of which, of course, can be identity in our sense).[19] The two varieties are (in Scotus's terminology) formal sameness and adequate sameness. Two items are adequately the same if and only if their definitions coincide exactly—adequate sameness is identity in our sense. If the definition of one item

[17] See e.g. Scotus, *Ord.* II, d. 1, qq. 4–5, nn. 200–40 (Vatican VII, 101–20); for an excellent discussion, see Mark G. Henninger, *Relations: Medieval Theories 1250–1325* (Oxford: Clarendon Press, 1989), 71–4.

[18] I discuss this in detail in Section 3 of my article, "Duns Scotus on Universals, Sameness, and Identity," forthcoming in a volume on universals edited by Gabriele Galluzzo.

[19] For all of what follows in this paragraph, see the summary, with references and complete quotations, in my "Scotus's Parisian Teaching on Divine Simplicity," in O. Boulnois et al. (eds.), *Duns Scot à Paris: actes du colloque de Paris, 2–4 Septembre 2002* (Turnhout: Brepols, 2004), 534–43.

does not include that of another item with which it is really the same, then that first item is formally distinct from the second. Conversely, if the definition does include that of the other item, then the first is formally the same as the second. So while adequate sameness is Leibniz-style identity, formal sameness is not. (I return to the non-symmetrical relation of formal sameness below.) Clearly, items which satisfy the criteria for formal distinction will satisfy the criteria for non-adequate sameness (Scotus's preferred term for the distinction between two items that are really the same but fail to be adequately the same). In what follows, I refer to texts in which Scotus talks about a formal distinction between two things—paradigmatically, for my purposes here, two *properties* (items he labels "realities" or "formalities": *essential* properties of a thing)—and by and large Scotus in fact has in mind the notion of non-adequate sameness in the sense just outlined.

Scotus holds that the various components in a complete individual substance satisfy the fifth kind of unity, but not the sixth:

> Whatever is common and yet determinable can still be distinguished (no matter how much it is one thing) into several formally distinct realities of which this one is not formally that one. This one is formally the entity of singularity and that one is formally the entity of the nature. These two realities cannot be distinguished as "thing" and "thing".... Rather when in the same thing... they are always formally distinct realities of the same thing.[20]

The idea is that the complete individual substance—the item that is *per se* one—necessarily includes two entities formally distinct from each other: the individualized nature (the item that is denominatively one) and the individuator (the item that is primarily one).

2. ESSENCE AND EXISTENCE IN CREATURES: (1) FORMAL DISTINCTION

Now, thus understood, the theory that existence individuates would maintain that existence is the *actuality* of an essence, and thus determines the essence to actually existing as this or that (or these or those) individuals. Scotus presents the view—which he rejects—as follows:

> The ultimate distinction occurs through the ultimate act. But the ultimate act of individuals is according to their being of existence (*esse exsistentiae*), because everything other than that is understood in potency to that.[21]

[20] Scotus, *Ord.* II, d. 3, p. 1, qq. 5–6 (Vatican VII, 484; Spade 107).
[21] Scotus, *Ord.* II, d. 3, p. 1, q. 3, n. 60 (Vatican VII, 418; Spade 72).

The idea as Scotus understands it would be, I think, that a complete individual substance includes an individualized essence and actual existence (which on this theory would be the individuator): presumably on the grounds that all individualized essences exist, and that only actually existent substances include such essences.

Scotus rejects this view about individuation, since (he maintains) existence is no more determinate than essence: existence is common to different particulars in just the same way as essence is, and is differentiated by whatever features individuate essence. It thus cannot be the individuator responsible for making the nature denominatively one and the whole particular *per se* one:

> There is the same question about existence as there is about the nature: By what and from where is it contracted, so that it is "this"? If the specific nature is the same in several individuals, it has the same kind of existence in them. Just as it is proved... that the nature is not of itself a "this", so too it can be asked what it is through which existence is a "this", because it is not "this" of itself. So it is not enough to give existence as that by which the nature is a this.[22]

This way of arguing does not question the objector's view that existence should be thought of as the ultimate act of an individual (to which everything else in the individual is in some way in potency), or that there is some kind of distinction between essence and existence.

Scotus is quite explicit as to the kind of distinction that obtains in this case: it is a *formal* distinction: "'This man' does not formally include existence any more than 'man' in general does."[23] To fail to include something formally is to be formally distinct from it, as we can see from the definition of formal inclusion:

> To include something formally is to include something in its essential notion, such that, if we can assign a definition to the including thing, what is included would be the definition or a part of the definition.... And a definition does not indicate merely a concept caused by the intellect, but the quiddity of a thing.[24]

A presupposition of the claim that "this man does not formally include existence" is that there can be something like a "definition" of a particular. Now, while Scotus holds that individuals cannot be defined, he maintains nevertheless they are "*per se* intelligible,"[25] and are such that "some notion

[22] Scotus, *Ord.* II, d. 3, p. 1, q. 3, n. 64 (Vatican VII, 419; Spade 73).

[23] Scotus, *Ord.* II, d. 3, p. 1, q. 3, n. 63 (Vatican VII, 419; Spade 73). Note that it is not the individual essence itself—the item that is denominatively one—that is properly distinguished from existence: it is the whole individual, including the individuator.

[24] Scotus, *Ord.* I, d. 8, p. 1, q. 4, n. 193 (Vatican IV, 261–2).

[25] Scotus, *Ord.* II, d. 3, p. 1, qq. 5–6, n. 193 (Vatican VII, 486; Spade 108).

is able to express whatever accords with the nature of the individual."[26] The reason for this is that he believes that the individuator—the item that is primarily one and explains individuation—is a haecceity: haecceities cannot be defined, but they can, in principle, be known, and the individual thus have a proper "notion." (Thus, the concept of the individual is prior to any accidental modification of that individual: so the concept that Scotus has in mind is not just a definite description, but some concept that rigidly designates the individual as a composite of essence and individuator.)

All of this has a direct bearing on the essence/existence question: claiming that essence does not include existence, and additionally that the individual does not include its existence (as Scotus claims), is a way of holding that existence does not enter into the definition of the essence; or, in the case at hand, that it does not enter into the definition (if such there were) or notion of the individual itself (i.e. the essence along with the individuator). The reason for this is that if existence entered into the notion of the individual then (Scotus maintains) the individual would be a necessary existent. Thus, in one passage Scotus argues that God formally includes existence: it is part of his essence, of what it is to be God—presumably since God is a necessary existent:

> This man is an individual in the genus of substance, and he does not include actual existence, because only God intrinsically includes actual existence.[27]

So Scotus accepts this kind of distinction—between the individual and its existence—because he sees no other way of maintaining the *contingent* nature of creaturely existence (I return to this claim in a moment, since it is not obviously true). As Scotus puts it, existence is, in this very restricted sense, something like a necessary accident of the individual substance:

> This distinction [between the individual and existence] is so to speak accidental in a certain sense.[28]

What Scotus means is that, as such, existence is included neither in the essence or quiddity of the individual, nor in the individual itself, represented in its notion (and hence existence is an accident of some kind, and the individual a contingent existent). Conversely, the definition of God includes all the divine attributes and existence, and this makes God a necessary existent (something I return to in a moment).

The claim about creatures is not that (e.g.) an existent human being does not include existence, but that "this human being" does not include

[26] Scotus, *Ord.* II, d. 3, p. 1, qq. 5–6, n. 194 (Vatican VII, 487; Spade 108).

[27] Scotus, *Reportatio* II, d. 12, q. 7, n. 1 (Wadding XI, 330b).

[28] Scotus, *Ord.* II, d. 3, p. 1, q. 3, n. 65 (Vatican VII, 420; Spade 73–4).

existence. What could Scotus mean by this mystifying claim (distinguishing between e.g. Socrates and existent-Socrates)? Scotus attempts to explain what he has in mind by appealing to the notion of a "categorial hierarchy":

> The ultimate distinction in a categorial hierarchy is the individual distinction, and it occurs through the ultimate act that pertains to the categorial hierarchy. But actual existence does not by itself pertain to this hierarchy. Actual existence is the ultimate act, but it is posterior to the whole categorial hierarchy.[29]

And a little earlier in the same discussion of individuation:

> In a categorial hierarchy, there are contained all the things that pertain by themselves to that hierarchy, disregarding whatever is irrelevant to that hierarchy. For according to the Philosopher, in *Posterior Analytics* I [ch. 20 (82a21–24)], "there is an end-point in each category, at the high end and at the low end." Therefore, just as there is found a highest in a genus, considering it precisely under the aspect of essence, so there are found intermediate genera, and species and difference. There is also found there a lowest, namely, the singular—actual existence being disregarded altogether.[30]

The background is Porphyry's tree: any categorial item falls under a highest genus—the category itself—and this genus can be successively divided—by specific differences—until we end up at the "most specific species": the natural kinds (substance-kinds and accident-kinds, whatever they be) that exist in the world. Scotus here extends this hierarchy to include the individual—including the individual essence—and still distinguishes the individual from its actual existence since, as I just noted, individuals are contingent, and (according to Scotus) thus require something additional in order to exist. (Talk of a categorial hierarchy here makes it clear, incidentally, that Scotus makes the same kinds of claims about the individuation and existence of accidents too—not only is an accident individuated by a haecceity intrinsic to it, it includes its own existence, distinct from that of the substance in which it inheres.)[31]

The claim about the exclusion of existence from the categorial hierarchy, incidentally, explains why the early commentators interpreted what Scotus says about the relation of essence and existence in terms of a modal distinction: existence is posterior to any and every quiddity, and modes are things that, as Meyronnes puts it, when they come "to some form or quiddity," do "not alter its formal notion." But Scotus does not make this

[29] Scotus, *Ord.* II, d. 3, p. 1, q. 3, n. 65 (Vatican VII, 420; Spade 73).

[30] Scotus, *Ord.* II, d. 3, p. 1, q. 3, n. 63 (Vatican VII, 419–20; Spade 73).

[31] On their individuation, see section 2 of my "Duns Scotus on Sameness"; on their existence, see Scotus, *Ord.* III, d. 6, q. 1, nn. 27 and 37 (Vatican IX, 241, 243); and particularly *Ord.* IV, d. 12, p. 1, q. 1, n. 17 (Vatican XII, 304).

modalization claim about essence and existence explicitly, and he refers to the existence—like the haecceity—not as a modalization of an essence but as something formally distinct from it.[32] (Note that, even given all this, Scotus does not accept a realm of *possibilia*: real but non-actual essences or individuals—something I return to in Section 5.)

The claim that "the distinction [between the individual and existence] is so to speak accidental in a certain sense" suggests a way in which we might picture the metaphysical make-up of the existent individual, though this is not something that Scotus explores explicitly. My suggestion is this, and it parallels what Scotus says about the unity of the nature in the particular. In the unity case, Scotus suggests that the individuator is primarily one, the whole individual substance *per se* one, and the particularized nature denominatively one. If existence is "so to speak accidental" to the individual, it might be reasonable to propose that the individual—say Socrates—is denominatively (i.e. accidentally) existent (existent in virtue of some feature extrinsic to Socrates, or to the categorial hierarchy), even though, of course, existence is not accidental to, or extrinsic to, existent-Socrates, and existent-Socrates exists *per se*, not denominatively. The crucial thing, at any rate, is that what it is to be Socrates does not include existence—on pain of Socrates's being a necessary existent.

There seems to me to be an obvious objection to all this: why should Scotus take the requirement of creaturely contingency to require any kind of extramental distinction between essence and existence? Claiming that existence cannot be included in the concept of thing, on the face of it, merely means that the question of existence is always and only a question of whether or not such-and-such a concept is realized, and as such existence is a property of a concept (viz. its realization), not of a real thing. Seen in this way, the question about the existence of an individual, for Scotus, would be about whether or not such-and-such a notion of an individual is realized, and the point of the distinction between essence and existence is that existence in contingent cases can never be included in any such notion. Still, on the face of it claiming that a notion or concept is realized does not seem to require anything more than a conceptual distinction between the notion and existence (i.e. existence is not included in the relevant *concept*). And this seems to undermine Scotus's key argument, to the effect that

[32] Although Scotus does not refer to existence as a mode, he does on occasion refer to the haecceity as an "individual degree" of the nature: see Scotus, *Quaestiones super libros metaphysicorum Aristotelis* [= *In metaph.*] VII, q. 13, n. 136 (*Opera Philosophica* IV, 265). For a defense of a modalization understanding of haecceities in Scotus, see Peter King, "Duns Scotus on the Individual Differentia and Common Nature," *Philosophical Topics* 20 (1992), 50–76.

contingency requires more than a merely conceptual distinction between essence and existence. But this conclusion would perhaps be too quick. Scotus's position here is based on some kind of isomorphism between our conceptualizations and the real items that they pick out: if the concept of the individual does not include existence, then the individual—the item in the categorial hierarchy—cannot do so either.[33] Of course, what Scotus needs to do is to justify the reality of the categorial hierarchy in some sense independently of existence. A first step is to highlight our ability (or that of some idealized cognizer) to *identify* individuals irrespective of their existence, or to make *de re* modal claims about individuals irrespective of their existence. Scotus's account of individuation is clearly relevant here (since it is his generous account of individuation, allowing "notions" of individuals, prior to any accidental modification of those individuals, not a generous account of reality (e.g. as including *possibilia*), that sanctions this kind of modal practice). But, secondly, I think Scotus wants his account of the constitution of an existent individual to do some kind of explanatory work: our ability (or that of some ideal cognizer) to identify individuals irrespective of their existence means that, in an actually existent thing, there needs to be some feature in virtue of which it is the *individual* that it is, and some feature in virtue of which it is *existent*, and simply appealing to different ways of conceptualizing the same thing will not do this explanatory work.

So Scotus thinks of existence as some kind of property (a formally distinct constituent) of an existent individual—albeit, on this showing, a very odd kind of property. A property is that in virtue of which something is, or is such-and-such: a property is, in the medieval jargon, a formal cause, an *id quo*, not an *id quod*. As Scotus puts it,

> Any nature, as it exists in itself and as a nature, is communicable . . . to many *supposita* . . . as *that in virtue of*, as a form in virtue of which the singular or *suppositum* is a being with a quiddity, or one having a nature.[34]

And Scotus talks of existence in just this way. Existence is that "in virtue of which (*quo*)" things exist. For example, Scotus argues that concrete parts of a substance exist in virtue of the existence of the whole substance in a way analogous to that in which a whole exists in virtue of that existence:

[33] This isomorphism is not unprincipled, as I hope to show in the rest of this paragraph. Scotus always works hard to distinguish cases in which there is some kind of isomorphism, and cases in which there is not: this, I take it, is part of the philosophical task of attempting to cut at the joints.

[34] Scotus, *Ord.* I, d. 2, p. 2, qq. 1–4, nn. 379–80 (Vatican II, 346).

My foot exists through my existence. For this reason, the existence of my foot is not other than that by which (*quo*) I exist, but is merely a partial existence within that by which I exist.[35]

But existence is an odd kind of property in the sense that it is excluded from the entire categorial hierarchy—from the entire realm of quiddities and haecceities.

Despite this, Scotus is nevertheless happy to affirm, as in the second of the passages quoted in this section, that there are different kinds of existences, and numerically distinct existences, and that the kinds of existences, and numerical distinction of existences, exactly track the distinctions in kinds and individuals that they presuppose:

The being of existence (*esse exsistentiae*), in the sense in which it is distinguished from the being of essence (*esse essentiae*), is not of itself distinct or determinate. For the being of existence does not have its own differences other than the differences of the being of essence, because in that case one would have to posit a proper hierarchy of existences other than the hierarchy of essences. Rather the being of existence is precisely determined from something else's determination [i.e. by the determination of the being of essence].[36]

Distinctions between kinds of existences, and the individuation of existences, are parasitic on distinctions between essences, on the one hand, and individuals, on the other, in the categorial hierarchy. Making distinction and individuation parasitic on the categorial hierarchy does not amount to making essence prior to existence *tout court*: indeed, I will give important evidence in Section 6 below to show that in some sense existence is prior to essence—that, despite its status as an (odd) feature or property of an existent, an *id quo*, existence includes the *positing* of the individual, prior to any further determination.

Thus far I have by and large spoken merely of a distinction between essence and existence. But I just quoted a passage that speaks more particularly of the being of existence—*esse exsistentiae*—and contrasts it with the being of essence—*esse essentiae*—and before I continue we need to get clear on this terminology, terminology that seems to have been introduced into the debate by Henry of Ghent.[37] As we saw above, Scotus talks about an essence's *primary entity*: that which is "the *per se* object of the intellect and is

[35] Scotus, *Ord.* III, d. 6, q. 1, n. 36 (Vatican IX, 243).

[36] Scotus, *Ord.* II, d. 3, p. 1, q. 3, n. 61 (Vatican VII, 418–19; Spade 72–3).

[37] The distinction first occurs in Henry, *Quodlibet* [= *Quod.*] I, q. 9 ((Paris, 1518), fos. 6v–7r), some twenty-five years or so earlier than the major text examined in this section.

per se, as such, considered by the metaphysician and expressed by the definition." This entity is referred to by Scotus as the essence's *esse essentiae*:

About *esse essentiae*, there is the true account of the Philosopher, *Topics* I,[38] "A definition is an utterance that indicates the what-it-is-to-be of a thing," and of Porphyry,[39] "The being of any thing is one and the same, and does not receive any intensification or diminution."[40]

And Scotus holds that this kind of *esse* differs from the essence as such "merely in our mode of conceiving it":[41] it is perhaps possible to think of an essence independently of its *esse essentiae*, or under a different description, but for sure the essence and its *esse essentiae*, its primary entity, are (in our Leibnizian sense) identical. But what is of interest here is the distinction between essence/*esse essentiae* and *esse exsistentiae*. One important clarification: just as the essence only has entity *when it actually exists* in the existent particular, so too it only has *esse essentiae* in that case too. I return to this towards the end of Section 5, discussing Scotus's interpretation of some claims made by Henry of Ghent. The important claim is that an existent individual includes *esse essentiae*, an existent particularized nature (i.e. the item with *esse essentiae*, denominatively one), an existent individuator, and *esse exsistentiae*.

3. ESSENCE AND EXISTENCE IN CREATURES: (2) REAL DISTINCTION REJECTED

Thus far I have argued that Scotus accepts a formal distinction between essence and existence, and between an individual and its existence. Some medieval thinkers hold that there is some kind of *real* distinction between essence and existence. Aquinas, for example, holds something like this, affirming both a real distinction of essence and existence, and their real composition in a particular substance;[42] and he is followed in a rather different way by Giles of Rome.[43] Nowhere, however, in the texts that

38 Aristotle, *Topics* 1.4 (101b39).

39 Porphyry, *Isagoge* 3 (ed. Minio-Paluello 16 (3a47–8)).

40 Scotus, *Lectura* [= *Lect.*] III, d. 6, q. 1, n. 29 (Vatican XX, 177).

41 Scotus, *Ord.* III, d. 6, q. 1, n. 7 (Vatican IX, 226).

42 For real distinction, see e.g. Aquinas, *In de hebd.* (Leonine L, 273); for real composition, see e.g. Aquinas, *Summa theologiae* [= *ST*] I, q. 50, a. 2 ad 3.

43 On Giles, see conveniently John F. Wippel, "The Relationship Between Essence and Existence in Late-Thirteenth-Century Thought: Giles of Rome, Henry of Ghent, Godfrey of Fontaines, and James of Viterbo," in P. Morewedge (ed.), *Philosophies of Existence Ancient and Medieval* (New York: Fordham University Press, 1982), 134–41.

I have considered thus far—Scotus's central discussion of the essence/existence question—does Scotus tackle this view. The closest he comes is the following rather fleeting comment, elsewhere in his *corpus* (I italicize the relevant clauses):

> For just as *being* (*ens*) and *one* are divided into simple and complex, so to be (*esse*) and to be one (*esse unum*) are divided into simple and complex. . . . In this way there is one existence (*esse*) of the whole composite, even though it includes many partial existences, just as a whole is one being (*ens*) which has and includes many partial beings. *For I do not know that fiction that existence is something* (*quid*) *that supervenes on essence*, and that is non-composite even though the essence is composite.[44]

Clearly, Scotus could not accept a real distinction between essence and existence, or between the individual and its existence, since (as I showed in Section 1) Scotus holds that real distinction requires separability, and Scotus does not hold that an essence or individual has any reality independent of its existence—something I return to in Section 5 below. So it is perhaps no surprise that he does not consider the view at great length. (Obviously, Aquinas does not share Scotus's account of distinction and sameness—but this is an issue for another time.)[45]

In this passage, Scotus's disagreement with Aquinas has nothing much to do with the supposed separability of really distinct components. Rather, Scotus is attempting to argue against Aquinas's claim that unity of existence requires unicity of substantial form. According to Aquinas, we can infer from the fact that a substance is just one existent that a substance includes just one substantial form, since, as he maintains, unity of existence is parasitic on unicity of form.[46] Scotus disagrees: there can be more than one substantial form in a composite substance, and there is no one-to-one correspondence between existence and substantial form.[47] Just as one composite can include prime matter and more than one substantial form, so too the one existence of the composite can itself be composite, embracing both prime matter and any (and all) of the substantial forms of the composite. Scotus does not deny that one substance is one existent, with one existence; but by denying the simplicity of existence, he believes

[44] Scotus, *Ord.* IV, d. 11, p. 1, q. 2, a. 1, nn. 250–1 (Vatican XII, 255).

[45] Likewise, Aquinas's composition claims are very different from Scotus's (claims to which I return in Section 5), not least because Aquinas denies any reality to the essence independent of its actual existence: on this question, Aquinas is far more nominalist than Scotus. See Aquinas, *De ente* 3 (Leonine XLIII, 373).

[46] See e.g. Aquinas, *ST* I, q. 76, a. 4 c.

[47] Scotus, *Ord.* IV, d. 11, p. 1, q. 2, a. 1, nn. 285–7 (Vatican XII, 267–8). On this, see my *The Physics of Duns Scotus: The Scientific Context of a Theological Vision* (Oxford: Clarendon Press, 1998), chap. 4.

himself to have undermined Aquinas's reasoning from unity of existence to unicity of substantial form. But the passage tells us something substantive about Scotus's views on essence and existence, and it is this: that the individuation and specification of *esse* tracks the individuation and specification of essence—as we saw above. We should not take the text as evidence that Scotus denies any kind of distinction between essence and existence.

4. ESSENCE AND EXISTENCE IN GOD

In creaturely cases, then, an individual's existence is formally distinct from the individual: existence is a property in the sense that it is an *id quo*, though excluded from the categorial hierarchy and "so to speak accidental" to the individual. What about the divine case? I think there is a sense in which Scotus would affirm something similar in the case of God too: that God's existence is formally distinct from God. The cases are different in various respects, of course, the most significant one of which is that Scotus holds God's essence and existence to be formally and adequately the same; the distinction between God's existence and God himself is a simple consequence of a conceptually prior distinction between God's essence and God himself. Thus, as we saw above, Scotus explicitly maintains that God "intrinsically includes actual existence." At heart, then, a good part of the issue has to do with claims that Scotus makes about divine simplicity—in particular, the distinction between God's essence and God himself. It is Scotus's loosening of the concept of divine simplicity (compared to some of his rivals) that allows him to block the inference from identity of essence and existence in God to the identity of God with his existence, or with his essence. So I deal first with various aspects of the simplicity issue, and then go on to relate the discussion specifically to the question of the adequate sameness (identity) of God's essence and existence, and the formal distinction between God's existence and God himself.

That Scotus posits a formal distinction between the various divine attributes is something that has been frequently noticed in the literature:[48] it is, indeed, a highly distinctive and characteristic feature of his theology. Less frequently observed is Scotus's claim that the divine essence is formally distinct from the divine attributes too. Scotus makes this latter point as part

[48] For recent examples, see e.g. Martin M. Tweedale, *Scotus vs. Ockham: A Medieval Dispute Over Universals*, 2 vols. (Lewiston: Edwin Mellen, 1999), 559–74; and my *Duns Scotus on God* (Aldershot: Ashgate, 2005), 103–13.

of a complex exegesis of some claims made by the Greek Church Fathers, mediated to him specifically through John of Damascus. The central claim, going back at least as far as Gregory of Nyssa, is that there is a distinction between God's essence and those things that are "around" the essence—the divine attributes. John of Damascus claims that the divine essence is like an "infinite and indeterminate sea (*pelugus*) of substance,"[49] and Scotus interprets this to mean that the divine essence somehow explains all of the other divine attributes (the things around the essence), which are likened to *propria* of that substance.[50] An interpretation that Scotus is anxious to block would maintain that the divine essence is such a "sea" because it is *formally the same* as these various attributes—which in this context he understands to mean adequately the same: *identical.* Rather, Scotus maintains, God is something that formally includes the divine essence and attributes; the divine essence is formally distinct from the attributes, even though it somehow explains the presence of the attributes.[51] And on this showing, the divine essence is formally distinct from God, and non-adequately the same as God, too.

Now, this has a bearing on the question of God's existence in its relation to the divine essence and to God. On the first of these, Scotus is happy to claim that the divine essence is (formally or adequately) identical with (God's) *esse*, such that there is merely a rational distinction between the two:

> The Damascene claims that, of all the names said of God, the most proper is "he who is" (*qui est*), because *esse* means "a certain sea of infinite substance," whereas the other [names] . . . mean those things which stand around (*circumstant*) the nature.[52]

Here the divine *esse* is identified with the divine substance, and this substance is contrasted with those things that "stand around the nature"—from which we can infer too that the divine substance is identical to the divine nature. And God's *esse* is formally the same as his essence,[53]

[49] John of Damascus, *De fide orthodoxa* 4 (ed. Buytaert 21, ll. 43–5).

[50] Scotus, *Ord.* I, d. 8, p. 1, q. 4, nn. 200–1 (Vatican IV, 265–6).

[51] Scotus, *Ord.* I, d. 8, p. 1, q. 4, n. 199 (Vatican IV, 264–5).

[52] Scotus, *Ord.* I, d. 8, p. 1, q. 4, n. 198 (Vatican IV, 264). For the claim about a merely rational distinction between essence and *esse*, as between all concrete and abstract items in God, see *Ord.* I, d. 8, p. 1, q. 4, nn. 191, 203 (Vatican IV, 260, 267). As is clear from the quotations just given, Scotus changes John's "infinite . . . sea of substance" to "sea of infinite substance." There are reasons for this, but as far as I can see nothing of importance turns on them for my purposes here, and I do not offer any comment.

[53] Note that this does not violate Scotus's claim that existence must lie outside the categorial hierarchy, and thus outside essence. According to the medievals, God lies outside any categorial hierarchy: see e.g. Scotus, *Ord.* I, d. 8, p. 1, q. 3, n. 95 (Vatican IV, 198).

since (Scotus avers) God to be wholly actual, both in the sense of not being able to be affected by anything (not being the end term of any power—not being in "objective potency"), and of not being subject of accidental modifications (not being in "subjective potency"—I return to these two kinds of potency in Section 5 below). Since God lacks these potencies, he is, if he exists at all, a necessary existent.[54] Now, the lack of these potencies is understood by Scotus to entail that no constituent of the divine could include such a potency:

> A necessary existent (*necesse esse*) includes nothing that is not either a necessary existent or a ground of existing necessarily (*ratio necessario essendi*).[55]

Just as in the creaturely case, existence does not line itself up, as it were, alongside the quidditative or qualitative properties of God: it pervades them all, in one of two ways—either because they are themselves necessary, or because they are a ground of existing necessarily. In line with this, Scotus very occasionally talks of God as "a being that is *ipsum esse*"—existence itself—though one senses that he does so only in the course of refuting the views of an opponent who uses this kind of language (language that is, of course, strongly associated with Thomas Aquinas).[56] And I take it that the distinction between the divine essence and God's other features helps us to understand what Scotus means by distinguishing between those things in God that are necessary existents from those things in God that are grounds of existing necessarily: the latter (I assume) will be the divine essence/*esse*, and the former the things around the essence—God's wisdom, goodness, and blessedness, to take Scotus's examples.[57]

All of this implies that there is a distinction between God's essence/existence, God's attributes, and God himself. God *includes* the divine essence/existence, and also the divine attributes (the things that stand around the nature). So, like the divine nature or essence itself, God's *esse*

[54] This inference, which I do not discuss here, forms the key conclusion in Scotus's complex proof for God's existence: see *Ord.* I, d. 2, p. 1, qq. 1–2, nn. 57–9, 70 (Vatican II, 162–5, 169–71).

[55] Scotus, *Ord.* I, d. 2, p. 1, qq. 1–2, *text. int.* (Vatican II, 172, ll. 16–17).

[56] Scotus, *Ord.* I, d. 3, p. 2, q. un., n. 326 (Vatican III, 197). The opponent is Richard of Conington, a Franciscan colleague of Scotus's and a close follower of Henry of Ghent. For the identification, see the report of his opinion in a question by an anonymous early Scotist edited by Stephen F. Brown and Stephen D. Dumont, "Univocity of the Concept of Being in the Early Fourteenth Century: III. An Early Scotist," *Mediaeval Studies* 51 (1989), 56–7, ll. 588–97. For Aquinas's assertion of God as *ipsum esse subsistens*, an entailment from God's pure actuality, see e.g. Aquinas, *ST* I, q. 4, a. 2 c, and of course see too the crucial discussion of the identity of God's essence and *esse* in Aquinas, *ST* I, q. 3, a. 4 c.

[57] See Scotus, *Ord.* I, d. 8, p. 1, q. 4, n. 199 (Vatican IV, 265).

must be formally included in God himself, but not be adequately or formally the same as God (since God includes other features formally distinct from his essence and *esse*). And since the divine essence is that in virtue of which (*id quo*) God is divine,[58] I assume that the divine *esse* is such too. This does not exactly make existence a property of God's, but—as in the case of an existent creature—it does make existence something that is formally included in God without being identical to him (since God includes other features too). Unlike a creature, of course, God's existence is simply identical with his essence. These issues are deep and hard; it is perhaps a mark of Scotus's basic indifference to the identification of God and his *esse*, made so centrally by Aquinas, that the reader has to put so much effort into uncovering anything at all of what he actually thought on the question.

5. ESSENCE, EXISTENCE, AND THREE VARIETIES OF POTENCY

In texts I discussed in Section 2, Scotus claims that essence is potential to the actuality of existence, or that existence is the ultimate act of a thing. In this section, I consider what Scotus has to say about this. Scotus never discusses the issue systematically, but in one late text—questions 1–2 of book IX of the questions on Aristotle's *Metaphysics*—he introduces three relevant senses of potency and relates one of these to the question of essence and existence; and elsewhere he shows too how the remaining two senses line up with the essence/existence issue. I consider the three senses in turn. In doing so, I clarify what Scotus has to say about the ways in which essence as potency does or does not enter into any kind of composition with existence as actuality; and I show too that (as we might expect from the discussion thus far) Scotus explicitly rejects any kind of real but non-actual *possibilia*—items in the categorial hierarchy, individual or common, distinct from their existence, would be natural candidates for such items.

The kind of potency relevant to this discussion is labeled "metaphysical potency," and in the *Metaphysics* text Scotus discerns three possible varieties:

> [Metaphysical potency] is understood in three ways. [1] In one way it is opposed to the impossible, not as it implies the way of composition... but as it means the disposition of something non-complex.... And in this way the possible is co-extensive with the whole of being, for nothing is a being whose notion includes

[58] See e.g. Scotus, *Ord.* I, d. 23, q. un., n. 16 (Vatican V, 357).

a contradiction. [2] In another way potency is understood as it is opposed to the necessary . . . ; and in this way the necessary is said to be what has of itself indefectible entity, and possible being that [has] defectible [entity]. [3] In the third way metaphysical potency is taken most strictly, as it is incompatible with act in the same respect (*circa idem*).[59]

These potencies are features of *things*, and are all distinguished from logical possibility, which Scotus identifies as a property of *propositions* (complexes or, as Scotus refers to them in this passage, (syntactic) *composites*), and which he understands in much the same way as we do (hardly a surprise, since Scotus is most likely the originator of the terminology of logical possibility).[60] All three of these varieties of metaphysical potency—the details of which I outline below—are relevant to the question of essence and existence, and in this section I discuss them in turn. I do so in reverse order, since it is the third kind of metaphysical potency that Scotus explicitly relates to the essence/existence relation. I do not think that anything I discuss in this section creates problems for the basic picture sketched in the sections above, and neither do I think that it adds anything vital. But my aim is completeness: to deal with texts that on the face of it are hard to integrate into the overall picture, and to show that when properly interpreted they do not raise any difficulties.

a. Metaphysical potency (type 3): Objective potency

The third kind of metaphysical potency—that which is "incompatible with act in the same respect"—is labeled by Scotus "objective potency,"[61] and the most extensive and straightforward discussion of it occurs in a long treatment of the nature of prime matter in the (early) *Lectura*:[62]

Something is said to be in potency in two ways: in one way, because it is the end term of a power (*potentia*), or is that to which the power is directed, and this is said to be objectively in potency (as the Antichrist, or whiteness that is to be generated, is said in one way to be a being in potency). In the other way, something is said to be in potency as the subject of a potency, or that in which the potency is. And in this

59 Scotus, *In metaph.* IX, qq. 1–2, n. 21 (OP IV, 515).

60 For logical possibility, see Scotus, *In metaph.* IX, qq. 1–2, n. 18 (OP IV, 514). On Scotus's role in the development of the notion, see Simo Knuuttila, *Modalities in Medieval Philosophy* (London: Routledge, 1993), 139–49.

61 See Scotus, *In metaph.* IX, qq. 1–2, nn. 43–4 (OP IV, 525–6).

62 The discussion has no parallel in later texts, since the relevant section of the *Ordinatio* was not completed, and since the relevant section of the *Reportatio* discussion deals not with the nature of matter but with the question of individuation.

way something is said to be in potency subjectively, because it is in potency to something but not yet perfected by it (as a surface that is to be made white).[63]

The idea is the Aristotelian one that something that is not but can be ϕ is potentially ϕ ("subjective potency"), generalized to include the further claim that something that is not at all but that will be *exists* potentially ("objective potency"). As Scotus understands it, objective potency is among other things the "pure potency" that his opponents ascribe to prime matter, and he objects that, as thus understood, prime matter will be nothing at all, and thus cannot be a part of a composite in the way that prime matter is supposed to be:

Those who say that matter is in potency in the first way say that it is simply speaking a non-being.... So matter is not a being in potency in the first way.... How can matter be a real part of an actual being if it is merely a potency to being? Because that which is the end term of a power is not a real part of an actual being while it is thus in potency.[64]

Prime matter, according to Scotus, must have *subjective* potency—it must be able to be a substrate for properties, or for substantial form—and thus have some kind of real actuality of its own.[65]

Scotus makes the non-composition claim very vividly: objectively potential individuals are *not* components of their actualizations:

For it is not from the fact that something was previously in potency and is now in act that there is one thing by the unity of composition (because whiteness is not more composite if it was previously in potency and is now in act than it would be if it was always in simple act; and if it were created, it would first be in itself wholly in potency and later in act).[66]

As Scotus makes clear in the *Metaphysics* text, objective potency thus understood "is incompatible with act in the same respect." (This incompatibility claim is important for my purposes here, and I return to it below.)

The burden of the *Metaphysics* discussion is to work out the relationship between essence (I assume: individualized essence, but probably nothing turns on this) and objective potency. The specific question Scotus sets out to answer is whether objective potency requires any kind of grounding.[67] The reason for the question is that objective potency is a relation (it is an ordering to something actual—i.e. the complete existent thing): hence the

63 Scotus, *Lect.* II, d. 12, q. un., n. 30 (Vatican XIX, 80).
64 Scotus, *Lect.* II, d. 12, q. un., nn. 31–3 (Vatican XIX, 80–1).
65 Scotus, *Lect.* II, d. 12, q. un., nn. 37–8 (Vatican XIX, 82).
66 Scotus, *Lect.* II, d. 12, q. un., n. 61 (Vatican XIX, 92).
67 Scotus, *In metaph.* IX, qq. 1–2, n. 27 (OP IV, 518).

worry about its being grounded, since real relations, according to Scotus, need to be grounded in something non-relational—they cannot be free-floating. Scotus considers two solutions, and both of them, in different ways, make explicit the connection between this discussion and the relation of essence and existence.

At issue, then, is the ground of the potency relation that has as its end term the actually existent individual. An assumption made in the whole discussion is that the potency cannot be grounded simply in the (future) existent individual as such, and the reason for this is that, as just noted, relations require *relata*, and in the case of real relations the *relata* cannot (it was held) be simply identical with each other. Here, the future existent is one *relatum*; the question is the identity of the other one. The first solution claims that objective potency is grounded on essence (whether common or individual—Scotus's example (again) is the future essence of (the soul of) the Antichrist). The idea is that the relevant potency is grounded in the essence, but that the complete future existent—including its *esse*—is objectively possible in virtue of the same potency: the ground of the possibility is the essence, and the end term of the relation—the thing that is really *possible*—is the complete existent. This view thus requires a distinction between essence and existence (or, more exactly, between the individual and the existent individual): one grounds the relation, and the other is the end term of the same relation; one is ordered to actuality, and the other is the actuality to which the first is ordered.[68]

The second solution claims that there is no ground for objective potency: objective potency is like a free-floating privation,[69] and the claim that objective potency has no ground entails that the "potency of the essence" is a merely rational relation to "*esse* as the end term" of that relation.[70] (The relation is rational because there are no real *relata* on this view at all; objective potency is just a way of thinking about the creature—i.e. as future, or as to-be-caused.) Scotus claims that, on this view, "the essence has absolutely no entity other than when it actually exists,"[71] and that if one take the further step of denying that essence has any entity of its own at all—if one hold that "essence and existence do not differ other than in

[68] Scotus, *In metaph.* IX, qq. 1–2, n. 27 (OP IV, 518).

[69] Scotus, *In metaph.* IX, qq. 1–2, n. 35 (OP IV, 522). I owe this talk of "free-floating privations" to John Boler, "The Ontological Commitment of Scotus's Account of Potency in his *Questions on the Metaphysics*, Book IX," in L. Honnefelder, R. Wood, and M. Dreyer (eds.), *John Duns Scotus: Metaphysics and Ethics* (Leiden: Brill, 1996), 153. Boler provides an excellent account of the grounding issue, fuller than mine here, though he does not explicitly relate it to the essence/existence question.

[70] Scotus, *In metaph.* IX, qq. 1–2, n. 36 (OP IV, 523).

[71] Scotus, *In metaph.* IX, qq. 1–2, n. 35 (OP IV, 523).

reason," as Scotus puts it—then one is likely to want to hold the second view (that objective potency is not grounded in essence, or, indeed, in anything at all).[72] After all, on the view that there is no distinction between essence and existence, there is and will be no essence, *distinct* from the concrete existent individual, in virtue of which that existent individual is the end term of a power; thus it cannot be the essence that grounds the contingency of that individual. So, on the second view about the grounding of objective potency, what explains the possibility of an individual (its being the future or possible end term of a power) is simply a free-floating, ungrounded, privation.

Clearly, the first view is compatible with the claim that there is a distinction between essence and existence: indeed, as I just presented it, it presupposes this claim. As it happens, Scotus prefers the second view on the grounding question: "this second view seems to be able to be shown (*videtur...probabilis*)."[73] But while the claim that there is no distinction between essence and existence entails the second view on grounding, the opposite entailment does not hold: the fact that there is no ground for objective potency does not entail that the distinction between essence and existence is merely rational, and we should not take the text as evidence that Scotus accepts merely a rational distinction between essence and existence. After all, the second view suggests that essence has "no entity other than when it actually exists"; but this does not mean that the existent comprises just one entity—it certainly could be a composite that includes an essence-entity and something else besides, even though it is not in virtue of essence that the (future) existent will be the end term of a power.

Scotus does not say why he prefers the second view on the grounding question. But one obvious reason springs to mind. Objective potency is the potency attaching to what will be but is not. If objective potency is grounded in essence, it will be tempting to think that objective potency is an essential feature of a thing: that the thing is logically inevitable, so to speak. And Scotus would certainly want to reject this, not least because he believes that God's creation is radically contingent. So much for this whole discussion: all it shows is that Scotus's negative views on the grounding of objective potency are not taken by him to entail that there is no distinction between essence and existence, even though someone denying any such distinction ought indeed to accept the negative view on the grounding of objective potency.

[72] Scotus, *In metaph.* IX, qq. 1–2, n. 36 (OP IV, 523).
[73] Scotus, *In metaph.* IX, qq. 1–2, n. 36 (OP IV, 523).

b. Metaphysical potency (type 2): Contingency

I just noted that one of the features of objective potency is that it cannot be a component of anything. But at one point, Scotus seems to deny this claim—and this will take me on to a brief consideration of the second sense of "metaphysical potency" mentioned in the *Metaphysics* text that opens this section—the potency that is "opposed to the necessary." The context is a rejection of a view, that Scotus ascribes to Henry of Ghent, which identifies objective potency with *esse essentiae*, and which infers from this identification that possible but non-actual essences must have some kind of reality of their own, independent of actualization. The argument ascribed to Henry is that objective potencies cannot be free-floating, and thus that they require a subject—in this case, real but non-actual essences, real items with *esse essentiae* but not *esse exsistentiae*.[74] Scotus suggests in reply that we do not need it to be the case that *esse essentiae* implies some kind of reality wholly independently of *esse exsistentiae* in order for it to ground a potency. What we need, rather, is composition

> not of two positive things (*re et re positivis*), but from a positive thing and a privation, namely from some entity that it has and the lack of some degree of perfection of entity.[75]

Here *essence* is actual, and the subject of a privation, a lack of perfection: and this privation is the grounded (objective) potency, grounded (according to Scotus) in an existent essence.[76]

Note already that this seems to be a different sense of "objective potency" from that which I outlined above. Clearly, what bothers Scotus about Henry's view is that it maintains that, if there is *any* sense in which an essence is potential, then it must have some reality wholly independent of instantiation. Scotus goes on to note that anything that lacks perfection includes

[74] Scotus, *Ord.* II, d. 1, q. 2, n. 78 (Vatican VII, 42), referring to Henry, *Summa quaestionum ordinariarum* a. 1, q. 4 (Paris 1520, I, fo. 128rS). Scotus does not mention objective potency here; but he does in the reply (Scotus, *Ord.* II, d. 1, q. 2, n. 94 (Vatican VII, 49–50)), from which I infer that he understands Henry to be talking in some sense about objective potency.

[75] Scotus, *Ord.* I, d. 8, p. 1, q. 2, n. 32 (Vatican IV, 166)—a text he refers to as his refutation of Henry's attempt to argue in favor of the independent reality of essence: see Scotus, *Ord.* II, d. 1, n. 94 (Vatican VII, 50).

[76] Scotus, *Ord.* I, d. 8, p. 1, q. 2, n. 32 (Vatican IV, 166). I suppose this is the closest Scotus gets to thinking of degrees of actuality in this context: but note that the degree of entity is restricted by the potency that the essence grounds, and the question of degrees here has nothing to do with actual existence.

a composition of potency and act objectively: for whatever is a being, and lacks some perfection of being, is simply speaking possible, and simply speaking the end term of a power.[77]

The contrast is with the divine case: "infinite being, which is necessary being, cannot be the end term of a power."[78] So the sense of "potency" here is contingency, or contingency coupled with the relation of being the end term of a power—all of which Scotus sums up in the term "defectible" (what can be made and destroyed). On the face of it, this seems to concede something to Henry, as Scotus presents Henry's view: namely, that we can speak of composition between objective potency and actuality—in contrast to claims made in passages quoted above. But it seems to me that there is an important point being made in the passage that claims composition: essence explains or grounds *contingency*, and creatures are composites of something that explains contingency (essence/categorial hierarchy) and something that explains actuality (existence). And this is the second sense of "metaphysical potency" in the *Metaphysics* text; it is what is "opposed to the necessary." I take it that this is the sense relevant when Scotus claims—as he does in texts quoted in Section 2 above—that essence is potential to the actuality of existence. Scotus insists, for example, that when Avicenna asserts that "equinity is just equinity," many extraneous features of the essence (such as unity, actuality, and so on) are excluded, but *possibility* (contingency/defectibility) is not.[79] So I take it that in the passage in which Scotus claims that existent individuals are composites of objective potency and actuality he is using "objective potency" loosely, to refer to the potency that is identified with contingency: something that explains contingency (i.e. an item located properly in the categorial hierarchy) can enter into some kind of composition with actuality: actuality, or existence, is what (formally) explains the fact that such-and-such a contingent thing exists. This deals with the issue of the incompatibility of objective potency and act "in the same respect." In the passage that affirms composition, Scotus is simply not talking about objective potency in this strict sense, but with potency in some looser sense. And note, nevertheless, that Scotus *is* making composition claims: an existent substance is indeed a composite of the individual substance and its existence, or of the potential and the actual (or of the contingency-grounder (essence) and an actualizer (existence)). And I take it that this composition is between two formally distinct components (the individual substance and its existence).

[77] Scotus, *Ord.* I, d. 8, p. 1, q. 2, n. 33 (Vatican IV, 166).
[78] Scotus, *Ord.* I, d. 8, p. 1, q. 2, n. 33 (Vatican IV, 166).
[79] Scotus, *Ord.* I, d. 3, p. 2, q. un., n. 324 (Vatican III, 195).

c. Metaphysical potency (type 1): The non-contradictory

So what about this first kind of metaphysical potency? As Scotus presents it, this is (part of) the domain of the non-contradictory. But it is distinguished from logical possibility, as noted above: logical possibility is a property of syntactic complexes, whereas this kind of metaphysical potency "is opposed to the impossible, not as it implies the way of composition . . . but as it means the disposition of something non-complex."

Now, there are issues to sort out here, both terminological and substantive, if we are to arrive at a reasonably complete understanding of Scotus on essence. As in the *Metaphysics* passage quoted at the beginning of this section, Scotus persistently ascribes some kind of entity to *possibilia*, whether or not such things are actual ("In this way the possible is co-extensive with the whole of being, for nothing is a being whose notion includes a contradiction"). This reflects his persistent teaching on the matter: the domain of *being* (*ens*) or *thing* (*res*) in its broadest sense includes anything that does not involve a (logical) contradiction:

> In this most general understanding [of 'being' or 'thing'] . . . anything conceivable, which does not include a contradiction, is said to be a thing or a being.[80]

Does this not suggest a realm of real but non-actual *possibilia*? The quick (and correct) answer is, No, since Scotus is clear that the possible but non-actual is no less *nothing* than the metaphysically impossible (the relevant passage is complex; for ease of exegesis I number the sentences and italicize the crucial clause in sentence [11]):

> [1] Eternally, *not being something* is in man, and *not being something* is in chimera. [2] But the affirmation which is *being something* is not repugnant to man; rather, the negation is in man on account of the negation of any cause positing [man in existence]. [3] And [*being something*] is repugnant to chimera because no cause could cause it to be something. [4] But why [*being something*] is not repugnant to man and is repugnant to chimera is because this is this and that is that, . . . because . . . whatever is formally repugnant to something of itself is repugnant to it, and what is not formally repugnant to something of itself is not repugnant to it. [5] Neither should it be supposed that [existence] is not incompatible with man because man is a being in potency, and that it is repugnant to chimera because chimera is not a being in potency. [6] Rather, *vice versa*, it is because [existence] is not incompatible with man that man is possible by a logical possibility, and because [it is repugnant] to chimera [chimera] is therefore impossible by the impossibility opposed [to logical possibility]. [7] And objective potency follows this possibility, if we suppose the

[80] Scotus, *Quod.* 3, n. 2 (Wadding XII, 67).

omnipotence of God, which relates to everything possible (provided that is other than himself). [8] Nevertheless, this logical possibility, absolutely, in virtue of itself, can obtain even if, *per impossibile*, no omnipotence is related to it. [9] Therefore the reason that is entirely first, not reducible to any other, why existence is not repugnant to man is because man formally is man (and this whether really, in reality, or intelligibly, in the intellect). [10] And the first reason why existence is repugnant to chimera is [that chimera is chimera]-as-chimera. [11] So the negation that is nothingness (*nihileitas*) is differently in man and in chimera, eternally, and nevertheless *it is not on account of this that the one is more nothing than the other.*[81]

Note, first, that this passage is strictly speaking about metaphysical possibility, not logical possibility: the relevant modalities are features not of syntactic complexes but of non-propositional intensions (*man*, *chimera*)—the modalities are "disposition[s] of something non-complex." These metaphysical possibilities ground logical possibilities, as we shall see.

Here is a discussion of the passage, sentence by sentence. [1] Scotus begins by noting that it is not the case that human beings and chimeras have always existed. [2] But it is possible that there are human beings, and the reason why human beings have not always existed is simply that there was no cause that eternally created them. [3] And (at a first pass at dealing with the question) it seems that chimeras cannot exist because nothing can cause them. [4] But, Scotus tells us, this is not quite right: existence is formally repugnant to chimera, and not to man, simply because each is the kind of thing it is.[82] [5] And this incompatibility is not explained by the fact that man is a being in potency, and chimera not. [6] Rather, it is logically possible that there are human beings, and not logically possible that there are chimeras. Logical possibility is *de dicto*, and across all possible worlds (as we would say): it is true that, possibly, there are human beings, and not true that, possibly, there are chimeras. And this is explained by the fact that the essence, *man*, is what it is, and the "essence", *chimera*,[83] is what it is—the logical possibility of "there are human beings" is grounded in the metaphysical possibility or potency that attaches to—is included in—the essence *human being*. [7] Objective potency is the potency that relates to

[81] Scotus, *Ord.* I, d. 36, q. un., nn. 60–2 (Vatican VI, 296–7). Scotus goes on to consider an alternative account, but he considers it less "real," and I ignore it here (see Scotus, *Ord.* I, d. 36, q. un., n. 63 (Vatican VI, 297)).

[82] Scotus clearly imagines that chimeras are lion, goat, and serpent *all over*, so to speak, and thus that it is logically impossible that there is any such thing.

[83] I put "essence" in scare quotes because Scotus denies that, strictly speaking, there are essences of *impossibilia*: see e.g. Scotus, *Ord.* I, d. 3, p. 2, q. un., n. 319 (Vatican III, 193).

some power, and Scotus notes that this potency, which, given divine power, is a feature of *man*, is grounded in the essence *man* (supposing what Scotus claims in [4] and [6]). (Here Scotus presupposes the first view on the grounding of objective potency laid out in the *Metaphysics* questions. On the second view, nothing is different other than the denial that this potency is grounded at all. But the clarification makes no difference to the view that it is logically possible that there are human beings, or that human beings are metaphysically possible but contingent beings: this possibility is indeed grounded in the essence, even if objective potency is not.) [8] Hence it is logically possible that there are human beings even if there is no power that as a matter of fact can bring them about. Hence, further, it is logically possible that there are human beings even if the essence *man* has no objective potency. (I take it that objective potency is a property of the essence *man* in worlds in which there is a God, but not in worlds that lack God. Scotus says *per impossibile* since he thinks there are no such worlds; but let that pass.) [9] and [10] basically repeat [6]: [6] was the conclusion that [7]–[8] aimed at showing. [11] is the crucial conclusion for my purposes here: in the absence of any existing human beings, and any existing chimeras, the essences of these are *nothing*. Clearly, the metaphysically impossible is nothing (the "essence" of chimera); and the possible but non-existent is *no less nothing* than this. The assumption, of course, is that everyone can agree that the logically contradictory or metaphysically impossible is indeed nothing: the aim is to show that all of Scotus's talk of possible essences is not supposed to commit him to the view that they have some minimal actuality.[84] There is *no* sense in which possible but non-actual essences exist, or are real, despite some of Scotus's language. And this shows that Scotus is committed to actualism: the possible has no kind of existence at all, and *ens* should not be taken to imply or require any kind of existence. Possible items in a categorial hierarchy are not already somehow "waiting" for actualization, and it is not in this sense that essence is prior to existence.

[84] Oddly, this is not an assumption that all of Scotus's opponents would share: Richard of Conington seems to reject it, allowing some kind of "somethingness" (*aliquitas*) even to *impossibilia*: see the refutation of Richard's view at Scotus, *Ord.* I, d. 3, p. 2, q. un., n. 313 (Vatican III, 190). The author of Scotus, *Collatio* 35 (Wadding III, 417b–20b)—certainly not Scotus and quite probably Richard of Conington, as I hope to show elsewhere—embraces this view enthusiastically: see the end of the second reply in *Collatio* 35, n. 10 (Wadding III, 419b–20a), where the author ascribes essence/quiddity, *aliquitas*, and *esse significabile* to *goat-stag*.

6. ESSENCE, EXISTENCE, AND EFFICIENT CAUSATION

In fact, given all this, it is hard to see how Scotus might think of essence as in any sense *prior* to existence, as though there were a realm of *possibilia* awaiting actualization. So I suppose this shows that Scotus's priority claims—e.g. that existence tracks essence—should not be understood in this way. In fact, there is some evidence in favor of the view that we might think of *existence* as in some way prior to *essence*. I suggested above that there might be a sense in which existence includes the *positing* of a thing, and I would like to explore this a little further here. Henry of Ghent holds that *esse exsistentiae* adds to the individual a relation to divine efficient causality,[85] and in the *Lectura*, Scotus endorses something like this (again, I italicize the crucial claims):

> Actual existence (*esse actuale*) is not the ultimate actual intrinsic item [i.e. intrinsic to the essence], but rather follows the distinction of things in the categorial hierarchy. Therefore, distinction through actual existence (*esse actuale*) is through existence (*exsistentiam*) in some way *in so far as the thing is compared to an agent*, and for this reason the distinction obtains *as a thing relates to extrinsic causes*, and is not a thing in potency to that [viz. the agent] as to some other existence (*esse*) within the categorial hierarchy.[86]

This gives us something akin to Henry's view—existence follows a relation to an efficient cause, the positing of the existent individual. In fact, this passage does not mention God (as *per* Henry's view), and seems to suggest that the different existences of distinct substances result from those substances' distinct relations to different efficient causes.

Now, Scotus's account of the causal relation between a substance and the agent or agents that brought it about provides some kind of clue as to how he might understand the tie between the substance and its dependence relation, and thus between a substance and its existence. He claims that, standardly, relations are indeed in some sense posterior to the substances they relate, since the relations are features or properties of the substances: a relation "is neither naturally prior nor naturally simultaneous with that thing which it is in."[87] But in cases in which the relation is necessary for the

[85] See e.g. Henry, *Quod.* I, q. 9 (fo. 7r). For a useful discussion of Henry of Ghent on essence and existence, see Wippel, "The Relationship Between Essence and Existence," 141–2.

[86] Scotus, *Lect.* II, d. 3, p. 1, q. 3, n. 60 (Vatican XVIII, 245–6). See too Scotus, *Ord.* II, d. 1, q. 2, n. 62 (Vatican VII, 35–6).

[87] Scotus, *Ord.* II, d. 1, qq. 4–5, n. 262 (Vatican VII, 129).

existence of the substance, all this shows, Scotus holds, is that there cannot be any kind of real distinction between the substance and the relation: they are merely formally distinct,[88] and there can be some kind of logical or conceptual ordering between them (some kind of *formal* ordering in terms of formal causes or *id quos*), such that the substance is logically prior to the relation, without this requiring that the one is not a feature or property of the other: claiming that the substance is logically prior to the relation does not mean that the substance does not really depend on its cause, and in this sense really presuppose, for its existence, its relation to the cause.[89] As Scotus lays out the formal distinction between the relation and the existent substance, he claims that the substance "contains" the relation,[90] and we might think that this is analogous to the case in which an existent substance "contains" its existence (though Scotus does not talk about existence in this passage, albeit that the passage is about the nature of creaturely dependence on God).[91]

Talk of features and properties is a way of talking about *formal* causes, or things akin to formal causes. We might worry that a simple appeal to *efficient* causality would be sufficient to account for actual existence, without thinking of existence as *id quo*—a property in virtue of which something exists. Well, perhaps, in some sense, it could be. I just suggested that Scotus sees *esse exsistentiae* as corresponding to relation between a thing and its cause, and we saw above, too, that Scotus accounts for both objective potency and contingency as something's being the (possible) *end term of a power*, or, in other words, the effect of a cause. We should think of this more perspicuously as a particular's having a set of relations to the items necessary and jointly sufficient for the existence of that particular. But these relations are, in Scotus's metaphysical analysis of reality, features or properties of the particular thing, in the way outlined a moment ago. And this might be all he needs for a formal explanation of existence and actuality: a contingent thing's actuality is its existential dependence, or something that corresponds precisely to this dependence—and of course existential dependence is a relation (to an efficient cause or causes), and thus in some sense a property of an existent individual.

88 See Scotus, *Ord.* II, d. 1, qq. 4–5, n. 272 (Vatican VII, 135).

89 Scotus, *Ord.* II, d. 1, qq. 4–5, n. 262 (Vatican VII, 129).

90 Scotus, *Ord.* II, d. 1, qq. 4–5, n. 275 (Vatican VII, 136).

91 Note too that such necessary relations are, like existence, seen by Scotus as falling outside the categorial hierarchy: they are trans-categorial or transcendental, in Scotus's language, since they will not fit into any of the Aristotelian categories (they are relations that are not accidents): on this, see Henninger, *Relations*, 78–85.

(A problem: a thing's relations to its efficient causes—and certainly to the things on which it actually depends—are constantly changing, and this might suggest that a thing's existence cannot be identified as its dependence on the collection items necessary and jointly sufficient for its existence. Perhaps Scotus could fall back onto the notion of dependence on the first cause, in the way that Henry suggests. I do not know: it is clear, however, that he has not devoted a great deal of thought to the matter.)

7. CONCLUDING COMMENTS

Given that Scotus is such a clear and careful thinker, and given that his account of essence and existence is so full of *aporias* and obscurities, it seems that he has not given the issue much sustained attention, and that it is not close to the heart of his metaphysical thinking. Indeed, apart from the brief discussion of individuation he gives the matter no real consideration at all. Evidently, Scotus devotes a lot of attention to topics in the general neighborhood: the distinction between objective and subjective potency; the question of the divine attributes; the formal distinction; Henry's view (as Scotus sees it) on the independent reality of items with merely *esse essentiae*. And he has learned from his opponents, too: for example, the view that *esse exsistentiae* involves a relation to an efficient cause. But he does not make any effort to tie the issue explicitly into the nature of God as *ipsum esse subsistens*—albeit that he discusses this view in relation not to Aquinas but to Richard of Conington and the Greek Patristic tradition. (Surprisingly, relevant texts from Augustine do not figure in the discussion at all.)

Neither does Scotus use talk of any kind of composition of essence and existence as a basis for the doctrine of creation, as Aquinas does. One of Aquinas's key arguments in favor of the view that only God can create is that causal relations between creatures explain the fact that an effect is of such-and-such a kind, but cannot explain the *existence* of the creature, since existence is the universal (most general) effect, and must be explained by the universal cause (i.e. God).[92] Scotus rejects this kind of argument,[93] and claims instead that God's creative power can be inferred from the fact that, as the first efficient cause, he can produce at least some things *immediately*, and thus without "presupposing" anything else.[94] And Henry of Ghent talks of the relation to God, as the first efficient cause, as the ground of *esse*

[92] See Aquinas, *ST* I, q. 44, a. 2 c.

[93] He cites a version of the argument at *Ord.* II, d. 1, q. 2, n. 63 (Vatican VII, 36).

[94] Scotus, *Ord.* II, d. 1, q. 2, n. 68 (Vatican VII, 37–8).

exsistentiae. But, as we saw above, Scotus holds that, to the extent that *esse* involves a relation, the relation it involves is a relation to (any kind of) agent or efficient cause, not just to God.

I had originally planned to try to place Scotus's views in some kind of context, by briefly considering the theories of his opponents in more detail. This proved an impossible task, requiring, as it would, a book-length study to make and defend all the claims that would have to be made and defended to provide a convincing account of these positions and their relation to Scotus. So, while there is a great deal more that could be said, I leave the issue here.[95]

University of Notre Dame

BIBLIOGRAPHY

Avicenna. *Liber de philosophia prima*, ed. S. van Riet, 3 vols. (Louvain: Peeters, 1977–83).

Boler, John. "The Ontological Commitment of Scotus's Account of Potency in his *Questions on the Metaphysics*, Book IX," in L. Honnefelder, R. Wood, and M. Dreyer (eds.), *John Duns Scotus: Metaphysics and Ethics* (Leiden: Brill, 1996), 146–60.

Brown, Stephen F. and Stephen D. Dumont. "Univocity of the Concept of Being in the Early Fourteenth Century: III. An Early Scotist," *Mediaeval Studies* 51 (1989), 1–129.

Cross, Richard. *The Physics of Duns Scotus: The Scientific Context of a Theological Vision* (Oxford: Clarendon Press, 1998).

—— "Scotus's Parisian Teaching on Divine Simplicity," in O. Boulnois et al. (eds.), *Duns Scot à Paris: actes du colloque de Paris, 2–4 Septembre 2002* (Turnhout: Brepols, 2004), 519–62.

—— *Duns Scotus on God* (Aldershot: Ashgate, 2005).

Francis of Meyronnes. *In libros sententiarum* (Venice, 1520).

—— *Tractatus formalitatum* (Venice, 1520).

Gilson, Etienne. *Being and Some Philosophers*, 2nd edn. (Toronto: Pontifical Institute of Medieval Studies, 1952).

Henninger, Mark G. *Relations: Medieval Theories 1250–1325* (Oxford: Clarendon Press, 1989).

Henry of Ghent. *Quodlibet* (Paris, 1518).

—— *Summa quaestionum ordinariarum*, 2 vols. (Paris, 1520).

[95] Thanks to Stephen Dumont and Tim Noone for conversations on this issue, to Andrew Helms, and to Garrett Smith for help with Meyronnes. I would like to thank, too, an anonymous referee for this paper, who forced me to present these rather difficult issues in a way that is, if not an easy read, at any rate more comprehensible than in my earlier draft.

Hoeres, W. "Wesen und Dasein bei Heinrich von Gent und Duns Scotus," *Franziskanishe Studien* 47 (1965), 121–86.

John of Damascus. *De fide orthodoxa*, ed. E. M. Buytaert (St. Bonaventure, NY: The Franciscan Institute, 1955).

John Duns Scotus. *Opera omnia*, ed. L. Wadding, 12 vols. (Lyons, 1639).

—— *Opera omnia*, ed. C. Balić et al. (Vatican City: Vatican Press, 1950–).

—— *Opera philosophica*, ed. G. J. Etzkorn et al. (St. Bonaventure, NY: The Franciscan Institute, 1997–2006).

King, Peter. "Duns Scotus on the Individual Differentia and Common Nature," *Philosophical Topics* 20 (1992), 50–76.

Knuuttila, Simo. *Modalities in Medieval Philosophy* (London: Routledge, 1993).

O'Brien, A. J. "Duns Scotus' Teaching on the Distinction Between Essence and Existence," *The New Scholasticism* 38 (1964), 61–77.

O'Meara, William. "Actual Existence and the Individual according to Duns Scotus," *Monist* 49 (1965), 659–69.

Porphyry. *Isagoge*, ed. L. Minio-Paluello, *Aristoteles Latinus*, I/6–7 (Bruges: Desclée de Brouwer, 1966).

Spade, Paul Vincent. *Five Texts on the Mediaeval Problem of Universals: Porphyry, Boethius, Abelard, Duns Scotus, Ockham* (Indianapolis: Hackett, 1994).

Thomas Aquinas. *Opera omnia iussu Leonis XIII P. M. edita* (Rome: Ex Typographia Polyglotta S.C. de Propaganda Fide, 1882–).

Tweedale, Martin M. *Scotus vs. Ockham: A Medieval Dispute Over Universals*, 2 vols. (Lewiston: Edwin Mellen, 1999).

Wippel, John F. "Essence and Existence," in N. Kretzmann, A. Kenny, and J. Pinborg (eds.), *The Cambridge History of Later Medieval Philosophy* (Cambridge: Cambridge University Press, 1982), 385–410.

—— "The Relationship Between Essence and Existence in Late-Thirteenth-Century Thought: Giles of Rome, Henry of Ghent, Godfrey of Fontaines, and James of Viterbo," in P. Morewedge (ed.), *Philosophies of Existence Ancient and Medieval* (New York: Fordham University Press, 1982), 131–64.

Wolter, Allan B. "Is Existence for Scotus a Perfection, Predicate, or What?" in Marilyn McCord Adams (ed.), *The Philosophical Theology of John Duns Scotus* (Ithaca, NY: Cornell University Press, 1990), 278–84.

Yaḥyā Ibn ʿAdī on the Location of God

Peter Adamson and Robert Wisnovsky

Aristotle's *Physics* says some puzzling things about God. One of the oddest is found in the last chapter of the last book.[1] Here Aristotle raises and answers the question of the location of the Prime Mover, writing:

Physics VIII.10, 267b6–9: [The mover] must be either in the center (ἐν μέσῳ) or in the circle (ἐν κύκλῳ). For they are the principles (αἱ ἀρχαί). But what is closest to the mover moves fastest, and such is the motion of the circle. Therefore the mover is there (ἐκεῖ ἄρα τὸ κινοῦν).

This passage occasioned a good deal of comment already in antiquity, as we shall see. In the present paper, we will be presenting a brief Arabic text that builds on the ancient debate. It is found in a Tehran codex, Madrasa-yi Marwī 19, which contains among other things, 53 works by the Christian philosopher Yaḥyā ibn ʿAdī (d. 363/974), a student of al-Fārābī who seems to have been for a while the most significant member of the Aristotelian school in Baghdad.[2] Of these 53 works, no fewer than 24 were previously thought lost. The contents of these "lost" treatises have already been described elsewhere,[3] and several of the newly discovered treatises have

[1] We are very grateful to Marwan Rashed, Fouad Ben Ahmed, and an anonymous referee for comments on the treatise and our interpretation of it. Peter Adamson would also like to acknowledge the support of the Leverhulme Trust and the assistance of David Bennett and Rotraud Hansberger, and Robert Wisnovsky would like to thank Ahmedreza Rahimiriseh and Reza Pourjavady for providing images of the Marwī codex, and Naser Dumairieh for his help with the Arabic text.

[2] Al-Masʿūdī for instance identifies Ibn ʿAdī as the outstanding instructor of philosophy in his day. See his *Kitāb al-tanbīh wa-l-iṣrāf*, ed. M. J. de Goeje (Leiden: Brill, 1893–4), 122.

[3] Robert Wisnovsky, "New Philosophical Texts of Yaḥyā Ibn ʿAdī: A Supplement to Endress' *Analytical Inventory*," in F. Opwis and D. Reisman (eds.), *Islamic Philosophy, Science, Culture, and Religion: Studies in Honor of Dimitri Gutas* (Leiden: Brill, 2012), 307–26. Cf. the fundamental study by G. Endress, *The Works of Yaḥyā ibn ʿAdī: An Analytical Inventory* (Wiesbaden: L. Reichert, 1977).

already been presented in greater detail.[4] Below, we provide an analysis, translation, and edition for a short piece in which Ibn ʿAdī asks, alluding to the passage of Aristotle cited above, "what is the meaning of Aristotle's assertion, in Book Eight of the *Physics*, that 'the mover is in the containing [sphere] (*al-muḥarrik fī-l-muḥīṭ*)'?" (§ 1).[5]

We will see that Ibn ʿAdī takes a rather deflationary view of the meaning of God's being "in" the sphere, one that avoids ascribing a specific location to God. This is in contrast to the views of Eudemus and Alexander, who actually assigned the Prime Mover a specific location (either the celestial equator or the surface of the sphere itself). Ibn ʿAdī's position is in this respect like that of Neoplatonist authors, who reject the idea of a literal location; here Simplicius is a good example, since he dismisses the very idea as inappropriate to the exalted status of immaterial causes. Ibn ʿAdī's own view is that God is in the sphere only in the non-spatial sense that an intelligible object is "in" an intellect. This is not prefigured in the Greek commentaries on our passage, which is all the more striking given that Ibn ʿAdī apparently knew those discussions.

1. THE ANCIENT CONTEXT

Physics VIII.10 is not the only Aristotelian passage to raise the question of God's location. In *De Caelo* I.9 Aristotle writes: "Clearly there is neither place, void, nor time outside [the heaven], so that things there are by their nature not in place (διόπερ οὔτ᾽ ἐν τόπῳ τἀκεῖ πέφυκεν)" (279a17–18). This is, if anything, even more puzzling than our *Physics* passage. Aristotle seems to recognize the existence of things with location outside the heaven—after all, they are "outside (ἔξωθεν)" and as at *Physics* VIII.10, Aristotle uses the word "there (ἐκεῖ)." Yet in the same breath, he also denies that they are in place—which stands to reason, since for Aristotle "place"

[4] Robert Wisnovsky, "Yaḥyā ibn ʿAdī's Discussion of the Prolegomena to the Study of a Philosophical Text," in M. Cook et al. (eds.), *Law and Tradition in Classical Islamic Thought* (Basingstoke: Palgrave Macmillan, 2012), 171–85; Stephen Menn and Robert Wisnovsky, "Yaḥyā ibn ʿAdī's *Essay on the Four Scientific Questions regarding the Three Categories of Existence: Divine, Natural and Logical. Editio princeps* and English Translation, with Historical-Philosophical Notes," *Mélanges de l'Institut dominicain d'études orientales du Caire (MIDEO)* 29 (2012) 73–96.

[5] Cited by section number from our translation and text. The treatise in question is numbered 2.21 in Endress 1977, and is number 41 in the listing found in the introduction to Saḥbān Khalīfāt, *Maqālāt Yaḥyā ibn ʿAdī al-falsafiyya* (ʿAmmān: al-Jāmiʿa al-Urdunniyya, 1988).

means the inner boundary of a containing body, and these entities have no containing bodies. Is it possible, then, to have a location without having a place? James Wilberding has recently explored Plotinus's similar claim that immaterial principles can have special locations in the universe assigned to them.[6] In the case of Plotinus, *nous* is likewise associated with the heaven, something Wilberding explains in terms of the heavenly body's high degree of receptivity for the influence of *nous*. One could see this as a deflationary account of location: the immaterial cause is not really "in" the heaven, but merely exercises its influence more at some places than others.

By contrast, several ancient Peripatetics adopted a stronger interpretation of Aristotle's location locutions. This becomes clear from Simplicius's commentary on the *Physics*,[7] which has recently been supplemented by Marwan Rashed's magisterial presentation of Byzantine scholia containing the comments of Alexander of Aphrodisias.[8] We learn from Simplicius that Eudemus took quite seriously the reference to a "circle" in Aristotle's text, and identified the location of the Prime Mover as the "greatest circle relative to the poles," i.e. the celestial equator, "for it moves most quickly, and the mover seems to act as a principle where it moves most quickly and easily" (1354.10–12). Eudemus's interpretation is not implausible, for the very reason he himself gives: Aristotle says in our passage that the mover should be located at the place with the fastest motion. In Aristotelian cosmology the outermost sphere of fixed stars has the fastest motion, since it rotates around the earth once a day. And of course the speed of rotation for any part of that sphere is faster as one moves away from its poles and towards its equator, with the fastest speed at the equator itself.

Against this, Alexander argued that Eudemus would violate the central claim that the Prime Mover is itself unmoved. For, Alexander writes, "if [the mover] were in some part of the outer circumference, it would be moved accidentally, given that the motion occurs through the parts of the sphere" (1354.17–19). Alexander prefers to hold that by "circle" Aristotle means the surface of the entire sphere and not only the equator. This has the advantage that in a sense, the heavenly bodies (including the outermost

[6] James Wilberding, "'Creeping Spatiality': The Location of *Nous* in Plotinus' Universe," *Phronesis* 50 (2005), 315–34.

[7] For the commentary on our passage see the edition of H. Diels in *CAG* vol. 10 (Berlin: George Reimer, 1895), 1353–5, and for an English translation, R. McKirahan, *Simplicius: On Aristotle's Physics 8.6–10* (London: Duckworth, 2001).

[8] Marwan Rashed, *Alexandre d'Aphrodise, Commentaire perdu à la Physique d'Aristote (Livres IV–VIII)* (Berlin: Walter de Gruyter, 2011).

sphere) do not move: as a whole they never shift from their location, but rather rotate always in the same place.[9] We quote here from § 821 in Rashed's edition:

Since what is moved accidentally is in something that is in a place, and since it is a part of that, it can rightly be said to be moved accidentally. But what is outermost in the heaven (*τὸ δὲ ἐξωτάτω τοῦ οὐρανοῦ*) is not in a place,[10] nor is the mover that is in it like a part of it; rather, it is [in it] as a substance in its own right (*ὡς οὐσία καθ' αὑτήν*), occupying the whole outer surface. Thus it does not move accidentally. For the outermost surface is, considered as a whole, unmoved.[11]

Notice, however, that Alexander is not identifying the location of the Mover with the sphere as such. Rather, he holds that the Mover is in the *surface* of the sphere (the scholium has *ἐκτὸς ἐπιφάνειαν*, whereas Simplicius uses the less perspicuous term *περιφέρεια*).

Alexander furthermore stresses that the Mover is not in the surface the way a form is in a subject. In a preceding comment (§ 818), we find:

One should not understand "in something (*τὸ ἔν τινι*)" as "in a place"—given that it was proved to have no parts—or as a form of that in which it resides (*ὡς εἴδους ὄντος τοῦ ἐν ᾧ ἐστιν*)—for then it would be the soul and actuality of the potentiality of the first body—but as a substance in a substance (*ὡς οὐσίας ἐν οὐσίᾳ*), immaterial in itself, and not as a form. For if the heaven is indeed ensouled and moves in accordance with the soul in it, which is its form, still in addition to being moved in accordance with the soul in it, it needs something else that provides it with a principle of motion, given that, for all ensouled things, there is something outside that is a cause and principle for them which produces motion in accordance with soul, in respect of place—if indeed impulse and desire for something bring to fulfillment the motion of ensouled things in respect of place.[12]

But what does it mean to be "in" something as a substance is in a substance? Rashed has argued that Alexander sees the surface or limit of a body as

[9] It is important for Alexander's refutation that the surface of the sphere is not, unlike the celestial equator, a "part" of the sphere, since the surface does not move whereas the equator does. He must therefore be thinking of the equator as a physical part which actually rotates.

[10] Again, because it has no containing body. For a collection of texts on the vexed question of whether the heaven has a place, see Richard Sorabji, *The Philosophy of the Commentators, 200–600 AD: A Sourcebook in Three Volumes* (London: Duckworth, 2004), vol. 2, § 13(b).

[11] See Rashed, *Alexandre d'Aphrodise*, 640–1; cf. Simplicius's quotation at 1354.12–25.

[12] Rashed, *Alexandre d'Aphrodise*, 639; cf. Simplicius 1354.25–34. Note that McKirahan, *Simplicius*, 144, mistranslates the key phrase in Simplicius which states that God is not "in" anything as a form (he writes "or as if there is a form in which it is" instead of "or as if it were a form of that in which it is").

being itself a kind of substance, insofar as it is a part of a substance. Thus a good comparison for the Mover's relation to the sphere is the way a color relates to a colored body, albeit that a color is of course not a substance. This has the advantage that it excludes accidental motion from the Mover (just as when a blue body rotates, blue does not rotate).[13] In the latter half of the scholium, Alexander also makes clear why he is so resistant to the suggestion that the Mover is in the sphere as a form: the sphere already has a form, namely its soul.[14] To explain the sphere's motion we need not only a soul, but also "something outside" which can serve as its final cause.

It is also worth touching on Simplicius's own solution to the problem, since this will give us a third interpretation with which we can compare Ibn ʿAdī's. Simplicius finds Alexander's solution wanting:

1355.15–28: Or is the contribution conceived by Alexander also insufficient to show that it is not even moved accidentally, given that it [i.e. Alexander's contribution] proceeds on the notion (ἐννοία) that the first mover is in the heaven? "For if," he says, "it is not in a part of the periphery but in it as a whole, since the whole [periphery] does not move or change from its place, but remains in the same spot (ἐν τῷ αὐτῷ), [the mover] would not move accidentally."[15] If then [the periphery] as a whole does not move, but the first mover is said to be in that which is moved most quickly, it is clear that it is not in the whole periphery. Furthermore, if it is in the whole [periphery] in the sense that it is allocated (κατατεταγμένον)[16] to it, but the whole [periphery] does move in respect of its parts, it is clear that it too will move accidentally in respect of the parts. But if it is present to (πάρεστι) the whole without relation (ἀσχέτως) and transcendently (ἐξῃρημένως), then what prevents (since it is present also to all the parts all at once, without relation, transcendently, without partition or motion) that it is not moved accidentally along with the motion of those [parts]? Eudemus firmly lays out the problem: "If," he says, "the first mover is without parts, and not in contact with the moved, how is it related to it (πῶς ἔχει πρὸς αὐτό)?" Therefore, how can that which is without parts and not in

[13] Rashed, *Alexandre d'Aphrodise*, 157–8.

[14] As Rashed, *Alexandre d'Aphrodise*, 640, notes, this hylomorphic aspect of Alexander's discussion is quietly eliminated in the quotation by Simplicius.

[15] Diels and McKirahan both take the Alexander quotation to continue on for the next three sentences, but it seems clear that Simplicius's rival view—which introduces the Neoplatonic technical vocabulary of "allocation," and the notion of unrelatedness, in reaction to Eudemus's formulation of the *aporia*—begins with the next sentence.

[16] As we learn from Simplicius's *Categories* commentary (at 53, 79) "allocation" means the immanence of a form in a particular. Simplicius is thus complaining that God should not relate to the sphere (or its surface) the way a form subsists in a particular. This is ironic given that Alexander had denied precisely this in respect of God's relation to the sphere. On this vocabulary, which may go back to Porphyry, see e.g. R. Chiaradonna, "Essence et prédication chez Porphyre et Plotin," *Revue des Sciences philosophiques et théologiques* 82 (1998), 577–606, at 591–2.

contact with the moved, but is instead without relation to it and transcendent, be moved along with the moved, so that it would be moved accidentally?

His critique invokes the same point stressed by Eudemus, namely that Aristotle uses fastest motion as a criterion for the Mover's location—if the sphere is immobile as a whole, Aristotle cannot possibly mean that the Mover is in the whole sphere, or its surface. Simplicius prefers to solve the difficulty by simply denying that the Mover is "related" to the sphere at all. It exists on a different, more transcendent level. Simplicius's solution would certainly show that the Mover does not move; whether it can give any substance to the idea that the Mover is "in the circle" is more doubtful.

2. IBN ʿADĪ'S INITIAL SOLUTION (§ 1, 6–8)

As it happens one of the most valuable documents regarding the activities of the Baghdad school is devoted to the *Physics*. This is an Arabic translation interspersed with comments by members of the school, including occasionally Ibn ʿAdī himself.[17] It also contains Arabic translations of otherwise lost comments by John Philoponus[18] and Alexander.[19] This means that Ibn ʿAdī would likely have known Alexander's discussion of VIII.10, though this part of Alexander's commentary is not quoted in the Baghdad school's version of the *Physics*. In the Arabic translation, the Aristotelian passage with which we have been concerned reads as follows:

Necessarily, [the mover] must be either in the center or in the circle, because these two are the principles. But the things closest to the mover have the quickest motion, and the motion of the universe is like this. So the mover is there.[20]

[17] Abdurrahman Badawī (ed.), *Arisṭūṭālis: al-Ṭabīʿa*, 2 vols, (Cairo: al-Dār al-Qawmiyya li-l-Ṭibāʿa wa-l-Nashr,1964–5). The contents are summarized and discussed in Paul Lettinck, *Aristotle's Physics and its Reception in the Arabic World* (Leiden: Brill, 1994).

[18] Unfortunately these do not preserve remarks by Philoponus on our passage. For an English translation of the Philoponus sections see Lettinck and J. O. Urmson (trans.), *Philoponus On Aristotle Physics 5–8 with Simplicius On Aristotle on the Void* (London: Duckworth, 1994); E. Giannakis, *Philoponus in the Arabic Tradition of Aristotle's Physics*, D. Phil. Thesis (Oxford, 1992). See further E. Giannakis, "The Structure of Abū l-Ḥusayn al-Baṣrī's Copy of Aristotle's *Physics*," *Zeitschrift für Geschichte der arabisch-islamischen Wissenschaften* 8 (1993), 251–8.

[19] Elias Giannakis, "Fragments from Alexander's lost Commentary on Aristotle's Physics," *Zeitschrift für Geschichte der arabisch-islamischen Wissenschaften* 10 (1995/6), 157–87.

[20] *fa-qad yajibu ḍarūratan an yakūna immā fī-l-wasaṭi wa-immā fī-l-dāʾirati wa-dhālika anna hādhayni humā al-mabdaʾāni lākinna aqraba l-ashyāʾi min al-muḥarriki*

As we will see, Ibn ʿAdī's treatise is largely devoted to the meaning in this passage of "in" (*fī*, corresponding to Greek ἐν). Perhaps surprisingly, he does not comment at all on *hunāka*, corresponding to Greek ἐκεῖ. In fact the little treatise begins from a rather loose reminiscence of our passage, rather than a strict translation: "the mover is in the container (*al-muḥarrik fī-l-muḥīṭ*)." Ibn ʿAdī clarifies that here "the mover" means "the Creator (*al-bāriʾ*)," while "the container" refers to "the celestial sphere (*al-falak*)"—presumably meaning only the outermost sphere. Thus, the challenge is to explain how the Creator is in the outermost sphere.

It should be noticed that Ibn ʿAdī does not directly address the possibility that God is in something other than the sphere itself—that is, in the celestial equator, as Eudemus argued, or the surface, as Alexander argued. However, we will see later on that Ibn ʿAdī was apparently aware of these discussions. His own solution is quite different:

§ 1: [God] is only "in" [the sphere] in the way that the object of intellection (*al-maʿqūl*) is "in" the subject of intellection (*al-ʿāqil*), so that it not be the case that He is "in it" in His own right.

An ambiguity arises in the final clause, which in the manuscript reads *allā/illā annahu bi-dhātihī fī-hi*. This clearly cannot be read as *illā annahu bi-dhātihī fī-hi* and understood as "except that He is 'in it [the sphere]' in His own right," because a good portion of the treatise is going to deny that God Himself is "in" the sphere. If we wish to retain the *illā*, we could understand the pronouns differently: "except that it [the object of intellection] is in it [the subject of intellection] essentially," the point being that by contrast, God is not in the sphere essentially.[21] This would be reasonable if Ibn ʿAdī meant an object of intellect *as such*—that is, the intelligible in my mind rather than the mind-independent entity which I am knowing. But on balance, it seems more economical to read the first word of the clause as *allā*, and to understand the pronouns as referring to God and the sphere: God must be "in" the sphere the way that an object of intellection is "in" the subject of intellection, so as to avoid the claim that God, Himself, is literally "in" the sphere.[22]

asraʿuhā ḥarakatan wa-ka-dhālika ḥarakatu l-kulli fa-l-muḥarriku idhan hunāka: Badawī, *Arisṭūṭālis: al-Ṭabīʿa* II: 932.10–13.

[21] A version of this reading has been suggested to us by Stephen Menn: it could mean, "unless [one were willing to say that] the object of intellection is in the subject of intellection," which would be a controversial claim.

[22] Another alternative would be to emend *allā/illā* to *lā*, which would give a similar sense to *allā*: God is "in" the sphere the way that an object of intellection is "in" the subject of intellection: that is, not in the sense that He Himself is "in" it. Cf. Ibn ʿAdī's *Essay on the Four Scientific Questions regarding the Three Categories of Existence: Divine,*

The solution is reprised below, after a clarificatory passage (§§ 2–5) which we will examine shortly:

§§ 6–8: The objects of knowledge exist in the knower. For the heavenly bodies know their mover, given that they are moved only out of their desire to receive Him, just as Aristotle says: the first mover moves them only as the object of desire moves what desires it. This can only happen with things that possess intellects.

This argument looks to go as follows:

(a) The heavens move out of desire for God.
(b) What moves out of desire has its object of desire as an intelligible.
(c) Therefore the heavens have God as an intelligible.
(d) Corollary: the heavens have intellects.

We are not yet told why the conclusion (c) should entail that God is "in" the sphere; this will be explained only at the end of the treatise (§ 28). Leaving that aside, the passage seems to be relatively uncontentious, with the exception of premise (b). This premise seems to neglect the possibility that something could move out of desire for something else without using, or even having, an intellective capacity. Yet irrational animals lack intellects and manage to conceive and act on desires. Perhaps he is thinking that strictly speaking animals do not engage in "action," since they lack practical intellect. Ibn ʿAdī in any case surely has in mind the passage where Aristotle himself identifies the objects of desire and of thought, in his discussion of the Prime Mover in the *Metaphysics* (XII.7, 1072a26–7).

3. CLARIFICATIONS (§§ 2–5)

In between these two statements of his solution, Ibn ʿAdī clarifies a pair of expressions used by "the philosophers" (*al-ḥukamāʾ*, i.e. Aristotle and his commentators). First, he remarks on the meaning of the term "vessel (*al-ināʾ*)." Presumably this is relevant to the characterization of the outermost sphere as a "containing [sphere] (*muḥīṭ*)." Ibn ʿAdī here quotes Aristotle's definition of "vessel" (*τὸ ἀγγεῖον*) as a "transportable place"

Natural and Logical, ed. and trans. Menn and Wisnovsky, § 12, 66a11–14, a passage copied in *Maqālat al-shaykh Yaḥyā ibn ʿAdī fī wujūb* [alt. *wujūd*] *al-taʾannus*, ed. and trans. Augustin Périer as "Traité de Yaḥyā ben ʿAdī sur le mode de l'Incarnation," in *Petits traités apologétiques de Yaḥyā ben ʿAdī (Texte arabe)* (Paris: Geuthner, 1920), 69–86 at 75.7–76.8. Here Ibn ʿAdī says that it would be manifestly absurd to claim that when a knower knows what "human" is, the thing that comes to be (*ḥadatha*) in the mind of the knower is the actual form–matter composite of a concrete individual human, complete with its matter and its body.

(*Physics* IV.2, 209b29: τόπος μεταφορητός). Second, he discusses the description of heavenly motion as the single, continuous motion of a magnitude. This remark is provoked by the application of these terms to the heavenly motion in the same final chapter of the *Physics* we are commenting on (μία, συνεχῆ, μεγέθους, at VIII.10, 267a21–2).

In both cases, Ibn ʿAdī wants to explain that these characterizations are not essential, but are ascribed "on the basis of the existence of something [else] in it (*min jihati wujūdi baʿḍi mā huwa fīhi*)" (§ 3). Thus a vessel is not a "moving place" essentially or in its own right, but only because something is contained (or perhaps, could be contained) within its inner surface (§ 4). Likewise the heavenly motion is not continuous in its own right. Rather, the motion's continuity is derived from the continuity of the heavenly body (§ 4). Nor is this continuity of magnitude essential, but rather derived in turn from the continuity of the heavenly body's parts (§ 5). The point of this is that a single heavenly sphere is not "continuous"—in the sense of "contiguous"—with anything else, since as a sphere, it has no edges that are in contact with another body. It can be called "continuous" only insofar as its own parts are touching one another (e.g. its top hemisphere would be touching its bottom hemisphere). Here one might worry that a nested heavenly sphere will in fact be touching both the sphere inside it and the sphere outside it. But he has just pointed out that this sort of contact, which is characteristic of a vessel, is also accidental. Finally, according to Ibn ʿAdī, the heavens do not even move essentially. This rather surprising claim is explained with the remark that they are said to move only "in view of the motion of their parts" (§ 4). This is an unmistakable reminiscence of Alexander's point that, whereas the parts of the sphere move in the daily rotation, the sphere as a whole does not move from where it is. The difference is that whereas Alexander wanted to show that the Mover is not moved even accidentally, Ibn ʿAdī is using the same rationale to say that the celestial sphere *is* moved accidentally, just not essentially.

Further light on this is shed by a comment found in the Baghdad *Physics.* The lemma is *Phys* IV.3, 210b18–21, where Aristotle argued that a thing cannot be in itself. In the comment, a member of the Baghdad school, Ibn al-Samḥ, provides examples to illustrate a point made by Philoponus:

Aristotle is showing that nothing can be "in itself (*fī dhātihī*)" either essentially (*bi-l-dhāt*) or accidentally. Clearly nothing can be in itself in a primary sense (*ʿalā-l-qaṣd al-awwal*), but only in a secondary sense.[23] The essential case [of something being

[23] Cf. Greek πρώτως vs. κατ' ἄλλο at Philoponus, *in Phys.* 530, rendered using the "first" and "second intention" terminology familiar from Porphyry (cf. προηγουμένως at Porphyry, *Isag.*, ed. Busse, 17.9) and used in the Baghdad school, e.g. by al-Fārābī in his

in itself] is, for instance, that Zayd is seeing himself, but in a secondary sense, and only because the seeing part of him is seeing in the primary sense. Or, Zayd is knowing himself, but only in a secondary sense, and only because of that which is knowing in a primary sense, that is, through his soul. In general, whatever is transferred from a part of something to the whole of that thing belongs to the whole in a secondary sense, and what is not transferred to it from its part belongs to it in a primary sense. The essential case is the opposite of the accidental case. The accidental case [of something being in itself] is when two accidents occur in a single subject, such that one of them is said of the other – then [one accident] is said of [the other accident] accidentally.[24]

As we just saw, Ibn ʿAdī makes a similar point regarding heavenly motion: the parts of the sphere are in motion, but the whole is not, so we speak of the sphere as "moving" only by "transferring from the part to the whole." However, Ibn ʿAdī does not adhere to the terminology used here in the Baghdad *Physics*. For Philoponus and Ibn al-Samḥ, the primary/secondary distinction is made *within* essential attributes, while "accidental" is reserved for coinciding features in the same subject:

Essential features: as a whole (primary)
transferred from a part (secondary)
Accidental features: coincidence of properties

In Ibn ʿAdī, by contrast, the features transferred from a part are simply labeled "accidental," with "essential" reserved for features possessed as a whole. We may conclude from this that he agrees with Alexander's analysis, despite the variation in terminology.

4. ONE CONTRARY IS ENOUGH

After these clarifications and the restatement of his view at §§ 6–8, Ibn ʿAdī quotes a passage from *Physics* book I, without giving us any clue how the quotation might be relevant to the topic at hand (§ 9). In the passage quoted (191a3–7), Aristotle writes: "it is clear that something must underlie the contraries, and that the contraries are two. But in another way this is

commentary on *On Interpretation* (see W. Kutsch and S. Marrow *Alfarabi's Commentary on Aristotle's Peri Hermêneias* (Beirut: Imprimerie Catholique, 1960), 105 and 206–7, and for a translation F. W. Zimmermann, *Al-Farabi's Commentary and Short Treatise on Aristotle's De Interpretatione* (Oxford: Oxford University Press, 1981), 100 and 200). More generally on these terms see Kwame Gyekye, "The Terms *Prima intentio* and *Secunda intentio* in Arabic Logic," *Speculum* 46 (1971), 32–48.

[24] Badawī, *Arisṭūṭālis: al-Ṭabīʿa* I: 299.18–26, cf. Lettinck, *Aristotle's Physics and its Reception*, 278.

not necessary, for one of the contraries will be sufficient for the change by its absence or presence." Ibn ʿAdī's version of the quotation is not identical to the translation in the Baghdad *Physics*, although both render the Aristotelian text accurately. (For instance, when Aristotle writes "in another way this is not necessary [τρόπον δέ τινα ἄλλον οὐκ ἀναγκαῖον]," Ibn ʿAdī has *wajh* for τρόπον and *fa-laysa dhālika bi-wujūb* for οὐκ ἀναγκαῖον, whereas the Baghdad *Physics* has respectively *nāḥiya* and *laysa hādhā bi-ḍarūrī*.) Following the quotation Ibn ʿAdī adds, "So [just] one of the two contraries is characterized as acting. The agent [acts] simply by virtue of what has been mentioned: its existence or lack" (§ 10). Apart from supplying the synonyms "existence and lack" (*wujūd, faqd*) for "absence and presence" (*ghayba, ḥuḍūr*),[25] the main contribution of this gloss seems to be identifying the efficacious contrary as an "agent" or "efficient cause" (*fāʿil*).

That may be a clue to what this little passage is doing here, in the midst of a discussion of God's relationship to the outermost sphere—though one cannot exclude that the passage has found its way into the text erroneously. If it does belong here, Ibn ʿAdī is presumably trying to safeguard God's status as a causal principle. He might be imagining a potential objection, along the following lines: "Aristotle says in *Physics* I that causation always involves two contraries operating on a subject. This is how change or motion is brought about. But God has no contrary, so He cannot be involved in the production of change or motion." Since Ibn ʿAdī has just explained how God causes motion (§§ 6–8), such an objection would make sense here. The response would then be to say that there does not need to be the possibility of a *contrary* to God; it is enough that God is present for Him to be causally efficacious. The gloss Ibn ʿAdī provides on the quotation would then have the further implication that God is here being seen as an efficient cause, and not just a final cause or object of desire, as could have been inferred from § 7, where he has written "the first mover moves them *just in the way* (*innamā*) that the object of desire moves what desires it." This translation of *innamā* (also used in § 27) seems preferable to rendering it as "only." It is hard to believe that Ibn ʿAdī wants to *exclude* that God is an efficient cause;[26] and as we've just seen he may be implying precisely that

[25] Commentary by means of synonymous paraphrase is standard exegetical practice for Ibn ʿAdī. It is highly characteristic, for instance, of his surviving commentary on *Metaphysics* Book α. On this text see Peter Adamson, "Yaḥyā Ibn ʿAdī and Averroes on *Metaphysics* Alpha Elatton," *Documenti e studi sulla tradizione filosofica medievale* 21 (2010), 343–74; C. Martini Bonadeo, "Un commento ad *alpha elatton* 'sicut litterae sonant' nella Baghdād del X secolo," *Medioevo* 28 (2003), 69–96.

[26] See for instance his treatise *On Unity* (ed. in Khalīfāt, *Maqālāt Yaḥyā ibn ʿAdī*, 375–404), in which he describes God's "generosity (*jūd*)" and "power (*qudra*)" in creating things, that is, voluntarily giving them existence after they did not exist (399–403).

God is such a cause at § 10. He makes no attempt in the present treatise to explain this in detail, and in particular to explain how God could be an efficient cause for the motion of the sphere without having some kind of spatial relation to it.

5. IS GOD "IN" THE CIRCLE IN HIS OWN RIGHT?

Ibn ʿAdī now takes up the point that seems to concern him most: denying that God is "existing in the circle in His own right (*bi-dhātihi*)." He has two worries about this claim. The first is the use of the word "circle (*dāʾira*)," which of course is present in the Aristotelian passage itself. He considers two possibilities: first, one might be using the word "circle" to refer to the celestial sphere, but that is dismissed on the basis that the sphere is ball-shaped and not only a circle (§ 11). Alternatively, Aristotle is using an analogy: one can call a sphere a "circle" because it relates to three-dimensional shapes the way the circle relates to two-dimensional shapes (§ 12). Although Ibn ʿAdī does not seem particularly enthusiastic about this proposal, he does not suggest anything better, and it is clear from what follows that he agrees Aristotle is talking about God's being in the celestial sphere and not in a circle. This passage may seem rather pedantic, but it takes on more significance in light of the material we examined in the Greek tradition.[27] By rejecting the talk of a "circle" as either misleading or metaphorical, Ibn ʿAdī has sided with Alexander against Eudemus, who took Aristotle to be speaking of the celestial equator. On the other hand, as we saw, Alexander said that the Prime Mover is in the surface of the sphere, rather than the sphere itself, and Ibn ʿAdī makes no allusion to this idea (he mentions "surfaces [*suṭūḥ*]" at § 12, but this is only a way of referring to two-dimensional figures in general).

Next, he comes on to the more significant question of whether God is "in" the sphere in His own right. He denies this, by means of an exhaustive discussion of all the meanings of the word "in." Unsurprisingly, he avails himself of Aristotle's own discussion of the senses of ἐν earlier in the *Physics* (IV.3). However his list of meanings does not conform exactly to Aristotle's:

God is characterized as a Creator and agent throughout his treatise on the *kalām* notion of "acquisition"; see Shlomo Pines and Michael Schwarz, "Yaḥyā Ibn ʿAdī's Refutation of the Doctrine of Acquisition (*Iktisāb*)," in J. Blau et al. (eds.), *Studia Orientalia Memoriae D. H. Baneth Dedicata* (Jerusalem: Magnes, 1979), 49–94.

[27] Our thanks to Marwan Rashed for discussion of this point.

Aristotle	Ibn ʿAdī
1 Part in whole	1 Genus in species
2 Whole in part	2 Whole in part
3 Species in genus	3 Part in whole
4 Genus in species	4 Thing in time
5 Form in matter	5 Thing in place
6 Deed in agent	6 Deed in agent
7 Thing in its goal	7 Thing in its goal
8 Thing in place/vessel	8 Form in subject
	9 Accident in substance
	10 Substance in accident
	11 Thing in a vessel

Aside from some re-ordering, Ibn ʿAdī seems to have added three senses (4, 9, and 10) and to have split up Aristotle's sense 8 into two entries.

It turns out that this gives us strong evidence that Ibn ʿAdī is using material from the Greek commentators. In a passage preserved in the Baghdad *Physics*, Philoponus notes in a comment on *Physics* 210a14 that Aristotle has missed out two senses of ἐν, namely Ibn ʿAdī's senses 4 and 8: being "in" a time, and being "in" a subject (τό τε ἐν χρόνῳ καὶ τὸ ἐν ὑποκειμένῳ).[28] Ibn ʿAdī has apparently understood the latter to refer to the relation between an accident and a substance; thus he speaks of *jawhar* rather than *mawḍūʿ* (§ 23). Philoponus also points out that Aristotle's sense 8 could be disambiguated into two distinct meanings: "in place" and "in a vessel,"[29] which explains why Ibn ʿAdī distinguishes senses 5 and 11. That leaves us with sense 10: a substance can be said to be "in" an accident. This corresponds to a passage found in the Baghdad *Physics* which preserves a remark by Alexander: "Another sense is the existence[30] of one thing in another in the sense of the existence of a subject (*al-mawḍūʿ*) in something else, as when Socrates is in 'good (*al-khayr*)'."[31] Notice that Ibn ʿAdī again makes the same variation from "subject" (*mawḍūʿ*) to "substance" (*jawhar*) (§ 24).

This gives us a grand total of 11 senses of "in (*fī*)," and Ibn ʿAdī shows (§§ 13–25) that God is not "in" the sphere in any of these senses. Although

[28] Philoponus, *In Phys.*, ed. Vitelli, 526.31–527.1, cf. Badawī, *Arisṭūṭālis: al-Ṭabīʿa* I: 298 (*fī l-zamān, fī l-mawḍūʿ*), and Vitelli 529.16–17, cf. Badawī, *Arisṭūṭālis: al-Ṭabīʿa* I: 299.13–14.

[29] Philoponus, *In Phys.*, ed. Vitelli, 529.13.

[30] Here we need to read *wujūd* for *jūd* in Badawī's edition.

[31] Badawī, *Arisṭūṭālis: al-Ṭabīʿa* I: 298.

this discussion is bracketed at both ends by passages which deny that God is in the sphere in His own right (§§ 11, 26), the arguments provided by Ibn ʿAdī show something stronger, which is that God is not "in" the sphere in any sense at all. At this point, we begin to realize why Ibn ʿAdī took the trouble to comment on our passage from the *Physics*: when Aristotle says that the Prime Mover is "in" the "circle," Ibn ʿAdī not only thinks we need to replace "circle" with "sphere," he also wants to take "in" to describe a relation that is not, strictly speaking, a possible meaning of the word "in"! His arguments against the appropriateness of the various senses of "in" are in most cases perfunctory: e.g. God cannot be in the sphere the way something is "in" time, because the sphere is not time (§ 19). One might be surprised that he is equally casual about the question of whether God is in the sphere as in a place or a vessel (§§ 20, 25), given the attention he has paid to Aristotle's definition of a "vessel" as a place earlier on (§§ 2, 4). He seems to assume that the outermost celestial sphere is a vessel for the contained, inner spheres, but not for God. This is reasonable enough, yet he is remarkably insouciant about the prospect of God's having a literal place, given the difficulties that this notion provoked in the Greek tradition. For Ibn ʿAdī, though, God's immateriality obviously rules out His having a place, so there is no need for detailed discussion.

More substantial are his arguments against God's being in the sphere as a genus in a species, as a whole in a part, or as a part in a whole (senses 1, 2, and 3). The idea that God *has* no genus is a familiar one in the Arabic philosophical tradition.[32] Ibn ʿAdī argues instead that God *is* not a genus, or at least, not related to the sphere as a genus relates to the species. This hardly seems to require refutation—he might have said simply that the sphere is not a species and leave it at that, much as he will do with the case of being in time. Instead, he invokes a criterion derived from Aristotle's *Categories*: if A is the genus of B, then A gives B its name and definition (§ 13, cf. *Cat.* 5, 2a20–1). In the next sentence, he calls again on this premise but drops the reference to "name." So it seems that it is the definition of God that is relevant here—which seems to presuppose that God is the sort of thing that can be defined. But all that Ibn ʿAdī needs here is the point that if God were the genus of the sphere then the sphere would have all His characteristics (*ṣifāt*). One of God's characteristics is to be incorporeal, but

[32] See for instance al-Kindī, *On First Philosophy*, in P. Adamson and P. E. Pormann (trs.), *The Philosophical Works of al-Kindī* (Karachi: Oxford University Press, 2012), § XIX.1; Avicenna, *The Metaphysics of the Healing*, tr. M. E. Marmura (Provo: Brigham Young University Press, 2005), VIII.4.14.

the sphere is a body (*jism*), which gives Ibn ʿAdī his desired conclusion. Given that, as already pointed out, Ibn ʿAdī could have reached the conclusion even more easily, it seems likely that this argument has been chosen in order to draw our attention to God's incorporeality. As we saw, the immateriality of the Prime Mover played a prominent role in the Greek discussion of the passage at hand (e.g. Alexander, § 818).

Ibn ʿAdī's most complicated arguments regarding the senses of "in" are devoted to the next two possibilities: that God is in the sphere as a whole or a part. Again, the Greek tradition of commentary may help explain this. Alexander worried that if, as Eudemus suggested, the Mover were in a part of the sphere (namely the celestial equator), then it would be moved accidentally along with the sphere. Of course there is a difference between being *in* a part of the sphere and *being* a part of the sphere, and it is the latter that is considered here by Ibn ʿAdī. Nonetheless, a version of Alexander's worry that God would be moved by the sphere becomes decisive in Ibn ʿAdī's discussion, which revolves around the claim that God cannot be causally dependent on the sphere.

He begins with a familiar distinction between homoiomerous (*mutashābih al-ajzāʾ*) and anhomoiomerous wholes, that is, wholes whose parts are uniform (e.g. flesh and bone) and those whose parts are non-uniform, i.e. discrete entities (e.g. the heart and the liver).[33] Against the possibility that God is like a homoiomerous whole, Ibn ʿAdī repeats that God does not share a definition with the sphere, whereas such wholes do share a definition with their parts. Again, this need mean only that such a whole will have its characteristics in common with its parts; for instance each part of a body of water will be wet. Next, against the prospect of God as an anhomoiomerous whole, we get the following argument:

> § 16: The whole needs its parts for its existence, whereas [the first mover] has no need of anything [else] for its existence, since it [sc. the first mover] is a cause of it [sc. that other thing]. If anything needs something [else] for its own existence, then that thing it needs for its existence is a cause of it.

This argument, of course, would also rule out the first alternative that God is a homoiomerous whole.

[33] For the distinction see Aristotle, Parts of Animals I.1, 640b19–20, Generation of Animals I.1, 715a10. For a strikingly similar discussion see al-Kindī's *That There are Separate Substances*, tr. Adamson and Pormann, 107–10. This brief treatise not only applies the distinctions between types of whole to the species–particular relation, but also invokes the name and definition test from the *Categories.*

But how do we know that God does not need the sphere for its existence? The premise is fairly uncontroversial, perhaps, but Ibn ʿAdī gives a rationale for it anyway, namely that God is the sphere's cause. When he uses the same point to argue that God is not a part of the sphere, he elaborates on this rationale:

§ 18: If it were the case that [the first mover] existed as belonging to (*li-*) the sphere and in it, then it would be wrong [to say] that the sphere desires it, since it is wrong [to say] that anything desires something that exists as belonging to it.

The point here is simply that the sphere could not desire the first mover if it already possessed the mover – but we know that God causes the sphere to move precisely because the sphere desires Him, as recalled at §7.[34]

6. CONCLUSION

Having ruled out the application of all 11 senses of "in" to the relation between God and the sphere, Ibn ʿAdī is ready to conclude that "the cause [sc. the Mover] does not exist in the container [sc. the sphere] in [its] own right (*bi-l-dhāt*)" (§ 26). As has already been noted, the phrase "in its own right," which has been absent from all the arguments regarding the senses of "in," now reappears in the conclusion.

We were already told (§§ 6–7), and are now told again (§§ 27–8), that God moves the sphere as a final cause, which means that He is an intelligible object for the sphere's intellect. Ibn ʿAdī now adds something significant: "the reality (*ḥaqīqa*) of the subject of intellection is that the image (*mithāl*) of the object of intellection is in it" (§ 28). Applying this to the case of God, this means that God is not "in" the sphere after all. Rather, an "image" of God is present in the sphere's intellect. It may well be that Ibn ʿAdī went on to spell this out explicitly in a final sentence, which has been cut off in the manuscript (see our note in the translation *ad loc*). The upshot is that, of the three positions we considered from the Greek tradition, the view of Simplicius is closest to anticipating Ibn ʿAdī's: God transcends the sphere and so is not "in" it, even in the rather extended senses of "in" recognized by Eudemus and Alexander.

This leaves us with a final question: given that Ibn ʿAdī seems to have known Alexander's *Physics* commentary, why might he have rejected

[34] Our thanks to Stephen Menn for discussion of this passage.

Alexander's view that God is in the sphere as a "substance in a substance"? The answer may lie with Ibn ʿAdī's theological commitments as a monophysite Christian.[35] Broadly speaking, he may have resisted the idea that God is specifically in the sphere, as opposed to equally omnipresent in all parts of the cosmos.[36] Furthermore, as we know from the apologetic works written by Ibn ʿAdī, he energetically attacked Nestorian conceptions of the Incarnation, which saw Christ as having two separate natures and two *hypostaseis*, divine and human.[37] In a refutation of the Nestorians, Ibn ʿAdī describes their position precisely as the view that Christ consists of "two substances (*jawharān*)"[38] which are united only by will. It may be that Ibn ʿAdī saw Alexander's account of God's presence in the sphere as uncomfortably close to the Nestorian account of how God is present to Christ's humanity. This would have been reason enough for him to distance himself from Alexander's interpretation, leaving him with the deflationary conclusion that God is in the sphere only in the sense that one can have something in mind.

Ludwig-Maximilians University Munich
McGill University

Translation

COMMENTARY ON BOOK EIGHT OF ARISTOTLE'S PHYSICS

(1) He said: If someone asks, what is the meaning of Aristotle's assertion, in Book Eight of the *Physics*, that "the mover is in the containing [sphere] (*al-muḥarrik fī-l-muḥīṭ*),"[39] let him know that he [Aristotle] means that "the mover" (and by "mover" he refers to the Creator,

[35] Again, our thanks to Marwan Rashed for suggesting this line of thought. For this side of Ibn ʿAdī's thought see Emilio Platti, *Yaḥyā Ibn ʿAdī: Théologien chrétien et philosophe arabe* (Leuven: Departement Oriëntalistiek, 1983).

[36] Our thanks to the anonymous referee for this point.

[37] Cf. Yaḥyā's Christological work *Maqālat al-shaykh Yaḥyā ibn ʿAdī fī wujūb* [alt. *wujūd*] *al-taʾannus*, ed. and trans. Périer, *Petits traités*. A significant portion of this work (Périer, 75.7–82.3) overlaps with the newly discovered philosophical treatise by Yaḥyā entitled *Essay on the Four Scientific Questions regarding the Three Categories of Existence: Divine, Natural and Logical* (ed. and trs. Menn and Wisnovsky, "Yaḥyā ibn ʿAdī's," n. 4).

[38] See Platti, *Yaḥyā Ibn ʿAdī*, *64, tr. at 190.

[39] The reference is to *Physics* VIII.10, 267b6–9.

exalted be His praise, and by "containing," he refers to the celestial sphere) is only "in" it in the way that the object of intellection (*al-maʿqūl*) is "in" the subject of intellection (*al-ʿāqil*), so that it not be the case that He is "in it" in His own right.

(2) The proof (*dalīl*) of this is that it is something widely acknowledged that philosophers (*al-ḥukamāʾ*) have used the expression "vessel (*al-ināʾ*)" in the sense of "a place which moves,"[40] and used the expression "motion" [of the sphere] in the sense of [something] single and uniform, and used the expression "heavenly orbs" in the sense of [something] moved.

(3) But they used each one of these [expressions] to describe what is described by it not with respect to its essence, but with respect to the existence of something in it (*min jihati wujūdi baʿḍi mā huwa fīhi*), to which this attribute may truly be applied.

(4) The vessel is not a place essentially, but in view of its inner concave surface; and the single motion is not essentially continuous, but [is continuous] in view of the magnitude to which [the motion] applies; and "moving" is correctly said to apply to the heavenly orbs not essentially, but in view of the motion of their parts.

(5) Again, the magnitude is said to be continuous not essentially, but in view of the continuity of its parts—one may only speak of "continuity" between at least two things, no matter how small they are, for a single thing is not rightly called "continuous."

(6) As for what Aristotle the philosopher says at the end of *Physics* Book Eight, that "the mover is in the containing [sphere]," this is correct just in the sense that the objects of knowledge exist in the knower.

(7) For the heavenly bodies know their mover, given that they are moved only out of their desire (*ishtiyāq*) to receive Him, just as Aristotle says: the first mover moves them just in the way that the object of desire moves what desires it.

(8) This can only happen with things that possess intellects.

(9) Aristotle said in the Book One of the *Physics* that "the contraries are two. But from another point of view this need not be the case, because one of two contraries may suffice to bring about change by its presence or absence."[41]

[40] A quote from *Physics* IV.2, 209b29: τόπος μεταφορητός.

[41] *Phys* I.7, 191a3–7.

(10) So [just] one of the two contraries is characterized as acting. The agent [acts] simply by virtue of what has been mentioned: its existence or lack.

(11) Furthermore, it is not correct for the first mover to be characterized as existing, in its own right, in the circle (*fī-l-dāʾira*). This is because it must either be said, in speaking of "circle," to refer to the highest "circular" sphere (and this is false, in view of the fact that the sphere is an orb [*al-falak kura*], not a circle), or

(12) be said that he [Aristotle] is deeming it permissible to call the sphere a circle in view of the fact that its status in respect of bodily things is the status of the circle in respect of planes (*suṭūḥ*) (if the person who asserts this is indulged in positing this facile [explanation], in view of what it entails).

(13) Clearly, it is not correct [to say] that [the mover] is in [the outermost sphere] the way that the genus is in the species. This is because the genus gives its name and its definition to its species,[42] whereas the first cause gives the celestial sphere neither its name[43] nor its definition, since one of its characteristics is not-to-be-a-body, and the celestial sphere is a body.

(14) Nor is it correct [to say] that it is in it the way the whole is in its parts.

(15) It is not like a homoiomerous whole, in view of the fact that its definition and the definition of sphere are not one and the same.

(16) Nor is it like an anhomoiomerous whole, in view of the fact that the whole needs its parts for its existence, whereas [the first mover] has no need of anything [else] for its existence, since it [sc. the first mover] is a cause of it [sc. that other thing]. If anything needs something [else] for its own existence, then that thing it needs for its existence is a cause of it.

(17) From this [sc. the supposition that it is a whole of heterogeneous (*anhomoiomerous*) parts] would follow that [the first mover both] has no cause and has a cause, and this is absurd.

(18) Nor is it correct [to say] that [it is in it] the way a part is in its whole. For if this were the case, and the part, without exception, necessarily existed whenever[44] the whole existed, and if it were the case that [the first mover] existed as belonging to (*li-*) the sphere and in it, then it would be wrong [to say] that the sphere desires it, since it is wrong [to say] that anything desires something that exists as belonging to it.

[42] Cf. *Categories* 5, 2a20–1.

[43] The marginal correction in the ms is right to emend *ashhar* to *ismahū.*

[44] Reading *idhā*; the ms. has *idhan.*

(19) Nor is it correct [to say] that [it is in it] the way something is in time. For the sphere is not time.

(20) Nor is it correct [to say] that [it is in it] the way something that has a place is in place. For [the first mover] is not a body, whereas everything that has a place is a body.

(21) Nor is it correct [to say] that [it is in it] the way what is acted upon is in the agent, or the way what has an end (*ghāya*) is in the end. For these are both causes, but [the first mover] has no cause.

(22) Nor is it correct [to say] that [it is in it] the way a form is in a subject. For the subject is a cause of the existence of the form, but [the first mover] has no cause.

(23) Nor is it correct [to say] that [it is in it] the way an accident is in a substance. For [the prime mover] is not an accident.

(24) Nor is it correct [to say] that [it is in it] the way a substance is in an accident. For the sphere is not an accident.[45]

(25) Again, it is wrong [to say] that [it is in it] the way something is in a vessel. For it is not a body, but whatever exists in a vessel is a body, because what is in a vessel is in the vessel as something that has a place is in a place.[46]

(26) Thus it has been shown that it is not correct to say that the [first] cause is in the containing [sphere] in any of the ways that a thing may be said to exist in its own right in another thing. Thus it has been shown that the cause does not exist, in its own right, in the containing [sphere].

(27) Since this is so, it has been shown that what is moved (namely, the heavenly body) is moved by the first cause just in the way the desiring thing is moved by the desideratum.

(28) And this, without doubt, necessitates that it [the heavenly body] is thinking about the first cause, and the reality of the subject of intellection is that the image of the object of intellection is in it. So it is thus plain and evident that the existence [of the Mover in the containing [sphere] is only like the existence of the object of intellection in the subject of intellection].[47]

[45] Following this the ms has two crossed-out words: *idh kāna*; the deletion is correct.

[46] Cf. § 20 above.

[47] We assume that several words have fallen out after the word *wujūd*, and that these would simply have spelled out the implication of the preceding sentence. A possible text is suggested in angle brackets in our Arabic edition of the text.

يحيى بن عدي

مقالة في تفسير فصل من المقالة الثامنة من السماع الطبيعيّ

(١) قال إنْ طلب طالب ما معنى قول الفيلسوف أرسطوطالس في المقالة الثامنة من السماع الطبيعيّ إنّ المحرّك في المحيط فلْيعلم أنّه إنّما يعني أنّ المحرّك و / هو يعني بالمحرّك الباري جلّ ثناؤه وبالمحيط الفلك وأنّه فيه كالمعقول في العاقل ألّا أنّه بذاته فيه (٢) والدليل على ذلك أنّه من المتعارف أنّ الحكماء قد / أطلقوا أنّ الإناء مكان متحرّك وقد أطلقوا أنّ الحركة واحدة متّصلة وأطلقوا أنّ الكرات السماويّة متحرّكة (٣) وإنّما وصفوا كلّ واحد من هذه لما وصف به / لا من جهة ذاته بل من جهة وجود بعض ما هو فيه يصدق عليه تلك الصفة (٤) وأنّ الإنا ليس بذاته هو مكان بل من جهة السطح المقعّر[١] منه الداخل / والحركة الواحدة ليس بذاتها هي متّصلة بل من قبل العظم الذي هي عليه والكرات السماويّة إنّما يصحّ أنْ يصدق عليها أنّها متحرّكة ليس بذواتها بل من / قبل تحرّك أجزائها (٥) وأيضاً العظم يقال إنّه متّصل لا من قبل ذاته بل من قبل اتّصال أجزائه وأنّ الاتّصال لا يصحّ إلّا بين شيْئيْن[٢] أقلّ ما يكون فإنّ الشيء الواحد / لا يصحّ أنْ يتّصل (٦) فأمّا قول الفيلسوف أرسطوطالس في آخر المقالة الثامنة من السماع الطبيعيّ أنّ المحرّك في المحيط فإنّما يصحّ بمعنى وجود المعلوم في العالم / (٧) إذْ كانت الأجرام السماويّة عالمة بمحرّكها إذْ كانت إنّما تتحرّك لاشتياقها إلى التقبّل به كما قال أرسطوطالس إنّ المحرّك الأوّل إنّما يحرّكها كما يحرّك المعشوق / عاشقه (٨) وهذا غير ممكن أنْ يوجد إلّا لذوي العقول (٩) وقد قال أرسطوطالس في المقالة الأولى من السماع الطبيعيّ إنّ الأضداد اثنان وأمّا على وجه آخر / فليس ذلك بواجب وذلك أنّه قد يكفي أحد الضدّيْن في أنْ يفعل التغيّر بحضوره وغيبته (١٠) فوصف أحد الضدّيْن بأنّه يفعل وإنّما الفاعل على ما ذكر / في وجوده وفقده (١١) وأيضاً فإنّه لا يصحّ أنْ يوصف المحرّك الأوّل أنْ يكون موجوداً في الدائرة بذاته وذلك أنّه لا يخلوا من أنْ يقال إنّه يشير بقوله الدائرة الفلك / الأعلى وهذا يبطل من قبل أنّ الفلك كرة وليس بدائرة وإمّا أنْ (١٢) يقال إنّما استجاز أنْ يسمّى الفلك دائرة من قبل أنّ منزلته في

[١] في الأصل: المعقر

[٢] في الأصل: سببيْن

المجسّمات منزلة الدائرة / في السطوح فإنْ سومح قائل هذا القول بوضع هذا اليسير[٣] بالنظر فيما يلزمه (١٣) فمن البيّن أنْ لا يصحّ أنْ يكون فيها كالجنس في الأنواع وذلك أنّ الجنس يعطي / أنواعه اسمه وحده وأمّا العلّة الأولى لا تعطي الفلك اسمه[٤] وحده إذْ كان من صفته أنّه ليس بجسم والفلك جسم (١٤) وكذلك لا يصحّ أنْ يكون فيه كالكلّ / في أجزائه (١٥) لا كالكلّ المتشابه الأجزاء من قبل أنّه ليس حدّه وحدّ الفلك حدّاً واحداً (١٦) ولا كالكلّ غير المتشابه من قبل أنّ الكلّ محتاج في وجوده / إلى أجزائه وهو غير محتاج في وجوده إلى شيء إذْ هو علّة له وكلّ ما هو محتاج في وجوده إلى شيء فذلك الشيء الذي هو محتاج إليه في وجوده /٢٨ب(١)/ هو علّة له (١٧) فيلزم من ذلك أنْ يكون لا علّة له وله علّة وهذا محال (١٨) ولا يصحّ أيضاً أنْ يكون كجزء في كلّه وذلك أنّه لو كان كذلك والجزء لا محالة إذاً[٥] كان / كلّه موجوداً يجب ضرورةً أنْ يكون موجوداً ولو كان موجوداً للفلك وفيه لم يصحّ أنْ يكون الفلك يتشوّقه إذْ لا يصحّ أنْ يشتاق شيء إلى ما هو موجود له / (١٩) ولا يصحّ أيضاً أنْ يكون كالشيء في الزمان إذْ كان الفلك ليس هو زماناً (٢٠) ولا يصحّ أيضاً أنْ يكون كالمتمكّن في المكان إذْ كان ليس بجسم وكان كلّ متمكّن جسماً / (٢١) ولا يصحّ أيضاً أنْ يكون كالمفعول في الفاعل ولا كذي الغاية في الغاية إذْ كانت هاتان علّتيْن وهو لا علّة له (٢٢) ولا يصحّ أيضاً أنْ يكون كصورة في موضوع / إذْ كان الموضوع علّة لوجود الصورة وهو لا علّة له (٢٣) ولا يصحّ أيضاً أنْ يكون كعرض في جوهر إذْ كان ليس هو عرضاً (٢٤) ولا يصحّ أيضاً أنْ يكون كجوهر في عرض / إذْ كان الفلك ليس هو عرض[٦] (٢٥) ولا يصحّ أيضاً أنْ يكون كالشيء في الإناء إذْ كان ليس بجسم وكلّ ما يوجد في الإناء هو جسم لأنّ ما في الإناء هو في الإناء / كالمتمكّن في المكان (٢٦) فإذْ قد تبيّن أنّه لا يصحّ أنْ تكون العلّة في المحيط بشيء من الوجوه التي يقال وجود شيء في شيء بذاته فقد تبيّن أنّ العلّة ليس / هو بذاته موجوداً في المحيط (٢٧) وإذْ ذلك كذلك فقد تبيّن أنّ المتحرّك وهو الجرم السمائيّ إنّما يتحرّك عن العلّة الأولى كحركة العاشق عن المعشوق / (٢٨) وكان ذلك موجباً لا محالة أنْ يكون عاقلاً للعلّة الأولى وكانت حقيقة العاقل هي أنْ يكون مثال المعقول فيه فقد ظهر ووضح أنّه إنّما وجود <المحرّك في المحيط كوجود المعقول في العاقل>

[٣] في الأصل: هذا ليسير

[٤] في الأصل: أشهر، وفوقها إشارة وفي الهامش كتب "اسمه"

[٥] في الأصل: إذاً

[٦] في الأصل: ~~إذ كان~~

BIBLIOGRAPHY

Adamson, Peter. "Yaḥyā Ibn ʿAdī and Averroes on Metaphysics Alpha Elatton," *Documenti e studi sulla tradizione filosofica medievale* 21 (2010), 343–74.

Aristotle. *Categoriae et Liber de Interpretatione*, ed. L. Minio-Paluello (Oxford: Oxford University Press, 1936).

—— *Physica*, ed. W. D. Ross (Oxford: Oxford University Press, 1950).

Avicenna. *The Metaphysics of the Healing*, tr. M. E. Marmura (Provo: Brigham Young University Press, 2005).

Badawī, Abdurrahman (ed). *Arisṭūṭālis: al-Ṭabīʿa*, 2 vols. (Cairo: al-Dār al-Qawmiyya li-l-Ṭibāʿa wa-l-Nashr, 1964–5).

Bonadeo, Cecilia Martini. "Un commento ad *alpha elatton* 'sicut litterae sonant' nella Baghdād del X secolo," *Medioevo* 28 (2003), 69–96.

Chiaradonna, Riccardo. "Essence et prédication chez Porphyre et Plotin," *Revue des sciences philosophiques et théologiques* 82 (1998), 577–606.

Endress, Gerhard. *The Works of Yaḥyā ibn ʿAdī: An Analytical Inventory* (Wiesbaden: L. Reichert, 1977).

al-Fārābī. *Commentary on Aristotle's Peri Hermêneias*, ed. W. Kutsch and S. Marrow (Beirut: Imprimerie Catholique, 1960).

—— *Commentary and Short Treatise on Aristotle's De Interpretatione*, tr. F. W. Zimmermann (Oxford: Oxford University Press, 1981).

Giannakis, Elias. *Philoponus in the Arabic Tradition of Aristotle's Physics*, D. Phil. Thesis (Oxford, 1992).

—— "The Structure of Abū l-Ḥusayn al-Baṣrī's Copy of Aristotle's *Physics*," *Zeitschrift für Geschichte der arabisch-islamischen Wissenschaften* 8 (1993), 251–8.

—— "Fragments from Alexander's lost Commentary on Aristotle's Physics," *Zeitschrift für Geschichte der arabisch-islamischen Wissenschaften* 10 (1995/6), 157–87.

Gyekye, Kwame. "The Terms *Prima intentio* and *Secunda intentio* in Arabic Logic," *Speculum* 46 (1971), 32–48.

Khalīfāt, Saḥbān. *Maqālāt Yaḥyā ibn ʿAdī al-falsafiyya* (ʿAmmān: al-Jāmiʿa al-Urdunniyya, 1988).

al-Kindī. *On First Philosophy*, tr. P. Adamson and P. E. Pormann, *The Philosophical Works of al-Kindī* (Karachi: Oxford University Press, 2012).

Lettinck, Paul. *Aristotle's Physics and its Reception in the Arabic World* (Leiden: Brill, 1994).

Al-Masʿūdī. *Kitāb al-tanbīh wa-l-iṣrāf*, ed. Michael Jan de Goeje (Leiden: Brill, 1893–4).

Menn, Stephen and Robert Wisnovsky. "Yaḥyā ibn ʿAdī's *Essay on the Four Scientific Questions regarding the Three Categories of Existence: Divine, Natural and Logical. Editio princeps* and English Translation, with Historical-Philosophical Notes," *Mélanges de l'Institut dominicain d'études orientales du Caire (MIDEO)* 29 (2012) 73–96.

Philoponus. *In Aristotelis Physicorum libros quinque posteriores commentaria*, ed. J. Vitelli (Berlin: Reimer, 1888).

Philoponus. *On Aristotle Physics 5–8 with Simplicius, On Aristotle on the Void*, tr. P. Lettinck and J. O. Urmson (London: Duckworth, 1994).

Pines, Shlomo and Michael Schwarz. "Yaḥyā ibn ʿAdī's Refutation of the Doctrine of Acquisition (*Iktisāb*)," in J. Blau et al. (eds.), *Studia Orientalia Memoriae D. H. Baneth Dedicata* (Jerusalem: Magnes, 1979), 49–94.

Platti, Emilio. *Yaḥyā ibn ʿAdī: théologien chrétien et philosophe arabe* (Leuven: Departement Oriëntalistiek, 1983).

Porphyry. *Isagoge et in Aristotelis Categorias commentarium*, ed. A. Busse (Berlin: Reimer, 1887).

Rashed, Marwan. *Alexandre d'Aphrodise, Commentaire perdu à la Physique d'Aristote (Livres IV–VIII)* (Berlin: Walter de Gruyter, 2011).

Simplicius. *In Aristotelis Physicorum libros quattuor posteriores commentaria*, ed. H. Diels (Berlin: George Reimer, 1895).

—— *On Aristotle's Physics 8.6–10*, ed. R. McKirahan (London: Duckworth, 2001).

Sorabji, Richard. *The Philosophy of the Commentators, 200–600 AD: A Sourcebook in Three Volumes* (London: Duckworth, 2004).

Wilberding, James. "'Creeping Spatiality': The Location of *Nous* in Plotinus' Universe," *Phronesis* 50 (2005), 315–34.

Wisnovsky, Robert. "Notes on Avicenna's Concept of 'Thingness' (*shayʾiyya*)," *Arabic Sciences and Philosophy* 10 (2000), 181–221.

—— "Yaḥyā ibn ʿAdī's Discussion of the Prolegomena to the Study of a Philosophical Text," in M. Cook et al. (eds.), *Law and Tradition in Classical Islamic Thought* (Basingstoke: Palgrave Macmillan, 2012), 171–85.

—— "New Philosophical Texts of Yaḥyā Ibn ʿAdī: A Supplement to Endress' *Analytical Inventory*," in F. Opwis and D. Reisman (eds.), *Islamic Philosophy, Science, Culture, and Religion: Studies in Honor of Dimitri Gutas* (Leiden: Brill, 2012), 307–26.

Yaḥyā ibn ʿAdī. *Petits traités apologétiques de Yaḥyā ben ʿAdī*, ed. A. Périer (Paris: Geuthner, 1920).

Briefly Noted

Joël Biard, *Science et nature: la théorie buridanienne du savoir* (Vrin, 2012). If Ockham was the venerable inceptor of nominalism, John Buridan was perhaps the one to give the theory its most compelling, comprehensive, and influential statement. Even while we await critical editions of Buridan's most important non-logical works (his questions on the *Physics*, *Metaphysics*, and *De anima*), Biard has given us a comprehensive, 400-page study of his conception of *scientia*. Beginning with the characteristics of *scientia*—certainty, universality, necessity—Biard moves on to the theory of language, the nature of demonstrations, and finally to the various sciences that Buridan works to develop. The discussion does not attempt to go deeply into any of the philosophical issues that arise, nor does it tend to provide much more than passing references to other fourteenth-century figures. But Biard displays a masterful familiarity with the entirety of Buridan's corpus, and extends his discussion to every corner of Buridan's thinking about *scientia*, from logic and language to mind and knowledge, and onward to physics and theology.

Richard de Mediavilla, *Questions disputées*, ed. Alain Boureau (Les Belles Lettres, 2011–), 6 vols. Hitherto available only in manuscript, Richard's *quaestiones* form an ordered series running from God through the angels and the fall of the devil, and on to human nature. Almost every question is richly philosophical in character. Boureau dates these questions, at least in their final form, to the last decade of the Franciscan's life, in the 1290s. He describes this as a working edition, but in fact it is surely good enough for the foreseeable future, given that the manuscript tradition is robust and consistent. On facing pages Boureau provides a French text, as if to celebrate the growing consensus that Richard hails from Picardy—that he is *de Menneville* and not *de Middleton*. The publication of this text is clearly a major scholarly achievement. But the translation raises questions. There is now an increasing tendency to publish modern translations along with editions, even of lesser-known texts. Is there a readership? Should we create a readership, by assigning these texts to our students? If we do, will that come at the expense of their reading other, more prominent and influential scholastic works? Might it be better to focus on translating the many quite fundamental texts—like the *Sentences*-commentaries of Aquinas, Scotus, and Ockham—that still remain untranslated?

José Filipe Silva, *Robert Kilwardby on the Human Soul: Plurality of Forms and Censorship in the Thirteenth Century* (Brill, 2012). This impressive debut monograph wants to resituate our understanding of Kilwardby, the Dominican who notoriously issued a "prohibition" of 30 philosophical doctrines at Oxford in 1277. Historians have long argued over whether these articles aim at Aquinas, given the way they target various theses associated with Aquinas's unitarian conception of the soul. Silva makes a strong case that Kilwardby did not have Aquinas in mind, but was rather thinking of much earlier views that insisted on the simplicity of the rational soul and its powers. The first half of the book makes the case for Kilwardby as a leading champion of the pluralist position, but argues that we think of him as still engaged with mid-century views and as largely out of touch with the innovative ideas of his decade-younger confrère. It was subsequent Franciscans, beginning with John Pecham, who made the 1277 Oxford articles into an attack on Aquinas, and subsequent Dominicans who took up the challenge. And it has been Thomistic scholarship from the last century that promoted this picture by framing a historical narrative of Aristotelians versus Augustinians (261). Kilwardby fits neatly into neither category, Silva tells us, but was instead simply behind the times. Or, as they evidently say on the streets of Porto, he was "a man wearing old shoes" (273).

Felicitas Opwis and David Reisman (editors), ***Islamic Philosophy, Science, Culture and Religion: Studies in Honor of Dimitri Gutas*** **(Brill, 2012).** Think of this volume's omnibus title not as something awkward but rather as a tribute to the wide-ranging erudition of its honoree. Philosophy gets pride of place here, both in the title and in the focus of many contributors, as befits Professor Gutas's own career-long dedication to understanding the Arabic tradition of *falsafa*. Among the distinguished contributors are Jules Janssens, Tony Street, Amos Bertolacci, Gerhard Endress, and Robert Wisnovsky. Best parenthetical remark: Charles Burnett and Gideon Bohak, in reporting on two astrological works unearthed in the famous Cairo Genizah, report that "we have examined all 140,000 [!?] Genizah fragments"—but alas they were able to find only four fragments from the two works in question. Best *ḥadīth*: Yahya Michot tells us that Ibn Taymīya's assessed the philosophers' treatment of the science of divinity by invoking the following: "What they say is like the meat of a lean camel at the top of a pathless mountain: it is not easily ascended and there is no fat to degustate." Only complaints: too little information about the life and work of Gutas, and no information at all about the *curricula* of the contributors. Sad postscript: The volume must serve as a tribute not only to Gutas but also to Reisman, who died in 2011.

John of Reading, ***Scriptum in primum librum Sententiarum*****, ed. Francesco Fiorentino (Vrin, 2011).** John of Reading is a minor Minor, but an interesting one: a Franciscan who had the good fortune to be active at Oxford circa 1320. Not much has survived: mainly one manuscript containing a series of twenty-five questions on the *Sentences* running through distinction three of book one. Only a few of these questions have previously been edited, in scattered venues. However, despite what the title of this edition promises, Fiorentino goes only part way towards rectifying the situation. The volume's contents are made clear neither on the title page nor in the table of contents nor in any other place one might think to look, but a reader possessing decent French and a free half an hour can discover from the lengthy introduction that in fact we are here given only the first five of the twelve questions from the prologue, and nothing from book one at all. The topics mainly concern the relationship between *scientia* and theology. Much of the interest comes from John's engagement with a host of famous and less famous figures, Franciscan and Dominican, from the preceding decade. *Caveat lector*: on the first four pages alone there are three serious errors: 100.5: Probatio maioris [*lege*: minoris]; 101.up4: Alio modo sumitur finis pro aliquo subtracto [*lege*: subiecto]; 102.13: <Sed> deo.

Notes for Contributors

OSMP welcomes submissions in all areas of medieval philosophy. Papers received will be evaluated in a timely manner, and an effort to provide significant feedback will be made in every case. To the fullest extent possible, all papers will be refereed according to a triple-blind process, so that neither editor nor referee will know the identity of the author, nor will the author know the identity of the referee.

In addition to articles, we welcome editions of texts and brief critical discussions of recently published work (both in *OSMP* and elsewhere). Book reviews, however, will be published only when solicited.

Submissions should be in English, without author's name or any other information that would impede blind refereeing. Papers may be of any length, and in particular we welcome the submission of longer works that fall outside the parameters of most journals. Contributors should bear in mind, however, that the lengthier the work, the higher the standard for acceptance.

Papers should be submitted as either .pdf or Word-compatible files. The formatting of the initial submission is immaterial, but accepted papers will ultimately need to adhere to *OSMP* style, as on display in this present volume. All submissions, as well as queries, should be addressed to osmp@colorado.edu.

Index of Names